MW00789057

Collectible Microcomputers

Michael Nadeau

4880 Lower Valley Road, Atglen, PA 19310 USA

Acknowledgments

I'm indebted to a number of people who helped me with this book. Vintage Computer Festival host Sellam Ismail lent his broad knowledge of collectible micros, offering suggestions and input on values. Sellam also has one of the largest computer collections that I'm aware of—more than 1,200 systems at last count—and he was kind enough to photograph some of them for this book. He also has a large software and literature archive.

Cameron Kaiser's knowledge of 8-bit Commodore systems could fill a book of its own. He operates two important Commodore Web sites: The Commodore Knowledge Base and The Secret Weapons of Commodore. Cameron's input added depth and texture to the Commodore section. For the Amiga portion of the Commodore material, I relied on the judgment of Gareth Knight, who maintains the Amiga Interactive Guide Web site.

Mike Stulir provided great insight on Atari systems. His Back In Time Web site is a fascinating resource for Atari fans. It not only has reliable information about the computers and game systems, but video and audio files of interviews Mike conducted with Atari luminaries such as company founder Nolan Bushnell.

Tom Owad's Applefritter Web site is one of the most trusted sources of vintage Apple information on the Web, and Tom was kind enough to send me his comments and additions for the Apple section of this book. Allison Parent contributed her knowledge of MITS Altair 8800 systems.

You can find the addresses for the above-mentioned Web sites in Appendix B: Resources.

I'd also like to thank Richard Berger of Canon Inc., who faxed me material from Canon's archives in Japan. And thanks also go to Karen Jacobs at CMP for helping obtain permission to use photos from *Byte* magazine.

Library of Congress Cataloging-in-Publication Data

Nadeau, Michael.
    Collectible microcomputers / By Michael Nadeau.
        p. cm.
    ISBN 0-7643-1600-1
    1. Microcomputers--Collectors and collecting--Catalogs. I. Title.
    QA76.5.N238 2002
    004'.074--dc21

                        2002008063

Copyright © 2002 by Michael Nadeau

All rights reserved. No part of this work may be reproduced or used in any form or by any means—graphic, electronic, or mechanical, including photocopying or information storage and retrieval systems—without written permission from the copyright holder.
"Schiffer," "Schiffer Publishing Ltd. & Design," and the "Design of pen and ink well" are registered trademarks of Schiffer Publishing Ltd.

Designed by Kevin Kelly
Cover by Bruce Waters
Type set in Futura Hv BT/Zapf Humanist BT

ISBN: 0-7643-1600-1
Printed in China

Published by Schiffer Publishing Ltd.
4880 Lower Valley Road
Atglen, PA 19310
Phone: (610) 593-1777; Fax: (610) 593-2002
E-mail: Schifferbk@aol.com
Please visit our web site catalog at **www.schifferbooks.com**
We are always looking for people to write books on new and related subjects. If you have an idea for a book please contact us at the above address.

This book may be purchased from the publisher.
Include $3.95 for shipping.
Please try your bookstore first.
You may write for a free catalog.

In Europe, Schiffer books are distributed by
Bushwood Books
6 Marksbury Ave.
Kew Gardens
Surrey TW9 4JF England
Phone: 44 (0)20-8392-8585
Fax: 44 (0)20-8392-9876
E-mail: Bushwd@aol.com
Free postage in the UK. Europe: air mail at cost

Contents

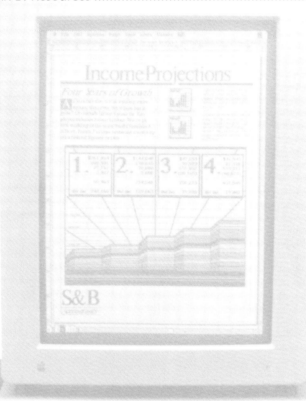

Chapter 1

Introducing
Collectible Microcomputers

Microcomputers have arguably had the greatest cultural impact on society of any product introduced in the last 30 years. Access to computer technology has changed the lives of millions by creating new career opportunities and improving the quality of life. Purchasing that first computer has become a right of passage akin to getting your first car. Brand loyalty can be fierce and long-lived.

It's no wonder, then, that people are beginning to acquire older microcomputers as a hobby. They might do it for the nostalgia, seeking out examples of the first computer or computer brand they owned. They might look for the computer they wished to have owned when it was new. Or perhaps they accumulate systems and related paraphernalia indiscriminately. Most people who collect micros have a technical background or otherwise have much experience with computers. Collectors might admire a given system's technical elegance—the way it executes a certain task or the manner in which the engineers designed it.

Collecting microcomputers is a hands-on hobby much like collecting old radios or antique cars. You have to be willing to tinker to get the full enjoyment of owning a vintage computer. That might include restoring a micro, repairing damaged circuits, and replacing lost components. Some collectors like to program older computers to perform useful tasks, while others acquire certain models to play the games or run applications developed for them.

As a collector, you likely have knowledge about certain brands or models of computers—how common or rare they are, the desirable peripherals, and their common ailments. However, computer collections can take on a life of their own. The more systems you own, the more the collection seems to attract others, like the gravitational pull of a planet drawing other heavenly bodies to it. You will eventually encounter or desire computers with which you are not familiar, and that's where this book comes in handy.

Collectible Microcomputers is a field guide for the vintage computer enthusiast and collector. It lists values, specifications, and key peripherals for more than 640 microcomputers made between 1971 and 1993. This book provides a little history about milestone computers and the companies that made them, and it also gives advice about collecting vintage micros. *Collectible Microcomputers* will help you identify and evaluate the systems you come across at flea markets, thrift stores, auctions, and elsewhere.

This book covers only desktop and portable microcomputers. What's a microcomputer? Good question. For the purposes of this book, I've defined it as any general-purpose, single-user computer for use in a home or professional setting. This includes:
*   early hobbyist computers
*   desktop business/professional computers
*   home computers
*   PC-compatibles
*   transportable computers
*   laptop computers
*   notebook computers

Collectible Microcomputers does not cover the following types of computers:
*   mainframe computers
*   minicomputers
*   multi-user systems
*   high-end workstations
*   game consoles
*   calculators
*   handheld computers
*   terminals

How to Use This Book

I suggest that you read Chapter 2, Tips on Collecting and Evaluating Microcomputers, even if you are an experienced collector. The chapter provides ideas on where to find older micros, but more importantly tells you what to look for in each general class of computer. It also offers advice on quickly assessing condition and value of your finds.

Chapter 3, Microcomputers A to Z, makes up the core of the book. It contains the model listings with specifications, values, and other information. In putting this chapter together, I made a number of assumptions and used certain conventions that you need to understand.

Data for each computer model is listed in up to six categories: Original Retail Price, Base Configuration, Video, Size/Weight, Important Options, and Value. I omitted categories for certain systems where they either were not relevant or the information was unknown. Whenever possible, I relied on original sources for this information, including sales literature, press releases, catalogs, advertisements, and documentation. Other important sources include magazine reviews and articles, collectors and other experts, early computer books, and my own recollections from my career as a computer journalist. In a few cases, I relied on information found on the Web, but only if I could verify the data from multiple sources or if original sources were cited. There are many great Web sites for vintage computer enthusiasts, and some of the best are listed in Appendix B.

Here's what you need to know about each category.

"Original Retail Price" is the manufacturer's price for the computer when it was first launched. Ranges are given where the vendor sold multiple standard configurations.

"Base Configuration" shows components and features sold with the lowest standard system. I've included only key items that will help you identify and evaluate a given system, including the CPU type, memory, ports and expansion slots, peripherals, software, and input devices. I also included the operating system even though it was an added-cost option for most computers, because you should know which operating system was most commonly used with a given micro.

"Video" lists the computer's maximum text display by number of lines and columns, and maximum graphics display by number of horizontal and vertical pixels. It also shows the maximum number of colors that can be displayed at one time.

"Size/Weight" provides the dimensions and weight of the computer's main unit. The category does not include the keyboard, monitor, or other devices unless they are integrated with the main processing unit.

"Important Options" lists the desirable peripherals, software, and enhancements sold separately by the computer's manufacturer. The items shown in this category tend to increase the value of a given system. Where known, model names or numbers for options are listed. I did not include items sold by third-party vendors.

"Value" provides a price range that you should use as a guide when buying, selling, or trading vintage micros. The low-end assumes a working computer in poor condition or that is incomplete. The high end assumes a working, complete (in terms of standard configuration) system in excellent, used condition. Expect to pay a premium for computers with desirable options or other extras, and for computers in

their original boxes and packing. See Chapter 2 for advice on evaluating vintage computers.

I used several sources to determine the value range. Online auction results were the most important source. I recorded sales of systems, noting condition and included items, for a period of about 18 months. I did not consider the shipping or other costs related to the sale. This gave me a reasonable baseline on the average value for most common systems.

For systems that were rarely or never offered online, I had to rely on other methods. In some cases, I used data for other similar systems. In other cases, I listened to the advice of people with knowledge of the particular brand.

Placing a value on vintage microcomputers is an inexact science, in large part because the hobby doesn't yet have a lot of history. Use the information on values in this book as it was intended: as a guideline only.

I used common computing acronyms and abbreviations throughout Chapter 3 for the sake of brevity. Appendix A is a glossary that provides definitions for any acronym, abbreviation, or computing term with which you are unfamiliar.

Want to Learn More?

Collecting vintage computers is a relatively new hobby, and one that is changing rapidly. Although this book will serve well as a guide for your collecting activities, many of you might want to learn more about a particular brand of computer or stay current on hobby trends and news. To go beyond what this book can offer, I have created another source of information about vintage computers and the computer collecting hobby.

In early 2002, I launched a monthly e-mail newsletter called the *Classic Tech E-letter*. It covers computing history from its earliest beginnings to the current day. The newsletter's scope will encompass all computing technology including calculators, micros, game systems, minicomputers, and mainframes. *Classic Tech* also presents news analysis of collecting trends, interviews with computing pioneers, and profiles of collectors. A classifieds section allows readers to sell items or help search for wanted items.

Classic Tech is free. To subscribe, send a message to eletter@classictechpub.com with the word "subscribe" in the subject line.

I Crave Feedback

Please send me your comments, stories, and any information you think might be worthwhile for future revisions of *Collectible Microcomputers*. Let me know, too, if you find a mistake, have information that contradicts what you find in these pages, or feel that the values I've assigned are off-base. I will post any necessary additional information or corrections on my Web site at http://www.classictechpub.com.

Send that input to my e-mail address at menadeau@attbi.com or through my publisher, Schiffer Publishing, at Schifferbk@aol.com

Chapter 2

Tips for Collecting
& Evaluating Microcomputers

Collecting vintage computers presents three types of challenges. First, finding less common older micros can be difficult, especially if you live in a rural area. Second, you need the ability to quickly evaluate systems that you find not only to determine value, but to identify problems or missing components. Finally, there's the issue of what to do with the micro once you acquire it. How do you prepare it for operation? What's the best way to store it? How do you maintain it?

The Hunt

For some people, the process of tracking down collectible micros is half the fun. Newcomers to the hobby, however, might be frustrated when their initial efforts to find interesting computers aren't as fruitful as they would like. Be patient; the computers are out there in your neighbors' closets, in back rooms of nearby businesses, and in the hands of fellow collectors.

You can find vintage computers almost anywhere, but the places and venues listed below are your best bets:

Yard and estate sales: For every collectible micro you'll find at yard sales, you'll see 10 five-year-old PCs. Nonetheless, yard sales are an excellent place to find older home computers and the occasional desktop micro or portable system. Estate sales are somewhat better hunting grounds. Always ask about software, manuals, cables, and other items belonging to the computers you find. It's common to find incomplete systems at yard sales, so you don't want to overlook associated items that are hidden in boxes or still tucked away in the garage.

Flea markets: Much like yard sales, flea markets are a good source for systems originally sold into the household. However, I've noticed recently that the larger flea markets will sometimes have a vendor or two who seems to specialize in older electronics. You want to learn more about these vendors, as they might have sources for the type of computer you are looking for. Get a name and number, and leave yours with the vendor along with a want-list.

Auctions: I like to check the auction listings in the Sunday papers for sales that might include old computers. The business liquidation auctions sometimes list older microcomputers, minicomputers, and workstations. You won't find leads in the auction listings frequently, but auctions are a good way to get a deal on interesting items. Your competition will be bidders looking for newer equipment to use or resell, or scrappers who buy older, large systems to strip them of their valuable metals. Ask to be put on the mailing list of any auctioneer you come across who sells older computers.

Scrappers/recyclers: Find out who scraps or recycles electronic equipment in your area. Call them and explain what you are looking for. They might tell you to take a hike, but many will gladly sell systems they take in if they can get more than scrap value for them. A few recyclers have Web sites that you can find with a simple search.

Schools: Is the local school district getting new computers this year? Find out what's happening to the old ones. Many schools still have Apple IIs, Macintoshes, TRS-80s, and even Commodore PETs in use or in storage. Administrators are often happy to sell them reasonably if they are out of service. Keep in mind, however, that micros from schools will be well used and valued at the low end of the price ranges listed in this book.

Fellow collectors: In many ways, other collectors will be your best source for vintage micros. Of course, you have to find them, first, and this is easy thanks to the Internet. Search the Web for references to the computers that interest you. Unless the computer is an obscure make, you will likely turn up a number of sites run by fellow enthusiasts. You might also join a mailing list such as the one at www.classiccmp.org. Collectors and experts you meet online are usually happy to offer advice and share their knowledge. As you build relationships with these people, you will likely be presented with opportunities to buy or trade for interesting computers.

Online auctions: I have mixed feelings about eBay and other auction sites as a source of vintage micros. On the plus side, it is easy to find common systems for a reasonable price, and you also have the occasional opportunity to acquire a rare system that would otherwise be unattainable.

Watch out for the negatives, however. People often get carried away in the bidding, especially for uncommon micros or micros that are in uncommonly good condition. You can easily overpay. Descriptions can be misleading. You don't know how much knowledge the seller has of the item, and it might not be what he thinks it is. Also, his idea of "excellent condition" might not match yours.

Shipping can be a problem, too, in terms of cost and potential for damage. Sending a seven-pound home computer is relatively inexpensive, but sending 50 pounds of an old CP/M system across country could easily be much more than the selling price. A poorly packed computer, especially if a monitor is included, might not survive the trip.

My advice is to be patient and get to know the sellers. If an item you want is going too high, back off. Many collectors who use eBay will decide on a top price before bidding and stick to it. Be aggressive about contacting the seller before the auction ends to clear up any questions you have about condition or the description. Ask exactly how the seller will ship the item. If the seller is unresponsive or cagey with his answers, don't bid.

If you buy regularly through auction sites, you will get to know and trust certain sellers. Some of those sellers will get to know your needs, too, and might deal with you off-line when they get an item that they know will interest you.

Serendipity: Over time, you will build a local reputation as the person who collects old computers. People might contact you because they have an old computer they want to dispose of or sell. In fact, many long-time collectors report that they have acquired some of their most interesting systems this way.

Sizing Them Up

Once you find a vintage micro, you will need to quickly evaluate it to determine its condition and how much you are willing to pay for it. Make sure you consider all the factors below.

Completeness: Look for systems that have all the items with which they were originally sold. Missing cables, manuals, software, and peripherals are common. External power supplies, if they are still with the machine, are often not working. It's relatively easy to find missing items for common systems, but might be impossible for scarce models. If you can, research the model to determine what its original components were.

Original packaging: A complete, well cared-for or unused system in its pristine box with all the packaging material intact is the Holy Grail of many collectors. Of course, you are likely to pay a premium for these systems. A box in poor condition rarely adds value to any system. A box in fair to good condition without the packing material will add only a modest premium to the computer's value. Don't forget to look for all the original papers, too, such as the warranty card, brochures, set-up instructions, and so on.

Extras: Hard-to-find, working expansion hardware and peripherals or desirable software can in some cases dramatically raise the value of a system. Look inside the computer for add-on cards, processor upgrades, and other desirable hardware enhancements.

Cosmetics: Keyboard wear, discolored or cracked plastic, and scratches are common. Some systems hold up better than others, but each model has its own wear characteristics. Look for user modifications to the enclosure and damage done by adhesive labels or other methods of marking—common with systems that come from schools or businesses. Missing keycaps, covers, and logos will detract from the value as well.

Cleanliness: Dirty systems require your time to clean, and the grime might hide defects. Look inside, too. Dust and rust can cause overheating and poor connections.

> **TIP:** The light-colored plastic cases of many systems are prone to permanent discoloration from exposure to sunlight. If you find a system that isn't discolored, store it out of direct sunlight or keep a cover on it. Sometimes, the discoloration is caused by residue such as that left by cigarette smoke. If you think this might be the case, try to clean a small inconspicuous area with a cleaner that has a mild abrasive. Some people use powdered cleaners such as Ajax or Comet, but toothpaste works, too. You can do the entire case if your test patch comes clean without damaging the finish. If it didn't, learn to live with the off-color.
>
> **TIP:** Some computer cases are dyed plastic, others are painted. Painted cases tend to have a glossy or textured surface. Be careful cleaning a painted surface, especially if the paint is already starting to wear off in places. Use a damp soft cloth and rub gently. If you must, use a mild cleanser such as dishwashing liquid.

Geography: If you live in Silicon Valley, then you have greater access to older micros than people living in, say, Newfoundland. Collectors living in rural areas often pay a premium for less common systems. Also, some systems bring a premium in certain regions. For example, many of the early British home computers sell for higher prices in Europe than in the U.S.

Rarity vs. Desirability

What makes an old computer valuable? Many people would answer "rarity," but at best that's only part of the answer. The same is true for desirability.

Rarity versus desirability, or in econospeak, supply versus demand, is a tricky equation for collectors of old computers. For starters, it's often difficult to know how rare or desirable a system might be. On any given day, for example, you can find a half-dozen or so Apple IIe systems for sale on eBay. Most will receive bids of no more than $20, but a few might sell for $100 or more. A dusty Altair 8800 might sell for a few thousand dollars, while a similar and much more scarce contemporary might sell for a few hundred dollars. Study the trends over time rather than the individual sales, and take the following attributes into account.

Nostalgia: What was coveted when it was new is likely to be in demand today. This is especially true of expensive systems that few could afford when new—the Apple Lisa, for example. Also, many people collect the systems that they first owned or used.

Historical significance: Milestone systems like the original IBM PC usually—but not always—command a premium. For a historically significant micro to have a higher-than-average value, it must be widely perceived to be a milestone system. Dozens of systems that were the first to use a particular CPU or technology remain obscure to most enthusiasts.

Tinkerability: Some people like to work with their old computers and look for systems they can upgrade or write interesting code for. Enthusiasts of early S-100 bus systems are often hands-on collectors.

Support: In general, systems for which there is a good supply of parts, software, peripherals, and documentation are better collectibles. An established knowledge base usually exists for these systems, too. The popular systems of the 1980s—Apple, Commodore, Tandy/Radio Shack, Atari—still enjoy good support. However, good support tends to increase the value more for scarce systems than for common ones. This is why collectors are willing to pay high prices for incomplete examples of computers like the Altair 8800 or the IMSAI 8080. A reasonably good supply of software and hardware exists for them.

The "cool" factor: A few systems are appealing because of their physical design or the technology they use. The NeXT Cube is cool, as is the Canon Cat. Even an obscure system can be cool. Few collectors would know an APF Imagination Machine or an Ampere WS-1 if they stumbled across one, but they would immediately find either system interesting.

A Word of Caution

The electronics found in most computers are durable. If they worked when put into storage, they will probably work when taken out of storage even years later. At worst, you might have to clean the contacts of add-on boards and connectors.

The one potential exception is with early computers that use electrolytic capacitors. Microcomputers produced between 1974 and 1978—before the mass market era—represent one of the most rewarding and most challenging areas for enthusiasts of old computers. Anyone wishing to own an early microcomputer today, however, should have at least a basic understanding of digital electronics and a good set of tools and test equipment. Most were fragile and cranky when new. The biggest concern, however, is with those capacitors. The electrolyte dries out over time, and if you apply current to one in a dried out state, it might explode. Take this warning to heart:

NEVER, EVER TRY TO RUN AN EARLY MICROCOMPUTER THAT HAS BEEN UNUSED FOR A LONG TIME WITHOUT FIRST TESTING ITS COMPONENTS.

You might be able to "reform" the electrolyte with a device called a Variac. A Variac brings up the voltage slowly so that the insulating oxide layer in the electrolyte can reform. Before you attempt this task, you should learn more about the process as my explanation is not meant as a tutorial. Also, examine the electrolytic capacitors (you can't miss them—they are the big cylindrical components) for leakage or bulging. If you observe either, then the capacitors must be replaced with either a NOS (new old stock) unit or modern equivalent.

An excellent discussion about electrolytic capacitors is available on the Web at http://www.nmr.mgh.harvard.edu/~reese/electrolytics/.

Chapter 3

Microcomputers A to Z

Access Matrix Corp. (San Jose, California)

Access Matrix claimed (questionably) that the Access was the first all-in-one portable, integrating a printer and acoustic coupler into the unit. Unfortunately, more components mean more potential points of failure. Keep this in mind if you come across one of these systems. In 1984, the company changed its name to Actrix Computer Corp. and the name of the computer to Actrix. At the same time it also offered an 8088 coprocessor option so the Actrix could run MS-DOS.

Access Matrix Access (Feb. 1983, transportable)
Original Retail Price: $2,495
Base Configuration: Z80A CPU; CP/M 2.2; 64K RAM; dual 5.25-inch floppy disk drives; integral 7-inch monochrome CRT; keyboard/keypad; two RS-232C, parallel, and IEEE-488 ports; MBASIC or C BASIC; application suite; integral printer and acoustic coupler; leather carrying case **Size/Weight:** 16.13 x 10 x 10.75 inches, 33 lbs. **Important Options:** 8088 coprocessor with MS-DOS (Actrix), battery pack **Value:** $15 to $35

Complete with built-in printer and acoustic couple, the Access ($15 to $35) from Access Matrix.

ACFA Inc. (Annapolis, Maryland)

ACFA stood for "Affordable Computer for All." The 6808 processor that the ACFA-8 used was part of Motorola's 6800 family. It was more often used for embedded processing tasks and rarely in microcomputers.

ACFA-8 (1979, desktop)
Original Retail Price: $595 kit, $695 assembled
Base Configuration: 6808 CPU, 16K RAM (48K max), cassette interface, color TV video interface, integral keyboard, TTY/RS-232 port, training manual
Value: $50 to $100

Acorn Computers Ltd. (Cambridge, U.K.)

Acorn would become one of England's and Europe's leading PC makers. Its earliest computers in the late 1970s were single-board trainers and Eurocard-based rack-mount systems designed for industrial and scientific applications. The System 3, for example, was an enhanced version of Acorn's 6502-driven System 1 computer trainer with a floppy disk drive and greater memory capacity in a desktop enclosure. A larger System 4 offered 14 slots and dual floppy drives, and the System 5 improved on the performance of the earlier versions.

Those early systems led to Acorn's first consumer-oriented computer, the Atom. It had better graphics capability than many of its competitors, and the Atom enjoyed a good production run until 1983. The company eventually developed a library of business, productivity, and game software for the Atom. Few were sold in the U.S., and although they are collected domestically, Atoms are more popular today in Europe.

In the early 1980s, Acorn had a U.S. subsidiary based in Massachusetts that sold to the North American market. The first system it sold was Acorn's BBC Microcomputer. The BBC got its name from the British Broadcasting Corporation, from which Acorn won the right to produce the system in a bidding process. The BBC wanted a computer that participants in its TV-based Open University could use.

For a low-cost computer, the BBC was unusual in that it was a multi-processor system; you could have in essence two computers that share common resources running in the same box. Acorn sold the BBC in two versions: The Model A came standard with 16K RAM, while the Model B had 32K RAM, better text and graphics capabilities, and RS-423, parallel, RGB, and I/O ports. Clearly, the Model B is the more desirable machine, and some were sold configured for the North American market starting in 1983. Acorn briefly offered a Model B+ in 1984 shortly before launching the BBC Master. The Model B+ had 64K RAM and a double-density floppy disk drive. Brits referred to the BBC as the "Beeb."

The BBC Master replaced the BBC Model B in Acorn's line in 1986. The series also included the BBC Master Turbo, which had a second 65C02 running at 4MHz, and the floppy-disk-based BBC Master 512, which had an 80186 coprocessor and 512K RAM. A Master Compact had similar specification in a smaller design.

In 1983, Acorn decided it needed an entry-level system and introduced the Electron. It wasn't much computer in its base configuration, but owners could buy expansion upgrades to achieve a system comparable to the BBC Model B, on which the Electron's design was based. Fully expanded and well-preserved Electrons bring a premium price, especially in the U.K.

While Acorn was getting a foothold in the consumer computer market, it hadn't forgotten the business user. Its Business Computer series, introduced in 1984, included seven models plus a terminal configuration. The Model PA (Personal Assistant) was the base configuration. Models 100 and 110 had a Z80 coprocessor running CP/M. Models 200 and 210 used a 32016 coprocessor running Xenix, and Models 300 and 310 used an 80286 coprocessor running CP/M, MS-DOS, or PC-DOS. The Business Computer internals were based on the BBC Model B+, and examples are scarce today.

Perhaps what Acorn is best known for today is not its computers, but its ARM series of RISC-based microprocessors. Acorn skipped straight from the 8-bit 6502 processors to the 32-bit ARM 2 CPU, which it developed, with the Archimedes line. In the process, the company leapfrogged many of its competitors in terms of pure processing power. The two models in the series were the Archimedes 305 with 512K RAM standard and the Archimedes 310 with 1MB RAM standard. A professional-class Archimedes 400 series was much like the 300, but with two more expansion slots and Acorn's Econet networking capability built in. It also had hard drive options and greater memory capacity.

Acorn System 3 (1979, early micro)
Base Configuration: 6502 CPU, DOS in ROM, four Eurocard slots, 8K RAM (32K max), 5.25-inch floppy disk drive, video and keyboard interfaces, BASIC in ROM
Value: $50 to $150

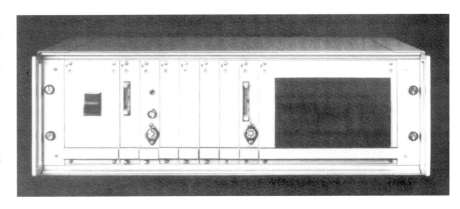

Acorn's System 3 ($50 to $150) was based on its System 1 computer trainer.

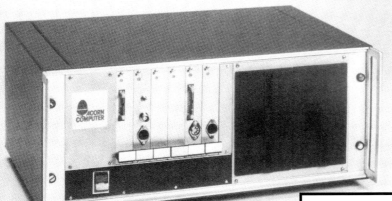

Acorn System 5 (1979, early micro)
Base Configuration: 2MHz 6502 CPU, seven Eurocard slots, 32K RAM, 5.25-inch floppy disk drive, video and keyboard interfaces **Important Options:** Versatile Interface card, Econet Interface card, ASCII keyboard, monochrome or color monitor, second floppy drive
Value: $65 to $175

The Acorn System 5 ($65 to $175) was designed for industrial and scientific applications.

Acorn Atom (1979, home computer)
Original Retail Price: £120 to £200 kit, £150 to £250 assembled
Base Configuration: 1MHz 6502A CPU; CUTS cassette routines; Eurocard slot; 2K RAM (40K max), 8K ROM (16K max); integral keyboard; serial, parallel, and PAL TV ports; Atom BASIC and assembler; manual; AC adapter; three-voice sound
Video: 256 x 192 graphics
Size/Weight: 15 x 9.5 x 2.5 inches
Important Options: DOS, 5.25-inch floppy disk drive, cassette recorder, color graphics card, word processor, GP-80 printer, Econet network interface
Value: $35 to $125

Acorn's Atom ($35 to $125) was one of the first home computers sold in the U.K.

Acorn BBC Microcomputer System Model A/Model B (Nov. 1981, desktop micro)
Original Retail Price: £299 to £399
Base Configuration: 2MHz 6502 CPU, MOS (Machine Operating System), extension bus; 16K or 32K RAM per CPU (64K max), 16K ROM, IEEE-488 and PAL TV interfaces, integral keyboard, BBC BASIC in ROM, user guide **Video:** 32-line x 40-column text, 320 x 256 graphics (Model A)/32-line x 80-column text, 640 x 256 graphics (Model B) **Size/Weight:** 16 x 13.5 x 2.5 inches **Important Options:** 6502 or Z80 coprocessor, CP/M 2.2, cassette recorder, 5.25-inch floppy disk drive, monochrome or color CRT display, game paddles, Videotext terminal, Econet network interface, voice synthesizer
Value: $25 to $80

> Acorn developed the BBC Microcomputer ($25 to $80) for use with a U.K. educational TV program.

Acorn BBC Master 128/BBC Master Turbo/BBC Master 512 (Jan. 1986, home computer)
Base Configuration: 2MHz 65C02 CPU, 4MHz 65C02 coprocessor (BBC Master Turbo)/8MHz 80186 coprocessor (BBC Master 512), ADFS, 128K RAM (512K max), 64K ROM, floppy disk drive (BBC Master 512)
Value: $15 to $60

Acorn Electron (Aug. 1983, home computer)
Base Configuration: 2MHz 6502 CPU; 32K RAM; 32K ROM; RGB, composite, and TV video ports; integral keyboard; game and cassette ports **Video:** 32-line x 80 column text, 640 x 256 graphics, eight colors **Important Options:** external 3.5-inch floppy disk drive, RS-232 and parallel interfaces, EPROM programmer
Value: $15 to $45

Acorn Business Computer Series
(1984, desktop)
Base Configuration: 2MHz 6502 CPU, operating system in ROM, 64K RAM (4MB max) **Important Options:** Z80, 32016, 80186, or 80286 coprocessor; CP/M, Xenix, MS-DOS, or PC-DOS; 10MB hard disk drive
Value: $20 to $55

Acorn Archimedes A300 Series
(1987, desktop)
Base Configuration: ARM 2 CPU, Arthur operating system and ADFS, two expansion slots, 512K RAM (1MB max), 512K ROM
Video: 640 x 512 graphics, 256 colors
Value: $15 to $45

The Acorn Archimedes A300 ($15 to $45) was one of a few micros to use a RISC processor. *Reused with permission CMP Media LLC, Byte.com (Byte Magazine), Manhasset NY. All rights reserved.*

Actrix Computer Corp. (see "Access Matrix Corp.")

Advanced Logic Research (ALR) (Irvine, California)

ALR's business strategy was to be the first to market with the latest and fastest possible PC-compatible designs. It often succeeded, and in July 1986 the Access 386 was the first 80386-based PC AT compatible sold, beating even IBM. In November, ALR upgraded the Access 386 to support the 80386's virtual 86 mode, which allowed for multitasking of MS-DOS applications. Despite being a milestone computer, the Access 386 has little recognition as a collectible.

ALR Access 386 (July 1986, desktop PC)
Base Configuration: 80386 CPU, MS-DOS, eight ISA slots, 512K RAM (2MB max), 5.25-inch floppy disk drive, 42MB to 80MB hard disk drive, keyboard/keypad, two serial and two parallel ports
Value: $5 to $25

Albert Computers Inc. (Thousand Oaks, California)

The Albert was unusual looking for an Apple IIe clone. It was a two-piece design with what the company called "stereo" styling. The company hedged its bets by offering a Z80 option for anyone wishing to use CP/M, and later sold multi-processor systems that could run AppleDOS, CP/M, or MS-DOS.

The company later developed other Albert models. The Albert Express appears similar to the original model. The Albert Executive and Alfred Professional Executive (Profex) offered more expansion options. A portable version of the Profex was also available, and the Albert Pup was a low-cost, entry-level model.

Albert Computers Albert
(April 1983, Apple II-class desktop)
Original Retail Price: $1,595
Base Configuration: 6502 CPU; AppleDOS 3.3 and Coyotesoft OS; 64K RAM (192K max); five Apple-compatible expansion slots; RGB video port; keyboard; RS-232, RS-422/432, parallel, microphone, and game ports, application suite **Video:** 24-line x 40-column text, 280 x 192 graphics, 16 colors **Important Options:** Z80 coprocessor, joysticks, 12-inch monitor
Value: $30 to $65

Alpha Digital Systems (ADS) (Boone, North Carolina)

Alpha Digital Systems (ADS) Alpha Z-80
(1977, early micro)
Original Retail Price: $495
Base Configuration: Z80 CPU, 12 S-100 slots, power supply
Important Options: 22-slot chassis
Value: $50 to $150

Alpha Microsystems (Santa Ana, California)

The AM100 was an early 16-bit microcomputer with a CPU based on the design of, but not compatible with, the DEC LSI-11. It was highly expandable and could be used in multi-user environments with enough memory and disk storage. The company is still in business as Optimal Systems Services, and it proudly claims the AM100 as the world's first multi-user, multitasking microcomputer.

Alpha Microsystems AM100 (early micro)
Base Configuration: WD16 CPU, S-100 bus, 16K RAM
Important Options: 8-inch floppy disk drive, hard disk drive, monochrome monitor
Value: $75 to $200

Ampere Inc. (Tokyo, Japan)

Ampere's WS-1 laptop was an oddball, but a cute oddball. When closed, its clamshell design resembled the wing of an airplane. Its case was designed by Kumeo Tamura, who also designed the Datsun 280Z sports car. The 68000 CPU and VMEbus were unusual for a laptop at the time, and the WS-1 featured an obscure multitasking operating system called BIG.DOS. Instead of bundling

The Albert ($30 to $65) Apple-compatible with the optional touch tablet and monitor.

BASIC as the standard programming language, the WS-1 has APL.68000, a variant of APL. The machine was called the BIG.APL in early references. The system was sold in the U.S. through Work Space Computer of Torrance, California. Its appealing design and unusual configuration make the WS-1 an interesting collectible. It will display well, but the parts, add-ons, software, or documentation needed to keep it working will be hard to find.

Ampere WS-1 (Nov. 1985, laptop)
Original Retail Price: $1,995 to $2,995
Base Configuration: 8MHz HD68000 CPU; BIG.DOS; VMEbus slot; 64K RAM (512K max); 128K ROM; integral microcassette drive; monochrome LCD; integral keyboard; two RS-232C, parallel, and microphone/speaker ports; APL.68000; application suite, AC adapter, modem, battery pack **Video:** 25-line x 80-column text, 480 x 128 graphics
Size/Weight: 13 x 11 x 3.6 inches, 9 lbs. **Important Options:** external dual 3.5-inch floppy disk drives
Value: $75 to $175

The Ampere WS-1 ($75 to $175) had the same designer as the Datsun 280Z sportscar.

Amstrad Consumer Electronics plc. (Essex, U.K.)

Amstrad was one of the world's leading PC manufacturers in the 1980s, having sold 1.7 million computers in 1986 alone. Most of the systems were sold in Europe and Asia, although the company had a sales organization, Amstrad Inc., in Irvine, Texas. Amstrad PCs were well designed and well-made, and would be a low-cost addition to your collection.

The company's CPC series was often sold under different brands from country to country in Europe. German models, for example, sold under the Schneider name. Amstrad sold a 72K version of the system as the CPC 472 in Spain. Nearly two million CPC 464s were sold, mostly in Europe, until its last year of production in 1990.

Although the 3-inch disks used in the CPC 664 model were double-sided, the drive could read only one side. You had to manually flip the disk to read the other side. Amstrad also sold the CPC 6128, which was identical to the CPC 664 but had 128K RAM and updated system software in ROM.

The 464 Plus featured a redesigned motherboard over the CPC464 that made use of ASICs to reduce chip count. It also had improved graphics. The Amstrad 6128 Plus was identical to the 464 Plus, but with 128K RAM and a 3-inch floppy disk drive in place of the cassette recorder.

In 1985, Amstrad introduced the PcW8256 and PcW8512. Both PcW series were also referred to as the Joyce computer, after the secretary of the company, and were sold with printers. The printers were designed to be used only with the PcW line, and in some cases were not even interchangeable within the product line. The PcW8512 had 512K and two floppy drives. Finding CP/M software on the 3-inch media was difficult and is more so now.

Although its internal design was similar to that of the PcW8256/PcW8512, the PcW9256/PcW9512 had a different enclosure with the drive bays positioned under the monitor rather than to the right. The 82-key keyboard was also different. The PcW256 was released after the PcW9512; it had 256K RAM and only one proprietary printer port, as Amstrad was trying to lower the cost of the system. Because the 3-inch floppy drives were no longer available, Amstrad was forced to switch to 3.5-inch drives with the PcW9256. Amstrad was one of the last CP/M holdouts, and the PcW16 and PcW10 machines introduced in the 1990s represented the last of the CP/M line.

Amstrad launched its first PC-compatible desktop, the PC 1512, in 1986. A PC 1640 followed it in 1987 and offered 640K of standard memory, a hard disk drive, and EGA capability. The Amstrad PC-20 was the same system as the Sinclair PC-200 with its own case and minus the capability to use a TV as a monitor.

The company's first portables, the PPC512/640 series, had an unusual design. Its full-size keyboard and keypad unfolds from the top of the unit. Then, a small LCD folds up. You can find PPC512/PPC640s moderately priced today, but pristine examples can fetch over $100, particularly in the U.K.

Amstrad CPC 464 (1984, home computer)
Base Configuration: 3.3MHz Z80A CPU, AMSDOS or CP/M, expansion bus, 64K RAM, 32K ROM, integral cassette recorder, integral keyboard/keypad, parallel and game ports, Locomotive BASIC in ROM, three-channel sound **Video:** 25-line x 80-column text, 640 x 200 graphics, 16 colors
Value: $12 to $35

Amstrad CPC 664/CPC 6128 (late 1985, home computer)
Base Configuration: 3.3MHz Z80A CPU, AMSDOS in ROM, CP/M 2.2 on disk, expansion bus, 64K RAM (128K max), 48K ROM, 3-inch floppy disk drive, parallel and game ports, Locomotive BASIC in ROM, three-channel sound **Video:** 25-line x 80-column text, 640 x 200 graphics, 16 colors
Value: $15 to $40

Amstrad 464 Plus/6128 Plus (home computer)
Base Configuration: 3.3MHz Z80A CPU; AMSDOS or CP/M 3.0; ROM cartridge slot; expansion slot; 64K RAM (128K max); integral cassette recorder (CPC 464 Plus)/ 3-inch floppy disk drive (CPC 6128 Plus); integral keyboard; parallel, three game, video, and light gun ports; Locomotive BASIC in ROM **Video:** 32 colors
Value: $12 to $38

Amstrad PcW8256/PcW8512 (Sept. 1985, desktop)
Original Retail Price: £399
Base Configuration: 3.4MHz Z80A CPU, CP/M Plus, external expansion bus, 256K RAM (512K max), 48K ROM, 3-inch floppy disk drive, integral monochrome CRT display, keyboard/keypad, proprietary printer port, LocoScript word processor, Mallard BASIC CP/M and BASIC manuals, dot-matrix printer **Video:** 32-line x 90-column text, 720 x 256 graphics
Value: $15 to $35

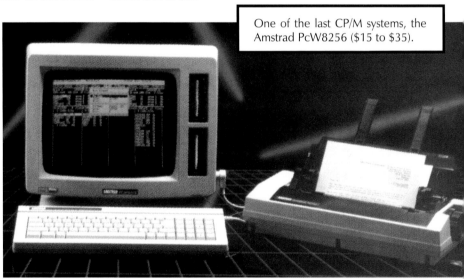

One of the last CP/M systems, the Amstrad PcW8256 ($15 to $35).

Amstrad PcW9256/PcW9512
(1987 [PcW0512]/1991 [PcW9256], desktop)
Base Configuration: 3.4MHz Z80A CPU, CP/M Plus, external expansion bus, 256K RAM (512K max), 3.5-inch floppy disk drive (PcW9256)/ 3-inch floppy disk drive (PcW9512), integral 14-inch monochrome CRT, keyboard/keypad, parallel and proprietary printer ports, LocoScript word processor, Mallard BASIC, dot-matrix printer (PcW9256)/daisy-wheel printer (PcW9512) **Video:** 32-line x 90-column text, 720 x 256 graphics
Value: $10 to $35

Amstrad PC 1512/PC 1640
(Sept. 1986 [PC 1512]/June 1987 [PC1640], desktop PC)
Original Retail Price: $799 to $1,499
Base Configuration: 8MHz 8086 CPU; MS-DOS 3.2 or DR-DOS with GEM; three ISA slots; 512K RAM (640K max); 5.25-inch floppy disk drive; 20MB hard disk drive (PC 1640), monochrome or RGB monitor; RS-232C, parallel, and game ports; word processor; mouse; user manual **Video:** CGA, EGA (PC 1640) **Important Options:** second floppy disk drive, printer
Value: $5 to $20

The Amstrad PC 1512 ($5 to $20) sold well in Europe.

Amstrad PC-20 (desktop PC)
Base Configuration: 8086 CPU, 512K RAM, 16K ROM, integral keyboard/keypad **Video:** MDA, 16 colors
Value: $7 to $22

Amstrad PPC512/PPC640 (Nov. 1987, transportable PC)
Original Retail Price: $799 (PPC512)/ $999 (PPC640)
Base Configuration: 8MHz V-30; MS-DOS 3.3; external expansion bus; 512K RAM (PPC512)/640K RAM (PPC640); 3.5-inch floppy disk drive; 9-inch monochrome LCD; keyboard/keypad; RS-232, parallel, and CGA video ports; AC adapter; battery pack; modem (PPC640) **Video:** CGA, MDA **Size/Weight:** 11.75 lbs. **Important Options:** dual 3.5-inch floppy disk drives, 20MB hard disk drive
Value: $30 to $125

APF Imagination Machine II (1980, home computer)
Original Retail Price: $599
Base Configuration: 6800 CPU, 9K RAM, 14K ROM, integral cassette drive, RF modulator, integral keyboard, RS-232C port, two integral game controllers with joysticks, BASIC, sound synthesizer **Video:** 16-line x 32-column text, 256 x 192 graphics, eight colors **Important Options:** Building Block expansion unit, external 5.25-inch floppy disk drive, modem
Value: $75 to $250

The distinctive PPC640 portable ($30 to $125) is popular with collectors today, especially in Europe.

APF Electronics Inc. (New York, New York)

Before home computers became popular, many electronics manufacturers produced processor-based game consoles that attached to a TV. APF was one of those manufacturers.

APF's Imagination Machine II was part game console, part home computer. In fact, the original Imagination Machine was a keyboard upgrade to the company's MP1000 game console. Much of the available software was either game-oriented or educational. The Building Block expansion unit provided a means to connect a printer, modem, or floppy disk drive. It also had a slot for an additional RAM cartridge.

The company produced an earlier computer, the PeCos (for Personal Computer) that used a proprietary programming language. It had a keyboard and two cassette recorder built into a wood-sided cabinet.

The only computer with color, sound, user programmability and expandability at $599.

An early home computer, the APF Imagination Machine II ($75 to $250) has a TV game console heritage.

Apple Computer Inc. (Cupertino, California)

If you're reading this book, you've probably already heard the story of Apple: Two guys named Jobs and Wozniak designed a complete, inexpensive microcomputer kit in a Los Altos, California, garage. That computer, the Apple I, created a small sensation when demonstrated at a Homebrew Computer Club meeting in 1975. The people who requested schematics at that meeting might be considered the first customers of Apple Computer, even though the company would not officially form until April 1976. Apple would go on to be one of the most successful microcomputer companies ever.

Only 200 Apple I systems were built by Apple, but it formed the basis for the hugely popular Apple II line. (I assume that some were built by hobbyists from schematics, but no known examples exist.) What made the Apple I interesting to hobbyists was its simplicity (fewer than 40 chips on the motherboard), its ability to run BASIC, and the fact that it was a complete, inexpensive computer on a single board. If a Holy Grail of vintage computing exists, the Apple I is it. The last one to publicly change hands sold for $25,000 at an auction held at the Vintage Computer Festival in 2000—a price that some Apple experts feel is excessive. That unit sold with a set of manuals, marketing literature, BASIC on cassette, and other collateral material that influenced its price. Sellam Ismail, who hosted the VCF Apple I auction, has tracked down 25 examples worldwide.

The earliest Apple IIs had gold ceramic Mostek memory chips and a white ceramic keyboard ROM. For fiscal 1978, Apple sold only 7,600 of the original Apple II computers and 35,100 more in 1979. Things picked up after that, as sales for all Apple II series systems reached 2 million in November 1984. In 1981, Apple created the Family System, an Apple II Plus with a floppy disk drive, joysticks, and a set of games and home productivity software. The Apple II Plus had an updated ROM with an enhanced Applesoft BASIC and system software.

The Apple IIe (for "enhanced") offered both upper- and lower-case characters and an expanded keyboard. Apple called the IIe the most extensive upgrade of the II line at the time. (There had been 13 major and minor revisions up to that point.) The circuitry was redesigned to use a quarter of the components found in the II Plus. In early 1987, Apple released a modest update of the IIe that featured an expanded keyboard with keypad and the same platinum-colored case as other Apple systems.

The Apple II, Apple II Plus, and Apple IIe designs were widely copied by other manufacturers. Some like the Franklin Ace series and the Video Technology Laser 128 systems are well known and collectible. Others are more obscure and include the Dick Smith Cat, Eurocon II, Microdigital TK3000 IIe, Orange, and Unitron U2200. All but the Laser 128 used illegally copied Apple system ROMs. Video Technology reverse-engineered the ROMs and was spared the legal trouble other clone makers faced.

Some people collect Apple clones, but their value is limited. Asian factories churned out clones under many brands with a form factor similar to the Apple systems. Most were poorly made and have little collector value. Better-made systems such as the Micro II, Microcom, and Syscom brands are valued in the $10 to $35 on average. Some clones including the CHE-1, Basis 108, and Spartan feature interesting designs or offer technical improvements over the Apple computers. These are valued slightly higher than other Apple II clones.

The Apple IIc was introduced as a "transportable" computer. Although small and with a handle, the IIc does not have as standard equipment an LCD screen usually associated with portable computers. It requires a separate CRT display or TV. Apple did offer an optional 24-line by 80-column LCD in late 1984, however. The IIc was based on the Snow White design, and Apple enlisted the famed frogdesign studio to help create it. In September 1986, Apple introduced an enhanced version of the IIc that could accept up to 1MB of additional RAM. Owners of earlier IIcs could upgrade their systems to take advantage of the extra memory. An Apple IIc+ model later offered a 3.5-inch floppy drive, a faster processor, and an internal power supply.

The Apple IIGS was the last hurrah for the Apple II line, and it offered much greater performance and more expansion options. It was compatible with nearly all Apple IIe software and hardware, and offered a graphical interface similar to the Mac's. A synthesizer chip was built into the system for more sophisticated sound capabilities. Two new graphics modes were available: 640 x 200 and 320 x 200 pixels, both with a palette of 4,096 colors. A limited run Woz Edition Apple IIGS will bring a premium price today, especially with its original authenticity papers. Apple discontinued the last of the II line in December 1992, but continued to sell the Apple IIe into 1993.

As the II line was establishing itself, Apple decided that it needed a more business-oriented offering: The Apple III. It was designed for and marketed to professionals and small businesses, and Apple supported it with a line of business applications and programming tools. It could, however, run most Apple II software in an emulation mode. Apple improved Apple III performance and reliability in late 1981. In 1983, Apple offered an Apple III Business System configuration that included the Monitor III, ProFile 5MB hard disk drive, 256K of RAM, and a software suite for $5,330. The most significant improvement that the Apple III Plus made over the III is the addition of an interlace video mode, which doubled screen resolution.

The Apple III did not sell as well as the company had hoped, and in 1983 Apple came out with a radically different (and more expensive) computer, the Lisa, aimed at the business market. Officially, Apple claimed that "Lisa" is an acronym that stands for Local Integrated Software Architecture. Legend has it, though, that the computer was named after either Steve Jobs's daughter or the daughter of one of the engineers.

The original Lisa, referred to as the Lisa 1 by collectors, was technologically innovative, but a commercial failure for Apple. It popularized the concept of the GUI (graphical user interface) and could perform pre-emptive multitasking, meaning it could run multiple programs at once. However, it was overpriced and lacked adequate software and hardware support. Apple was able to make lemonade out of lemons by using Lisa technology to develop the Macintosh, one of the most successful microcomputers ever made.

Faced with resistance to the Lisa 1's price, Apple unbundled the six business applications from the system in September 1983 and dropped the price by $3,000 to $6,995. Lisa 1s, especially unmodified early models, are highly sought after today. Finding complete working units is difficult. For example, the original Twiggy floppy disk drives were notoriously unreliable and were often replaced with a single 3.5-inch Sony drive. A Lisa with working Twiggy floppy drives will command a premium.

Launched with the Macintosh, the Lisa 2 came in three versions: The Lisa 2, Lisa 2/5, and Lisa 2/10. The 2/5 came with an external ProFile hard disk drive, and the 2/10 had an internal 10 MB hard disk drive. In early 1985, Apple renamed the Lisa 2/10 the Macintosh XL, a move that marked the end of the Lisa line. The Mac XL itself was discontinued in April 1985. Apple referred to the Lisa 2 and Macintosh series as Apple 32 SuperMicros.

In 1984, Apple introduced the Macintosh series, which would eventually acquire a cult following. The Mac vs. PC religious wars persist to this day, started no doubt by the infamous "1984" TV ad that launched the Macintosh. Many current and former Mac users hold the original model in great reverence. Despite capturing the public's attention, Mac sales were slow at first.

In some ways, the original Macintosh is the prototypical collectible microcomputer. Although much of the technology used in the Mac, including its GUI, was originally developed for the Lisa, it is a milestone system in every sense of the word. Most important, the Mac developed a devoted following—sometimes obsessively so. Early models are hard to come by, especially in good unaltered condition. The cases are often discolored, cracked, or damaged by prying tools used for repairs or upgrades. The keyboard or mouse is usually missing, as are the system software disks and manuals. Pristine, complete examples are uncommon and command a high price. Old Macs are in high demand in Japan, where prices can reach two or three times the values listed here.

The Mac 512K was a modest upgrade to the original model. Mac 128K systems were labeled as such after the 512K was introduced. The 512K Enhanced Mac replaced the 512K in April 1986. It had a double-density disk drive and improved system ROMs. Many original Macs were upgraded with 512K motherboards, and will not be valued as highly.

Apple's next major Mac revision was the Plus, which had a SCSI port and could accommodate up to 4MB RAM. Apple sold upgrade kits (essentially a replacement motherboard) for previous compact Mac models to bring them up to the Mac Plus level. Mac XL and Lisa 1 owners could trade in their systems for a Mac Plus. Apple also unbundled the MacWrite and MacPaint applications for the Plus and 512K Enhanced models, selling them separately for $125 each. The Plus was sold for four years and is one of the most common models found today.

The SE extended the life span of the original compact Mac design through expandability and better performance, especially in hard disk access times. The SE/30 then boosted performance even further, claiming as much as four times the speed of the Mac SE. The SE stands for System Expansion. The SE and SE/30 used the same design as the Macintosh Plus, but provided a slot to extend the system and an additional bay for a disk drive. SE owners could upgrade their systems to a Mac SE/30 with a kit (another motherboard replacement) from Apple. A platinum case replaced the cream color of older Macs, but it is just as prone to discoloration. The SE and SE/30 were well supported by third-party communications, graphics, and other hardware manufacturers.

The Macintosh II revitalized the Macintosh line with a more powerful CPU, six expansion slots, and color video. With greater on-board memory capacity, the Mac II could be beefed up for graphics-intensive applications such as desktop publishing or computer-aided design. It's not unusual to see Mac II series systems still in business use today. A number of third-party vendors produced accelerator boards—essentially processor upgrades—for the Mac II line, and they are desirable add-ons for enthusiasts today. In general, the more working expansion boards you find in an old Mac II, the better.

A lot of people thought that the Mac IIci and IIfx were overpriced when new, but everybody wanted one. The IIci boasted a 55 percent performance boost over its predecessors and could use higher capacity memory chips for a maximum 32MB of RAM. Today, you can get a good working unit with a monitor for well under $100—a deal especially considering that these machines are compatible enough and powerful enough for most of your everyday computing needs.

The Macintosh IIfx provided a twofold increase in performance over the IIci. Apple introduced a number of high-end graphics options for the Macintosh at the same time as the IIfx. The most powerful was the Macintosh Display Card 8*24 GC, which offered high-speed graphics and 24-bit color. Values for the IIfx are higher than for some of its contemporary Mac models because it remains a productive system today, especially if it contains processor and graphics upgrades.

Apple didn't have a true portable until the Macintosh Portable in 1989. Smaller than most luggables but still too big to be a laptop, the Portable was a "hate it" or "love it" system. Detractors said it was too expensive, big, and heavy. The use of a lead acid battery—an unusual choice—added heft and bulk to the system, but provided great battery life of between five and ten hours. Be careful to check the battery compartment when purchasing a Mac Portable that has been unused in a long time. The lead acid battery might have leaked and damaged the unit. Also, the optional keypad took the place of the trackball. Later models had a backlit LCD and are the more desirable systems.

Fans of the Portable liked the fact that it sacrificed little functional-

ity over the desktop Mac models. In fact, the Mac Portable is a comfortable and capable machine, but Apple would not have a successful portable until it launched its PowerBook line in 1991.

Where the Portable faced mixed reviews, the Macintosh Powerbook 100 was an instant hit. The well-known Mac interface in a notebook form factor was a strong enough combination to convert more than a few PC users. Perhaps because it is not very old, the original Powerbook is overlooked as a collectible and a good value at present.

Apple I (1976, early micro)
Original Retail Price: $666.66
Base Configuration: 6502 CPU, 8K RAM, BASIC, power supply **Size/Weight:** 6 x 8 inches (motherboard) **Important Options:** keyboard, monochrome monitor, dual transformers
Value: $12,500 to $25,000

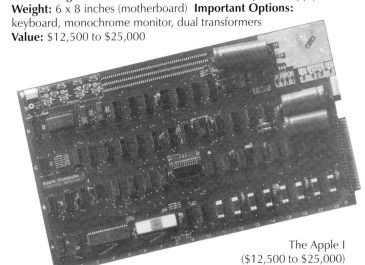

The Apple I ($12,500 to $25,000) was a complete computer on one system board, but you had to supply your own enclosure. *Reused with permission CMP Media LLC, Byte.com (Byte Magazine), Manhasset NY. All rights reserved.*

Apple II/Apple II Plus (June 1977 [Apple II]/June 1979 [Apple II Plus], Apple II-class desktop)
Original Retail Price: $1,298 to $2,638 (Apple II)/$1,330 (Apple II Plus)
Base Configuration: 1MHz 6502 CPU, eight expansion slots, 16K RAM (48K max), 8K ROM (12K max), composite video port, integral keyboard, game and cassette ports, BASIC (Apple II Plus) **Video:** 24-line x 40-column text, 280 x 192 graphics, 15 colors **Important Options:** lowercase upgrade, color monitor, external 5.25-inch floppy disk drive, serial interface, Silentype printer, game controllers, modem
Value: $75 to $250 (Apple II)/ $10 to $75 (Apple II Plus)

This photo from an Apple brochure shows an Apple II Plus ($10 to $75) with an Apple III monitor.

Apple IIe (Jan. 1983, Apple II-class desktop)
Original Retail Price: $1,395 to $1,995
Base Configuration: 6502A CPU, seven expansion slots, 64K RAM (128K max), 16K ROM, integral keyboard, Applesoft BASIC in ROM, owner's manual
Video: 40-column text, 280 x 192 graphics **Important Options:** ProDOS, external 5.25-inch floppy disk drive, 80-column card, 12-inch Apple II monochrome monitor, mouse
Value: $2 to $45

The Apple IIe ($2 to $45), in all its iterations, was the best-selling Apple II. This is one of the last revisions as it has a keypad.

Apple IIc (April 1984, Apple II-class desktop)
Original Retail Price: $1,295
Base Configuration: 1.02MHz 65C02 CPU; ProDOS; 128K (1.1MB max); 16K ROM (32K max); 5.25-inch floppy disk drive; integral keyboard; two serial, RCA video, headphone, mouse, and game ports; owner's manual on disk; AC adapter; setup and system utilities manuals
Video: 24-line x 80-column text, 560 x 192 graphics, 16 colors **Size/Weight:** 2.5 x 12 x 11.5 inches, 7.5 lbs. **Important Options:** external floppy disk drive; 9-inch monochrome, composite, or RGB monitor; RF modulator; LCD; mouse; AppleWorks 2.0; Scribe or ImageWriter printer; joysticks; modem; carrying case
Value: $10 to $50

The Apple IIc ($10 to $50) could be configured as a portable or a desktop (shown with the optional monitor) computer.

Apple IIGS (Sept. 1986, Apple II-class desktop)
Original Retail Price: $999
Base Configuration: 2.8MHz 65C816; ProDOS 16; seven slots; 256K RAM (8MB max); 128K ROM (1MB max); 5.25-inch floppy disk drive; NTSC, composite, and RGB video interfaces; keyboard/keypad; SmartPort; two serial and one game port; mouse; setup guide; owner's, AppleSoft BASIC, and system disk manuals; ProDOS training disk
Video: 640 x 200 graphics, 16 colors **Important Options:** LaserWriter or ImageWriter printer
Value: $10 to $75

Last of the Apple II line, the Apple IIGS ($10 to $75) can still be found in use in homes and schools today.

Apple III/Apple III Plus

(May 1980 [Apple III]/Dec. 1983 [Apple III Plus], desktop)
Original Retail Price: $4,340 to $7,800 (Apple III)/
$2,995 (Apple III Plus)
Base Configuration: 1.8MHz 6502A CPU; Sophisticated Operating System (SOS); four slots; 128K RAM (256K max); 4K ROM; 5.25-inch floppy disk drives; NTSC video interface; integral keyboard/keypad; RS-232C, printer, and two game ports; Apple II emulation and utilities disks; Business BASIC; Pascal; SOS and owner's manuals   **Video:** 24-line x 80-character text, 560 x 192 graphics, 16 colors   **Important Options:** external 5.25-inch floppy disk drive, 5MB ProFile hard disk drive, Monitor III monitor, Silentype printer, Apple Daisy-Wheel printer (Apple III Plus)
Value: $30 to $300

Not a hot seller when new, the Apple III ($30 to $300) is now popular with collectors (Monitor III shown here was an option). Clean, complete systems are hard to find.

Apple's original Lisa ($750 to $3,000), shown with the optional ProFile hard drive unit, set the technological and usability groundwork for the Macintosh.

Apple Lisa (Jan. 1983, desktop)
Original Retail Price: $9,995
Base Configuration: 68000 CPU, three slots, 1MB RAM, two 5.25-inch floppy disk drives ("Twiggy" drives), integral 12-inch monochrome monitor, keyboard/keypad, mouse, two serial and one parallel port, application suite
Video: 40-line x 132-column text, 720 x 364 graphics
Important Options: CP/M or Xenix, external 5MB ProFile hard disk drive, dot-matrix or daisy-wheel printer
Value: $750 to $3,000

Apple Lisa 2/Macintosh XL (Jan. 1984, desktop)
Original Retail Price: $3,495 to $5,495
Base Configuration: 5MHz 68000 CPU, three AppleBus slots, 512K RAM (1MB max), 3.5-inch floppy disk drive, integral 12-inch monochrome CRT, keyboard/keypad, mouse, two serial and one parallel port   **Video:** 720 x 364 graphics   **Size/Weight:** 13.8 x 18.7 x 15.2, 48 lbs.
Important Options:
CP/M or Xenix, 5MB or 10MB ProFile hard disk drive, two-port parallel interface, Lisa 7/7 application suite
Value: $50 to $500

The Apple Lisa 2/ Macintosh XL (left, $50 to $500) was discontinued shortly after the introduction of the Apple Macintosh (right, $35 to $400).

Apple Macintosh/Macintosh 512K

(Jan. 1984 [Macintosh]/Sept. 1984 [Macintosh 512K], desktop)
Original Retail Price: $2,495 (Macintosh)/
$3,195 (Macintosh 512K)
Base Configuration: 7.83MHz 68000 CPU, system software in ROM, 128K RAM (512K max) and 64K ROM, 3.5-inch floppy disk drive, integral 9-inch monochrome CRT, keyboard, mouse, two RS-232C/RS-422 ports, guided tour on disk, owner's manual
Video: 512 x 342 graphics **Size/Weight:** 9.75 x 9.75 x 13.5 inches, 22.7 lbs. **Important Options:** external 3.5-inch floppy disk drive, keypad, ImageWriter printer, carrying case, modem
Value: $50 to $700 (Macintosh)/$20 to $75 (Macintosh 512K)

The Apple Macintosh ($50 to $700) with all the originally offered options.

Apple Macintosh Plus (Jan. 1986, desktop)

Original Retail Price: $2,599 to $4,098
Base Configuration: 7.83MHz 68000 CPU, Macintosh System Software, 1MB RAM (4MB max), 3.5-inch floppy disk drive, integral monochrome CRT display, keyboard/keypad, mouse, SCSI port
Video: 512 x 342 graphics **Size/Weight:** 13.5 x 9.5 x 11 inches, 16.5 lbs. **Important Options:** 20MB hard disk drive, ImageWriter or LaserWriter printer
Value: $5 to $20

Apple Macintosh SE/Macintosh SE/30

(March 1987 [SE]/Jan. 1989 [SE/30], desktop)
Original Retail Price: $2,898 to $3,698 (SE)/$4,369 to $6,569 (SE/30)
Base Configuration (SE): 68000 CPU; System Software; SE-Bus slot; 1MB RAM (4MB max), 256K ROM; one or two 3.5-inch floppy disk drives; keyboard/keypad; SCSI, ADB, two RS-422, and sound ports
Base Configuration (SE/30): 16MHz 68030 CPU, System Software 6.0.3, 030 Direct Slot, 1MB RAM (8MB max), 3.5-inch floppy disk drive, keyboard/keypad, SCSI port, AppleTalk and HyperCard software **Video:** 512 x 342 graphics **Size/Weight:** 13.6 x 9.69 x 10.9 inches **Important Options:** 20MB hard disk drive (SE), 40MB or 80MB hard disk drive (SE/30)
Value: $5 to $25 (SE)/$12 to $50 (SE/30)

Three forms of the Apple Macintosh, from left to right: the Macintosh Plus ($5 to $20), the Macintosh II ($15 to $55), and the Macintosh SE ($5 to $25).

Apple Macintosh II (May 1987, desktop)
Original Retail Price: $3,898 to $5,498
Base Configuration: 16MHz 68020; System Software with Multifinder; six NuBus slots; 1MB RAM (8MB max); 3.5-inch floppy disk drive; keyboard/keypad; SCSI, two RS-422, sound, and ADB ports; AppleTalk and HyperCard software **Video:** 640 x 480 graphics, eight colors **Size/Weight:** 5.5 x 18.7 x 14.5 inches, 24 lbs. **Important Options:** A/UX, 40MB hard disk drive, graphics upgrade, 12-inch monochrome or 13-inch RGB monitor, laser printer
Value: $15 to $55

Apple Macintosh IIx (Sept. 1988, desktop)
Original Retail Price: $9,300
Base Configuration: 16MHz 68030 CPU, System Software 6.0.2, six NuBus slots, 1MB RAM, 3.5-inch floppy disk drive **Size/Weight:** 5.5 x 18.7 x 14.5 inches, 24 lbs.
Value: $20 to $65

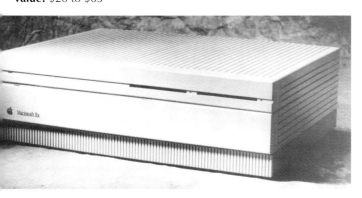

The speedy and expandable Apple Macintosh IIx ($20 to $65).

Apple Macintosh IIcx (March 1989, desktop)
Original Retail Price: $4,669 to $7,552
Base Configuration: 16MHz 68030 CPU; System Software 6.0.3; three NuBus slots; 1MB RAM (8MB max), 256K ROM; 3.5-inch floppy disk drive, keyboard/keypad; SCSI, two RS-232/422, two ADB, and sound ports; AppleTalk and HyperCard software **Video:** 640 x 480 graphics, eight colors **Size/Weight:** 5.5 x 11.9 x 14.4 inches, 14 lbs. **Important Options:** A/UX, 40MB or 80MB hard disk drive, graphics upgrade, 12-inch monochrome or 13-inch RGB monitor, laser printer
Value: $10 to $45

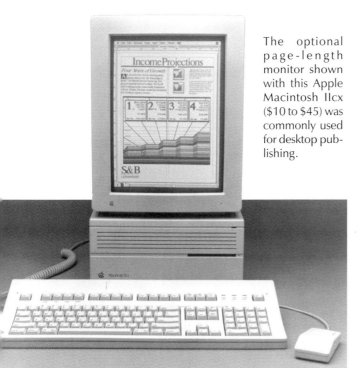

The optional page-length monitor shown with this Apple Macintosh IIcx ($10 to $45) was commonly used for desktop publishing.

Apple Macintosh IIci (Sept. 1989, desktop)
Original Retail Price: $6,269 to $9,152
Base Configuration: 25MHz 68030 CPU; System Software 6.0.4; three NuBus slots; 1MB RAM (32MB max); 512K ROM; 3.5-inch floppy disk drive; RGB or monochrome monitor; keyboard/keypad; mouse; SCSI port; AppleTalk and HyperCard software **Video:** 640 x 480 graphics, 256 colors **Size/Weight:** 5.5 x 11.9 x 14.5 inches, 16 lbs. **Important Options:** A/UX, 40MB or 80MB hard disk drive, LaserWriter printer
Value: $10 to $75

The Apple Macintosh IIci ($10 to $75).

Apple Macintosh IIfx (March 1990, desktop)
Original Retail Price: $8,969 to $10,969
Base Configuration: 40MHz 68030 CPU; System Software 6.0.5; six NuBus slots; Processor Direct Slot; 4MB RAM (128MB max); 3.5-inch floppy disk drive; keyboard/keypad; SCSI and ADB ports; AppleTalk and HyperCard software **Size/Weight:** 5.5 x 18.7 x 14.5 inches, 24 lbs. **Important Options:** A/UX, 80MB to 160MB hard disk drive, Macintosh Display Card 8*24 GC, LaserWriter printer
Value: $35 to $150

The powerful Apple IIfx ($35 to $150) is still productive by today's computing standards.

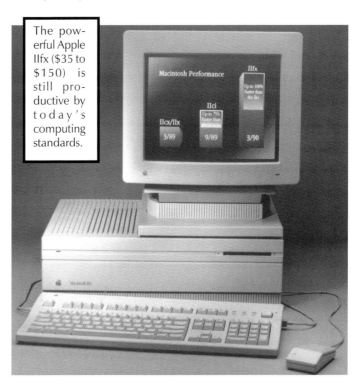

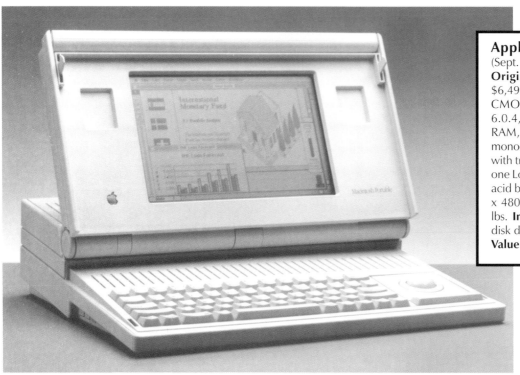

Apple Macintosh Portable
(Sept. 1989, transportable)
Original Retail Price: $5,799 to $6,499 **Base Configuration:** 16MHz CMOS 68000, System Software 6.0.4, Processor Direct Slot, 1MB RAM, 3.5-inch floppy disk drive, monochrome LCD, integral keyboard with trackball, mouse, two serial and one LocalTalk port, HyperCard, lead-acid battery, AC adapter **Video:** 640 x 480 graphics **Size/Weight:** 15.7 lbs. **Important Options:** 40MB hard disk drive, keypad, modem **Value:** $35 to $125

The Apple Macintosh Portable ($35 to $125) was big for a portable, but nearly as powerful as its desktop relatives.

Apple Macintosh Powerbook 100 (1991, notebook)

Original Retail Price: $2,500 **Base Configuration:** 16MHz 68000 CPU, MacOS, 4MB RAM (8MB max), 256K ROM, external 3.5-inch floppy disk drive, 20MB hard disk drive, 9-inch monochrome LCD, integral keyboard and trackball, lead-acid battery, AC adapter **Size/Weight:** 1.8 x 11 x 8.5 inches, 5.1 lbs. **Important Options:** 40- or 80MB hard disk drive, internal modem **Value:** $25 to $75

Applied Computer Techniques (ACT) Ltd. (Birmingham, U.K.)

ACT was a leading European computer manufacturer that started in 1965 with a computer time-share service. It sold the Victor 9000 in Europe as the ACT Sirius starting in 1982, but did not build its own computer until the Apricot, which it sold through its U.S. subsidiary, ACT North America. Later, the U.S. arm would become simply Apricot Inc.

The Apricot had an odd configuration. Is it a portable or a desktop PC? The Apricot folds up and can be carried by a handle, and you could use the system without a monitor by relying on the two-line LCD on the keyboard. Practically speaking, however, the Apricot is more of a desktop unit. ACT launched a true Apricot Portable the following year. The Apricot came standard with three operating systems, including MS-DOS and CP/M. It therefore had a huge software base. In 1984, the Apricot F1 appeared. It was more of a true PC-compatible.

Like the original Apricot, the Apricot Xi was designed to be transportable although it was not sold with an integrated display (unless you count the tiny two-line LCD built into the keyboard). In early 1986, ACT introduced the Apricot XEN, a PC AT compatible.

The Apricot Portable provided near desktop performance in a small package for the time. An unusual feature was the built-in voice recognition capability with a 4,000-word vocabulary. The intent was to ease data entry, but you had to create your own applications to take advantage of the feature. ACT bundled diary and drawing programs that used speech recognition.

ACT Apricot (Nov. 1983, desktop PC)

Original Retail Price: $2,495 to $3,190
Base Configuration: 5MHz 8086 CPU; MS-DOS 2.0, CP/M-86, and Concurrent CP/M-86; two proprietary slots; 256K RAM (768K max); two 3.5-inch floppy disk drives; keyboard/keypad; RS-232 and parallel ports; application suite; BASIC **Video:** 24-line x 80-column text, 800 x 400 graphics **Size/Weight:** 16.5 x 4 x 12.5 inches, 17.5 lbs. **Important Options:** UCSD p-System, 5MB or 10MB hard disk drive, 9-inch monochrome monitor, mouse, modem
Value: $15 to $45

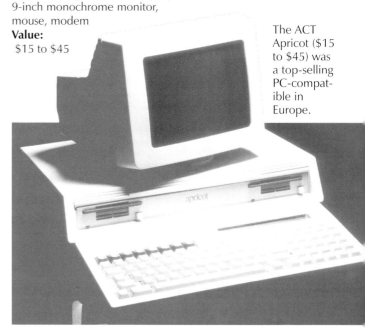

The ACT Apricot ($15 to $45) was a top-selling PC-compatible in Europe.

ACT Apricot F1 (July 1984, desktop PC)

Original Retail Price: $1,595 to $2,995
Base Configuration: 8086 CPU, MS-DOS, expansion slot, 256K RAM (768K max), 3.5-inch floppy disk drive, infrared keyboard/keypad, RS-232 and parallel ports, application suite **Size/Weight:** 7 x 4 x 18 inches, 13 lbs. **Important Options:** Concurrent DOS, expansion box, 10-inch color monitor, infrared mouse/trackball, carrying case **Value:** $7 to $30

ACT Apricot Xi (1985, desktop PC)
Original Retail Price: $4,495
Base Configuration: 8086 CPU, MS-DOS, 256K RAM (768K max), 3.5-inch floppy disk drive, 5MB hard disk drive, keyboard/keypad, application suite **Video:** 18.6 lbs. **Important Options:** CP/M-86 or Concurrent CP/M-86, 10- or 20MB hard disk drive, 9- or 12-inch monochrome or 13-inch color monitor, internal modem
Value: $7 to $30

ACT Apricot Portable (Oct. 1984, transportable PC)
Original Retail Price: $2,695 to $5,395
Base Configuration: 8086 CPU, MS-DOS, 256K RAM (1MB max), 3.5-inch floppy disk drive, monochrome LCD, infrared keyboard/keypad and mouse, RS-232C and parallel ports, application suite, voice recognition **Video:** 25-line x 80-column text, 640 x 256 graphics **Size/Weight:** 18 x 8 x 6 inches, 13 lbs. **Important Options:** 10MB hard disk drive, 10-inch color monitor, carrying case
Value: $25 to $75

Applied Technology Ventures Inc. (ATV) (Santa Ana, California)

"Designed for the 80s—with power, utility, comfort, and styling," as the ATV brochure on the Fox II reads. Today, the Fox II has the retro look that some collectors desire. The main unit holding the CPU and monitor sits on a pedestal with a white case and dark front panel. The hefty keyboard matches the front panel in color.

The pedestal mount for the monitor on this ATV Fox II ($17 to $45) gives it a retro look.

ATV Fox II (Nov. 1982, desktop)
Base Configuration: 4MHz Z80A CPU, CP/M, 80K RAM, two 8-inch floppy disk drives, 10MB hard disk drive, integral 12-inch monochrome monitor, keyboard/keypad, three RS-232C ports, BASIC, FORTRAN, COBOL, APL, Pascal, Macro Assembler **Video:** 24-line x 80-column text **Size/Weight:** 16 x 21 x 16 inches, 37 lbs.
Value: $17 to $45

Apricot Inc. (see "Applied Computer Techniques")

AT&T Information Systems (Morristown, New Jersey)

Long-time *Byte* magazine columnist Jerry Pournelle was fond of saying that AT&T couldn't market eternal life. The company had some of the world's top engineering talent and produced several excellent computers, but AT&T found it difficult to find success in the micro-computer market.

The Unix PC and Olivetti-manufactured PC 6300 were well-regarded when new and are interesting finds in good, unaltered condition. The AT&T Unix PC could be used as a standalone workstation or as a multi-user system. Its keyboard attached to the main CPU unit, covering the floppy drive. It could be used in that position or detached.

AT&T was known for its utilitarian, industrial computer designs. The Safari NSX/20 broke with that tradition. It was one of the sharpest looking notebooks at the time with a slim, well-chiseled form that sported a distinctive grey and green color scheme. The Safari was designed with communications in mind; it was optimized for AT&T Mail and AT&T EasyLink Services, which provided access to online news and databases (this was before the Web). While the Safari design team overcame the traditional AT&T stodginess, it couldn't overcome AT&T's awful marketing of the product. The Safari was available only a short time and did not sell well, but today it makes an excellent collectible.

AT&T PC 6300 (1984, desktop PC)
Original Retail Price: $2,811 to $4,985
Base Configuration: 8MHz 8086 CPU; MS-DOS 2.11, PC-DOS 2.0, or PC-DOS 2.1; seven ISA slots; 128K RAM (512K max); two 5.25-inch floppy disk drives; keyboard/keypad; serial and parallel ports **Video:** 640 x 400 graphics **Important Options:** Xenix 3.0, 20MB hard disk drive, mouse
Value: $10 to $45

Olivetti produced this PC 6300 ($10 to $45) for AT&T.

AT&T Unix PC (1985, desktop)
Original Retail Price: $5,095 to $6,590
Base Configuration: 10MHz 68010 CPU, Unix System V, three slots, 512K RAM (2MB max), 5.25-inch floppy disk drive, 10MB hard disk drive, 12-inch monochrome monitor, keyboard/keypad, mouse, parallel and RS-232C ports, development tools, utilities disk, internal modem **Video:** 29-line x 80-column text, 720 x 348 graphics **Important Options:** 20MB hard disk drive
Value: $20 to $65

AT&T Safari NSX/20 (1991, notebook PC)
Base Configuration: 20MHz 80386SX CPU, MS-DOS 4.01 with Windows 3.0a Productivity Pack, external AT bus, 2MB RAM (8MB max), 128K ROM, 3.5-inch floppy disk drive, 40- or 80MB hard disk drive, 10-inch monochrome LCD, integral keyboard, mouse, two RS-232C and one parallel port, Access Plus software, internal modem, carrying case, tutorial software, NiCad battery, AC adapter **Video:** VGA, EGA, CGA, and MDA **Size/Weight:** 12 x 9.5 x 1.8 inches, 6.5 lbs. **Important Options:** keypad
Value: $15 to $35

AT&T's Safari NSX/20 ($15 to $35) was one of the sharpest-looking notebook PCs ever made. It is an uncommon and often overlooked collectible.

Atari Corp. (Sunnyvale, California)

The Atari 400 put the company, which launched the video game industry with the introduction of Pong in 1972, on the home computer map. A big drawback for the 400 was its membrane keyboard. When a 400 keyboard goes bad, the only repair is to replace it, but 400 systems are still reasonably priced and plentiful. It would be easier to buy another working system than to fix the keyboard.

The Atari 800 is a refined 400 (although Atari released both simultaneously) that eliminated its biggest drawback, the dreadful membrane keyboard, and replaced it with a full-size, full travel keyboard. The 800 also had two ROM cartridge slots and systems expansion slots. It was also capable of composite video output.

Atari followed the 800 and 400 with the 1200XL, which was software compatible with the earlier models, more or less. Some programs written for the 400/800 will not run correctly due to differences in the 1200XL operating system, and some 400/800 ROM cartridges do not fit in the 1200XL slot. Atari discontinued 1200XL production in early 1984, making for a short production run. Word spread quickly among Atari fans of the systems above-mentioned shortcomings, and of its poorer video quality.

The Atari 600XL and 800XL replaced the Atari 400 and 800, respectively, and gave you a lot for your money. In fact, Atari had sold its entire inventory of both systems within months of their introduction. It was forced to stop taking orders, and then raised the price by $40 for each system. By late 1985, production of the 800XL had ended and Atari was selling remaining stock for less than $100.

The 65XE replaced the 800XL in Atari's line, and it could run all 800XL software. In fact, its electronics were nearly identical to the 800XL's. Atari sold the 65XE in Europe as the 800XE. The 130XE was software compatible with Atari's XL series. It is common to find XE systems with XL-style floppy drives, because Atari did not introduce the XF-551 drive until its stock of older units was sold out.

Although it couldn't match the capabilities of the Amiga, the 520ST offered exceptional sound and graphics at a low price. It was hard to find a more powerful computer than the Atari 1040ST in 1986 within several hundred dollars of its price. Atari introduced the 520STe and 1040STe in 1989. Both featured enhanced graphics and sound capability, as well as an improved joystick interface.

In the mid-1980s, Atari decided to take a crack at the business market with the Mega ST series. The Mega STs offered good performance and graphics, but its TOS (Tramiel Operating System, named after former Commodore CEO Jack Tramiel who had bought Atari after he was ousted from Commodore) operating environment was unknown to business buyers. The Mega STe used a case that was identical to that of the TT line, except that it was grey instead of off-white. In fact, the STe had more in common with the TT than the original Mega ST. Mega ST systems are much sought after by Atari collectors.

Atari followed up the Mega ST series with the TT 030 line. With a 32MHz 68000, the TT 030 was the fastest ever offered by the company. In addition to the systems standard RAM, Atari provided up to 16MB of FastRAM to further boost performance.

The last computer that Atari produced was the Falcon 030, a multimedia system that used a DSP coprocessor to boost sound and video performance. Because of its MIDI capability and 16-bit stereo sound, the Falcon 030 is still used by amateur and professional musicians.

Atari dabbled with selling PC-compatible desktop systems, primarily in Europe. All were fairly typical, but Atari collectors seek them out. That fact and their low production numbers make the Atari PC series more valuable than your typical clone.

The company also produced two TOS-based portables. The Stacy was a largish laptop that ran on 12 C-size alkaline batteries. The STBook isn't very old, but is sought after by Atari fans. It was a capable color notebook, but its Atari TOS operating system limited software options and allowed file transfer only with another TOS-based computer.

Atari 400 (Aug. 1979, home computer)
Base Configuration: 1.8MHz 6502 CPU, ROM cartridge slot, 8K RAM (16K max), TV adapter, integral membrane keyboard, serial and four game ports, owner's manual, AC adapter, music synthesizer **Video:** 24-line x 40-column text, 320 x 192 graphics, 16 colors **Size/Weight:** 13.5 x 11.5 x 4.5 inches, 5.75 lbs. **Important Options:** 410 Program Recorder; 830 Acoustic Modem; 822, 825, or 820 printer
Value: $10 to $50

A huge existing game library and availability of peripherals like those shown here made the Atari 400 (right, $10 to $50) and 800 (left, $10 to $45) successful, and today the two make excellent starter systems for new collectors.

Atari 800 (Aug. 1979, home computer)
Base Configuration: 1.8MHz 6502B CPU, two ROM cartridge slots, 8K RAM (48K max), 10K ROM, TV adapter, integral keyboard, serial and four game ports, Atari BASIC, owner's and two BASIC manuals, AC adapter, sound synthesizer **Video:** 24-line x 40-column text, 320 x 192 graphics, 16 colors **Size/Weight:** 16 x 12.5 x 4.5 inches, 9.75 lbs. **Important Options:** 410 Program Recorder; 810 external 5.25-inch floppy disk drive; monochrome or color monitor; 830 Acoustic Modem; 820, 822, or 825 printer
Value: $10 to $45

The Atari 1200XL ($25 to $75) had a short production run and is an uncommon find.

Atari 1200XL (late 1982, home computer)\
Base Configuration: 1.8MHz 6502C CPU, 64K RAM, ROM cartridge slot, integral keyboard, two game ports, four-voice sound **Important Options:** 1020 or 1025 printer
Value: $25 to $75

Atari 600XL (July 1983, home computer)
Original Retail Price: $199
Base Configuration: 1.8MHz 6502C CPU, operating system in ROM, expansion bus, 16K RAM (64K max), 24K ROM, TV adapter, integral keyboard, serial and two game ports, Atari BASIC in ROM, owner's manual, AC adapter, four-channel sound **Video:** 24-line x 32-column text, 320 x 192 graphics, 128 colors **Important Options:** CP/M; 1050 external 5.25-inch floppy disk drive; 1010 data recorder; keypad; trackball; 1020, 1025, or 1027 printers; joystick; 1030 modem
Value: $7 to $40

The Atari 600XL (left, $7 to $40) and Atari 800XL (right, $10 to $65) were hot-selling replacements for the Atari 400 and 800, respectively.

Atari 800XL (Aug. 1983, home computer)
Base Configuration: 1.8MHz 6502C CPU; operating system in ROM; Expansion Connection; 64K RAM; 24K ROM; TV adapter; integral keyboard; video, serial and two game ports; Atari BASIC in ROM; owner's manual; AC adapter; sound synthesizer **Video:** 24-line x 40-column text, 320 x 192 graphics, 128 colors **Important Options:** CP/M; 1050 external 5.25-inch floppy disk drive; 1010 data recorder; keypad; trackball; 1020, 1025, or 1027 printer; joystick; 1030 modem
Value: $10 to $65

Atari 65XE (1985, home computer)
Original Retail Price: $120
Base Configuration: 6502C CPU, 64K RAM, ROM cartridge slot, integral keyboard, BASIC in ROM, four-voice sound **Video:** 320 x 192 graphics **Important Options:** XF-551 external 5.25-inch floppy disk drive
Value: $5 to $35

Atari 130XE (early 1985, home computer)
Original Retail Price: $150
Base Configuration: 6502C CPU, ROM cartridge slot, 128K RAM, integral keyboard, BASIC in ROM, four-voice sound **Video:** 320 x 192 graphics **Important Options:** XF-551 external 5.25-inch floppy disk drive
Value: $8 to $40

The Atari 130 XE ($8 to $40).

Atari 1040ST/1040STe
(1986 [1040ST]/1989 [1040STe], home computer)
Original Retail Price: $999
Base Configuration: 8MHz 68000 CPU, TOS, ROM cartridge slot, 1MB RAM, 192K ROM, 3.5-inch floppy disk drive, monochrome monitor, integral keyboard/keypad, mouse, TV video port, MIDI interface, ST BASIC, Atari Logo, three-voice sound **Video:** 640 x 400 graphics, 16 colors **Important Options:** expansion unit, 10MB hard disk drive, RGB monitor, graphics coprocessor, SMM801 or SDM121 printer
Value: $20 to $50 (1040ST)/$25 to $65 (1040STe)

Atari Mega ST Series (1986, desktop)
Base Configuration: 8MHz 68000 CPU; TOS; ROM cartridge slot; Mega bus slot; 1MB RAM (4MB max); 3.5-inch floppy disk drive; keyboard/keypad; serial, parallel, mouse, game, and MIDI ports **Video:** 640 x 400 graphics **Size/Weight:** 12 x 12 x 3 inches **Important Options:** color monitor, laser printer
Value: $50 to $115

The Mega ST ($50 to $115) was Atari's first attempt at a business computer. *Photo courtesy of Sellam Ismail, Vintage Computer Festival.*

Atari 520ST/520STe (1985 [520ST]/1989 [520STe], home computer)
Original Retail Price: $800
Base Configuration: 8MHz 68000 CPU; TOS with GEM; 512K RAM; external 3.5-inch floppy disk drive; monochrome monitor; integral keyboard/keypad; mouse; RS-232C, parallel, and game ports; Logo and Atari BASIC; MIDI interface; three-voice sound; AC adapter **Video:** 640 x 400 graphics **Important Options:** SP354 or SF314 external floppy disk drive, hard disk drive, RGB monitor, SMM801 or SDM121 printer, modem
Value: $15 to $40 (520ST)/ $17 to $45 (520STe)

Atari Mega STe (1991, desktop)
Base Configuration: 16MHz 68000 CPU; TOS; ROM cartridge slot; VMEbus slot; 1MB RAM (4MB max); 3.5-inch floppy disk drive; 40MB hard disk drive; keyboard/keypad; two serial, parallel, game, and mouse ports **Video:** 640 x 400 graphics
Value: $75 to $225

Atari TT 030 (1990, desktop)
Base Configuration: 32MHz 68030 CPU; TOS 3.01 in ROM; VMEbus slot; ROM cartridge slot; 6MB RAM (26MB max); 3.5-inch floppy disk drive; keyboard/keypad; four serial, parallel, MIDI, SCSI, LAN, and mouse ports **Video:** VGA, 1280 x 960 graphics, 4,096 colors **Important Options:** hard disk drive
Value: $85 to $250

Few other home computers could match the Atari 520ST ($15 to $40) for computing power, shown here with the optional SC1224 monitor.

Atari Falcon 030 (1993, desktop)
Base Configuration: 16MHz 68030 CPU; Multi-TOS 4.01 in ROM; processor direct slot; ROM cartridge slot; 1MB RAM (14.3MB max); 3.5-inch floppy disk drive; integral keyboard/keypad; mouse; serial, parallel, MIDI, SCSI-2, LAN, DSP, and mouse ports
Video: VGA **Important Options:** hard disk drive
Value: $125 to $300

Atari Stacy (1989, laptop)
Base Configuration: 8MHz 68000 CPU; Rainbow TOS and GEM in ROM; ROM cartridge slot; 1MB RAM (4MB max); 192K ROM; 3.2-inch floppy disk drive monochrome LCD; integral keyboard/keypad and trackball; RS-232C, parallel, MIDI, mouse, and game ports; three-voice sound; AC adapter **Video:** 640 x 200 graphics, 16 colors **Size/Weight:** 15.2 lbs. **Important Options:** 20- or 40MB hard disk drive
Value: $225 to $500

Coveted by Atari enthusiasts, the Stacy laptop ($225 to $500).

Atari STBook (1991, notebook)
Base Configuration: 8MHz 68000; TOS in ROM; proprietary slot; 1MB RAM (4MB max); 512K ROM; 40MB to 120MB hard disk drive; color LCD; integral keyboard with pointing device; MIDI, RS-232, and parallel ports; file-transfer and organizer software; NiCad battery pack; AC adapter; sound synthesizer **Video:** 640 x 400 graphics **Size/Weight:** 8.5 x 11.4 x 1.4 inches, 4.2 lbs. **Important Options:** external 3.5-inch floppy disk drive, fax modem, MIDI/SMPTE adapter
Value: $175 to $475

Another Atari portable, the STBook notebook ($175 to $475).

Athena Computer & Electronic Systems (San Juan Capistrano, California)

When first launched, the Athena I had an unusual but interesting dual-processor design using NSC-800 CPUs, a low-power version of the Zilog Z80. What's more, it used solid-state storage in the form of fast dynamic RAM. It was a powerful system, but its small LCD and external floppy drive limited its usefulness. In 1983, the company switched to a single low-power Intel 80C86 CPU, the first computer to do so, and offered MS-DOS along with CP/M.

Athena I (1983, transportable)
Original Retail Price: $3,250 to $4,950
Base Configuration: dual 2.5MHz NSC-800 CPUs, CP/M 2.2, 68K RAM, 6K ROM, external 5.25-inch floppy disk drive, 128K (1MB max) solid state storage, monochrome LCD, keyboard, two RS-232 and one parallel port, JRT Pascal, owner's and software manuals, battery pack, AC adapter **Video:** 4-line x 80-column text **Size/Weight:** 3.37 x 11.87 x 14.5 inches, 15 lbs. **Important Options:** 12-inch monochrome monitor
Value: $20 to $50

An early LCD-based transportable, the Athena 1 ($20 to $50) came standard with everything in the photo.

Aval Corp. (Japan)

Aval sold the petite AVC-666 as a CP/M development system. The AVC-777 J2 was the transportable version of the AVC-666 and had a somewhat lower profile than many of its contemporaries.

Aval AVC-666 (1983, desktop)
Original Retail Price: $2,500
Base Configuration: Z80A CPU, CP/M 2.2, 64K RAM, two 5.25-inch floppy disk drives, keyboard, serial and parallel ports **Important Options:** 12-inch monochrome monitor
Value: $12 to $35

Aval AVC-777 J2
(1983, transportable)
Original Retail Price: $3,320
Base Configuration: Z80A CPU, CP/M 2.2, 64K RAM, two 5.25-inch floppy disk drives, integral 5-inch monochrome CRT, keyboard, two RS-232C and one parallel port, integral thermal printer, carrying case **Size/Weight:** 27.5 lbs. **Important Options:** external dual 8-inch floppy disk drives
Value: $20 to $45

It's not clear if the Aval AVC-777 J2 transportable ($20 to $45) was sold in North America.

AVT Trading A.G. (Zug, Switzerland)

The AVT COMP-2 was sold in Canada through Interactive Consulting Group and in the U.S. through Tano Corp.

AVT COMP-2 (Apple II-class desktop)
Base Configuration: 6502 CPU; seven Apple-compatible slots; 64K RAM (256K max); 16K ROM; composite, PAL, and NTSC video ports; keyboard; game port; Microsoft BASIC **Video:** 280 x 183 graphics **Size/Weight:** 14.8 x 19.4 x 6.2 inches **Important Options:** cassette recorder, 5.25-inch floppy disk drive, 80-column card, game paddles
Value: $10 to $40

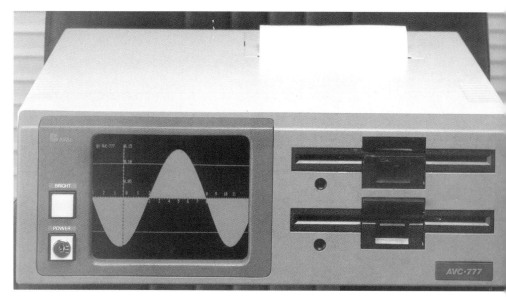

Basis Microcomputer GmbH (Muenster, Germany)

Basis was a European distributor for Apple until the company decided to set up its own sales operation on the continent. Basis's response was to build and sell what it believed to be a better Apple II. The company set up a U.S. subsidiary in California in 1982. The company headquarters appear to have moved to Hong Kong by the time it produced the oddly named Medfly system. Basis also made the Basis 203 CP/M systems and the Xenix-based Basis 216. The Basis 216 was unusual in that one of its processors was the seldom-used Zilog Z8001.

The dual-processor Basis 108 was hardware and software compatible with the Apple II and could also run CP/M applications. The 108 looked more like a typical CP/M machine than the Apple II, with a separate keyboard and an optional monitor in a retro-looking swivel frame. At least 25,000 Basis 108s were produced.

At the system level, the Medfly seems identical to the 108. A redesigned keyboard and ivory-color enclosure replaced the 108's beige components.

Basis 108 (Jan. 1982, Apple II-class desktop)
Original Retail Price: $2,150 to $4,245
Base Configuration: 1MHz 6502 and 2MHz Z80 CPUs; CP/M Plus; six Apple-compatible slots; 64K RAM (128K max), 2K ROM (12K max); keyboard/keypad; RS-232C and parallel ports; NTSC, RGB, and composite video ports; Perfect Software application suite; owner's manual
Video: 24-line x 80-column text, 280 x 192 graphics, six colors   **Important Options:** 5.25-inch floppy disk drive, 256K RAM disk board, 12-inch monochrome monitor, game paddles
Value: $20 to $65

Don't you just love that retro-looking monitor (an option) on this Basis 108 ($20 to $65)?

I'm betting that the Basis Medfly ($20 to $65) did not sell well in California.

Basis Medfly (Apple II-class desktop)
Base Configuration: 6502 and Z80 CPUs; CP/M 3.0; six Apple-compatible slots; 64K RAM (128K max); 2K ROM (12K max); RGB, composite, and NTSC video ports; keyboard/keypad; RS-232C and parallel ports
Video: 280 x 192 graphics   **Important Options:** external dual 5.25-inch floppy disk drives, 12-inch monochrome monitor, game paddles
Value: $20 to $65
Basis 208 (1982, desktop)
Base Configuration: Z80B CPU, CP/M, 10 proprietary slots
Value: $15 to $40
Basis 216 (1982, desktop)
Base Configuration: Z8001 and 68000 CPUs, Xenix, 10 proprietary slots
Value: $20 to $50

Bell & Howell Audio-Visual Products Division (Chicago, Illinois)

The Bell & Howell Microcomputer wasn't an Apple II clone; it was a relabeled Apple II made by Apple in a redesigned black or gray case. Bell & Howell had a long-established sales channel into the education market, and Apple was savvy enough to take advantage of it. Several modifications were made for use in schools. The back panel had an array of headphone and speaker jacks, as well as several volume controls. Three AC power outlets allowed you to plug in accessories to the computer, and a cover lock prevented tampering. Since Bell & Howell systems were sold exclusively to schools, surviving units have usually taken a beating. A pristine system would command a higher-than-average premium.

Bell & Howell Microcomputer (1980, Apple II-class desktop)
Base Configuration: 6502 CPU; eight expansion slots; 16K RAM (48K max); 12K ROM; TV video port; integral keyboard; RS-232C, parallel, and cassette ports; BASIC; two game paddles; reference and BASIC manuals   **Video:** 24-line x 40-column text, 280 x 160 graphics, 15 colors   **Important Options:** external 5.25-inch floppy disk drive, graphics tablet, modem, printer
Value: $20 to $55

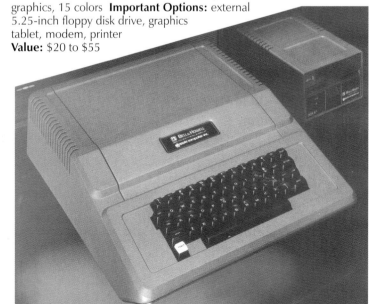

A standard Apple II modified for use in a classroom, the Bell & Howell Microcomputer ($20 to $55).

BMC Systems Inc.
(Century City, California)

There's no mistaking the if800 for anything else. Its unique all-in-one design places the CRT and drives above the main unit on two columns, with a built-in printer in the middle. Oki Electric built the if800 and sold it in Japan, although with a different configuration. The Sumicom 830 appears to be the same system as well.

BMC if800 (1983, desktop)
Original Retail Price: $4,995
Base Configuration: 4MHz Z80A CPU; CP/M; ROM cartridge slot; four expansion slots; 128K RAM (256K max); two 8-inch floppy disk drives; integral 12-inch color CRT; integral keyboard/keypad; RS-232C, IEEE-488, parallel, and light-pen ports; Oki BASIC; integral printer **Video:** 25-line x 80-column text, 640 x 200 graphics **Important Options:** 16-bit coprocessor; 16MB hard disk drive; parallel, IEEE-488, and ADC/DAC interfaces; light pen
Value: $22 to $65

Bondwell Industrial Co. Inc.
(Fremont, California)

Hong Kong-based Bondwell purchased home computer vendor Spectravideo in 1984. In 1985, Spectravideo changed its name to Bondwell and switched from making home computer systems to CP/M and PC-compatible desktop and portable computers. Bondwell's laptops were relatively inexpensive, and examples frequently pop up today.

Sold primarily as a word-processing system, the Bondwell 22 had an odd configuration. The main unit was a half-tower design with a small CRT imbedded at the top that displays the software menu. A standalone monitor is for text display. Because all the Bondwell 22 components are tightly integrated, an incomplete example would be of limited or no use.

The Bondwell 12 emphasized compatibility with Kaypro systems. A Bondwell 14 offered dual 360K floppy drives, twice the capacity of the Bondwell 12's drives.

The most exceptional feature of the Bondwell 2 CP/M laptop was its price—less than $1,000. The Bondwell 8 was the company's first PC-compatible laptop. Although inexpensive, it was a tad heavy for a laptop with mediocre viewing quality on the LCD.

Bondwell 22 (1984, desktop)
Original Retail Price: $3,500
Base Configuration: two Z80A CPUs, CP/M 3.0, 128K RAM, 4K ROM, two 5.25-inch floppy disk drives, integral 7-inch monochrome CRT and 12-inch monochrome monitor, keyboard/keypad with integral trackball, two RS-232C and one parallel port, daisy-wheel printer, application suite **Video:** 24-line x 81-column text (monitor)/24-line x 40-column text (integral CRT) **Important Options:** hard disk drive, modem, speaker-phone card
Value: $12 to $45

Bondwell 12 (1984, transportable)
Original Retail Price: $1,595
Base Configuration: 4MHz Z80A CPU, CP/M, 64K RAM, two 5.25-inch floppy disk drives, integral 9-inch monochrome CRT, composite video port, keyboard/keypad, two serial and one parallel port, speech synthesizer, BASIC, application suite, modem **Size/Weight:** 26 lbs.
Value: $12 to $35

A few early laptops were CP/M-based, like this Bondwell 2 ($5 to $25).

Bondwell 2 (1985, laptop)
Original Retail Price: $995
Base Configuration: Z80L CPU, CP/M 2.2, expansion slot, 64K RAM (256K max), 4K ROM, 3.5-inch floppy disk drive, monochrome LCD, serial and parallel ports, application suite, voice synthesizer, internal modem, battery pack, AC adapter **Video:** 25-line x 80-column text, 640 x 200 graphics **Size/Weight:** 11.2 x 12.2 x 3.1 inches, 11 lbs. **Important Options:** external 3.5-inch floppy disk drive
Value: $5 to $25

Bondwell 8 (1986, laptop PC)
Original Retail Price: $1,595
Base Configuration: 80C88 CPU, 512K RAM, MS-DOS 2.11, 3.5-inch floppy disk drive, monochrome LCD, RGB and composite video ports, integral keyboard, serial and parallel ports, GW-BASIC, internal modem, AC adapter **Video:** 25-line x 80-column text **Size/Weight:** 12.5 x 11 x 3.5 inches, 12 lbs. **Important Options:** external 3.5- or 5.25-inch floppy disk drive, carrying case
Value: $6 to $27

Designed primarily as a word processing system, the Bondwell 22 ($12 to $45) could perform most computing functions.

BT Enterprises (Bohemia, New York)

The BT Model III was a souped-up Tandy-made TRS-80 Model III. B.T. Enterprises installed a faster processor, high-quality drive controller with floppy and hard drives, and a real-time clock.

BT Model III Microcomputer (1983, desktop)
Original Retail Price: $3,995 to $4,295
Base Configuration: 4MHz Z80A CPU, DOSPLUS 4.0, 48K RAM, 5.25-inch floppy disk drive, 5MB hard disk drive, integral monochrome CRT, integral keyboard/keypad **Important Options:** 10- or 15.7MB hard disk drive
Value: $20 to $60

Bytec, Bytec-Comterm, Bytec/ Dynalogic (see "Dynalogic Info-Tech")

Byte Shop Inc. (El Camino, California)

The Byte Shop's main claim to fame is that it was the first computer retailer to order the Apple I computer. Owner Paul Terrell paid Jobs and Wozniak cash in advance for 50 assembled systems, and his order launched Apple as a real business.

The Byt-8 was the "house brand" system. It was also sold under the Olson name.

Byte Shop Byt-8 (1977, early micro)
Original Retail Price: $539 **Base Configuration:** 8080A CPU, S-100 bus, status LEDs, front panel switches
Value: $150 to $400

CAD/CAM On-Line Inc. (Chatsworth, California)

CAD/CAM On-Line originally intended the MiDAS[3] as a computer-aided design system, but soon made it available as a general-purpose, high-performance computer. Everything about this portable was industrial strength, including a titanium case, dual cooling fans, and a big gas plasma display. A military version of the MiDAS[3] was sold by Diversified Computer Consultants.

CAD/CAM On-Line MiDAS[3] Portable
(June 1987, transportable PC)
Original Retail Price: $6,495
Base Configuration: 12.5MHz 80286 CPU, MS-DOS 3.2, seven ISA slots, 1MB RAM (4MB max), 5.25-inch floppy disk drive, 30MB hard disk drive, 14-inch monochrome gas plasma display, keyboard/keypad, two serial and two parallel ports **Video:** 720 x 350 graphics **Size/ Weight:** 17 x 15 x 7.5 inches, 24 lbs. **Important Options:** Unix System V, tape backup drive, external battery pack
Value: $15 to $40

The CAD/CAM On-Line MiDAS[3] ($15 to $40) was designed for engineers.

Cado Systems Corp. (Torrance, California)

Cado sold its C.A.T. (Computer Aided Tutor) system to professionals and small businesses with the promise that the computer would teach the customer how to use it. The C.A.T. came with a set of tutorials that the user selected from a menu item. Cado introduced the C.A.T. around 1982.

Cado provided built-in lessons on using its C.A.T. system ($15 to $37).

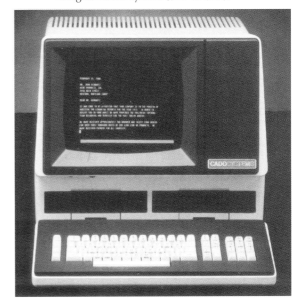

Cado C.A.T. (**Computer-Aided Tutor**) (desktop)
Base Configuration: two 5.25-inch floppy disk drives, monochrome monitor, keyboard/keypad, application suite, printer, tutorial software
Value: $15 to $37

Cambridge Computer Ltd. (Cambridge, U.K.)

For many mobile professionals, the Z88 was the perfect portable computer. It was small and light with a full-size keyboard and could run for hours on four standard alkaline batteries. Its OZ operating system was designed for mobile use, allowing for easy task switching among the built-in applications and maximizing system resources. A built-in utility allowed for easy file transfer with a PC. Z88 owners were often fanatical about the computers, and the systems are still in demand today. Be careful about the plastic covering the LCD, as it scratches easily.

The Z88 was designed by Sir Clive Sinclair, who kick-started the consumer microcomputer business in the U.K. with the Sinclair ZX80 in 1980.

Cambridge Computer Z88
(Sept. 1987, notebook)
Original Retail Price: $499
Base Configuration: Z80 CPU, OZ, three proprietary expansion slots, 32K RAM (3MB max), 128K ROM, EPROM card storage, monochrome LCD, integral keyboard, RS-232 port, application suite, BBC BASIC, AC adapter **Video:** 8-line x 106-column text **Size/Weight:** 11.5 x 8.25 x .87 inches, 1.88 lbs. **Important Options:** modem
Value: $35 to $100

Owners of the Cambridge Computer Z88 ($35 to $100) could transfer their work from the notebook to a PC.

Camputers (U.K.)

Camputers was one of many British companies that hoped to ride the coattails of Sinclair's success. It offered two home computer designs, the Lynx 48/96 and the faster and more upgradeable Lynx 128. Most Lynx systems were sold in the U.K.

Camputers Lynx 48 (1983, home computer)
Base Configuration: 4MHz Z80A CPU; 48K RAM (192K max); 16K ROM; RGB video port; integral keyboard; RS-232C, parallel, and cassette ports **Video:** 24-line x 40-column text, 256 x 248 graphics, eight colors
Value: $20 to $50

Camputers Lynx 128 (1984, home computer)
Base Configuration: 6MHz Z80B CPU; Lynx DOS; 128K RAM; 24K ROM; 5.25-inch floppy disk drive; RGB video port; integral keyboard; RS-232, parallel, cassette, and light-pen ports; Lynx BASIC in ROM, AC adapter **Video:** 24-line x 80-column text, 512 x 480 graphics, eight colors **Size/Weight:** 12.5 x 7.8 x 2.7 inches, 4.4 lbs. **Important Options:** cassette recorder, light pen
Value: $35 to $100

Canon USA (Lake Success, New York)

Although no longer a force as a computer manufacturer, Canon was a significant player in the early and mid-1980s in both Asia and North America. One of the earliest systems sold overseas was the CX-1 desktop with an all-in-one design. It did not sell well, perhaps because it used the proprietary MCX operating system.

The BX-3, introduced at about the same time, also used MCX. It had an all-in-one design as well, but with small LED display and built-in printer. A controller card for an external monitor was available as an option.

Faring better was the AS-100. Glance quickly at it and you might mistake the AS-100 for a microwave oven. Canon later upgraded the base memory for the AS-100 to 128K and bundled a suite of popular application software. Although the AS-100 ran MS-DOS, its PC compatibility was limited. Canon's AS-200 was more of a true PC Compatible. Canon introduced the A-200EX, a PC AT-compatible, in late 1986. Its value is similar to original AS-200. An AC-power-only A-200TP portable had an odd design where the LCD screen folded back on the top of the unit.

The TX-50 appeared between the introductions of the AS-100 and AS-200. It had an all-in-one design—unusual for a PC compatible—reminiscent of the Hewlett-Packard HP 85 and HP 86. Its 3-inch floppy limits what PC software can be used with the system. A TX-25 model was also available. Advertised as a "portable desktop," the TX-25 was part calculator and part microcomputer. Its display was a 20-character LED, but it had a typewriter-style keyboard, a proprietary 4-inch disk cartridge, and telecommunications capability.

Canon produced a number of MSX systems, which apparently were not sold in North America. They range from the tiny V-8 introduced around 1983 to the V-25 MSX-2 computer. In between were the V-10/V-20, which came with either black or white cases.

The system that Canon is best known for among collectors is the Cat. Jef Raskin designed the Canon Cat, and that's significant because he also led the original development team for the Apple Macintosh. He left before the Mac was completed to found his own company, Information Appliance, where he built a prototype of what was to be the Cat. Canon liked it and built the Cat under license. Unlike the Mac, the Cat is text-based and lacks a mouse. However, its approach to data storage and retrieval was innovative. The data appears in one long stream of text with page breaks between individual documents. A Leap function lets you search for particular items. This scheme wasn't for everyone, but the Cat had a dedicated group of devotees. Canon built an estimated 20,000 Cats, and some are still in everyday use.

The company's X-07 notebook was similar in configuration but smaller than the Tandy Model 100. It was expandable through credit-card-size plug-in cards.

Canon CX-1 (1981, desktop)
Original Retail Price: $4,995
Base Configuration: 6809 CPU, MCX, 32K RAM (128K max), two 5.25-inch floppy disk drives, integral 12-inch monochrome CRT and keyboard/keypad, RS-232C and parallel ports, CX-1 BASIC **Video:** 24-line x 80-column text **Size/Weight:** 20.9 x 25.2 x 13 inches, 55 lbs. **Important Options:** external dual 8-inch floppy disk drives, dot-matrix or thermal printer
Value: $25 to $75

Canon BX-3 (1981, desktop)

Base Configuration: 6809 CPU; MCX; 32K RAM (96K max); two 5.25-inch floppy disk drives; integral 28-character LED display and keyboard/keypad; RS-232C, parallel, and GP-IB ports; BX-3 BASIC; integral printer **Size/Weight:** 20.9 x 25.2 x 9 inches, 55 lbs. **Important Options:** external dual 5.25- or 8-inch floppy disk drives, CRT control board
Value: $20 to $50

Canon AS-100 (1982, desktop PC)

Base Configuration: 4MHz 8088 CPU, MS-DOS or CP/M-86, 64K RAM (512K max), integral 12-inch monochrome CRT, keyboard/keypad, RS-232 and parallel ports, Canon BASIC, GW-BASIC, utilities disk **Video:** 640 x 400 graphics **Size/Weight:** 15.75 x 13.5 x 16.87 inches, 43 lbs. **Important Options:** dual 8- or 5.25-inch floppy disk drives, 8MB hard disk drive, integral 12-inch color CRT, A-1201 or A-1200 printer
Value: $20 to $55

Canon's AS-100 ($20 to $55) is an important MS-DOS/CP/M hybrid, shown here with the optional color display, printer, and dual 5.25-inch floppy drives.

Canon A-200 Series (1985, desktop PC)

Original Retail Price: $2,195 to $2,695
Base Configuration: 7.16MHz 8086 CPU, MS-DOS 2.11, five ISA slots, 256K RAM (640K max), 16K ROM, two 5.25-inch floppy disk drives, monochrome monitor, keyboard/keypad, RS-232C and parallel ports, GW-BASIC **Video:** 25-line x 80-column text, 640 x 200 graphics **Size/Weight:** 17.37 x 15.62 x 5.5 inches, 25 lbs. **Important Options:** 10- or 20MB hard disk drive, color monitor
Value: $8 to $27

Canon A-200TP (1985, transportable PC)

Base Configuration: 4.77MHz 80C88 CPU, MS-DOS 2.0, external expansion slot, 256K RAM (640K max), 8K ROM, 5.25-inch floppy disk drive, composite video port, monochrome LCD, integral keyboard/keypad, RS-232C and parallel ports, GW-BASIC, modem **Video:** 640 x 200 graphics **Size/Weight:** 17.75 x 5.37 x 15.5 inches, 19.8 lbs. **Important Options:** expansion box, 10MB hard disk drive, carrying case
Value: $12 to $32

Although the Canon TX-50 ($12 to $40) was a PC-compatible computer, its calculator-style keyboard couldn't have been an advantage.

Canon TX-50 (1984, desktop PC)

Base Configuration: MS-DOS, 128K RAM (256K max), 3-inch floppy disk drive, integral 7-inch monochrome CRT, integral keyboard/keypad, integral printer **Important Options:** RS-232C and parallel interfaces
Value: $12 to $40

Canon V-8 (MSX home computer)

Base Configuration: Z80A CPU, 16K RAM, integral keyboard, Microsoft Extended BASIC, three-voice sound **Video:** 24-line x 40-column text, 256 x 192 graphics, 16 colors
Value: $7 to $30

Canon V-10/V-20 (1984, MSX home computer)

Original Retail Price: $225 (V-10)/$270 (V-20)
Base Configuration: Z80 CPU, two ROM cartridge slots, 16K RAM (V-10)/64K RAM (V-20), composite video port, integral keyboard, parallel port, eight-octave sound **Video:** 24-line x 40-column text, 256 x 192 graphics
Value: $10 to $35

The Canon A-200TP ($12 to $32) had an unusual configuration for a transportable.

Canon Cat (1987, desktop)
Original Retail Price: $1,495
Base Configuration: 5MHz 68000 CPU, 256K RAM, 3.5-inch floppy disk drive, integral 9-inch monochrome CRT, integral keyboard, RS-232C and parallel ports, word processor in ROM, FORTH, internal modem **Size/Weight:** 10.75 x 13.2 x 17.75 inches, 17 lbs. **Important Options:** printer
Value: $100 to $400

Canon X-07 (1983, notebook)
Base Configuration: NSC-800 CPU; expansion and cartridge slots; 8K RAM; 20K ROM; monochrome LCD; integral Chiclet-style keyboard; serial, parallel, and cassette ports **Video:** 4-line x 20-column text, 120 x 32 graphics **Size/Weight:** 7.8 x 5.1 x 1 inches, 2 lbs.
Value: $45 to $100

The Canon Cat ($100 to $400) stored all user data in one file.

Casio Inc. (Fairfield, New Jersey)

Casio's first full-size computer was the FX-9000P. It used a proprietary operating system and plug-in RAM and ROM packs. A battery-backed 4K RAM cartridge could be used as removable storage. The CP/M-based FP-1000/FP-1100 followed with a more standard desktop configuration.

The PC-compatible FP-6000 was not sold in North America, and it's not clear if its successor, the FP-4000, was sold there, either.

Casio is best known for its small computers, and in 1982 it beat NEC and Tandy to the market with its FP-200 notebook. The FP-200 had similar capabilities to the better-known aforementioned models but was not sold as widely.

Casio FX-9000P (1981, desktop)
Original Retail Price: $1,199
Base Configuration: Z80-compatible CPU, Casio OS, 32K RAM, integral 5-inch monochrome CRT, integral keyboard/keypad, RS-232C port, CA-BASIC in ROM **Video:** 16-line x 32-column text, 256 x 128 graphics
Value: $17 to $42

Casio FP-1000/FP-1100 (1983, desktop)
Base Configuration: 4MHz Z80A CPU, CP/M, two expansion slots, 64K RAM, 32K ROM, keyboard/keypad, parallel and cassette ports **Video:** 25-line x 80-column text, 640 x 200 graphics (PF-1000)/640 x 400 graphics (FP-1100), eight colors **Important Options:** external dual 5.25-inch floppy disk drives
Value: $15 to $40

Casio FP-6000 (1984, desktop PC)
Original Retail Price: $2,800
Base Configuration: 8MHz 8086 CPU, MS-DOS, 256K RAM (768K max), two external 5.25-inch floppy disk drives, external 10MB hard disk drive, 12-inch monochrome monitor, RS-232C port, C86 BASIC
Value: $15 to $40

Casio FP-200 (1982, notebook)
Base Configuration: 4MHz 80C85 CPU; three RAM/ROM card slots; 8K RAM (32K max); 32K ROM (40K max); monochrome LCD; integral keyboard; serial, parallel, and cassette ports **Video:** 8-line x 20-column text, 160 x 64 graphics **Size/Weight:** 12.1 x 8.6 x 2.2 inches
Important Options: keypad, floppy disk drive
Value: $30 to $125

Challenge Systems Inc. (Richardson, Texas)

Challenge Systems was known mainly as a maker of multi-user systems. The CS1000 was a standalone computer upgradeable to a multi-user system.

Challenge Systems CS1000 (1982, desktop)
Base Configuration: Z80 CPU, CP/M 2.2, 64K RAM (384K max), two 8-inch floppy disk drives, monochrome monitor, keyboard/keypad, RS-232C and parallel ports **Video:** 25-line x 80-column text **Important Options:** I/OS, 5- to 20MB hard disk drive, printer
Value: $17 to $42

The Challenge Systems CS1000 ($17 to $42).

Colby Computer
(Mountain View, California)

In addition to its PC-compatible transportable, Colby produced conversion kits that would let you turn any desktop PC into a portable computer.

Colby PC-3 (1984, transportable PC)
Original Retail Price: $2,795
Base Configuration: MS-DOS, three ISA slots, 128K RAM (1MB max), two 5.25-inch floppy disk drives, integral 9-inch monochrome CRT, keyboard/keypad, serial and parallel ports **Video:** 25-line x 80-column text **Size/Weight:** 8.5 x 16 x 16.5 inches, 26 lbs.
Value: $15 to $40

Coleco Industries Inc.
(West Hartford, Connecticut)

Built by the company that created the Colecovision game console and Cabbage Patch Dolls, the Adam was supposed to be the ultimate home computer, offering a complete package at a low price. The Adam was a good value, and it developed a loyal following. However, reliability issues and poor technical support kept that following smaller than Coleco had hoped for. Owners came to rely on grassroots support groups rather than the company for troubleshooting information. Coleco also tried to control third-party software development for the Adam, which only slowed the growth of the Adam software library.

All Colecovision game cartridges work with the Adam, and Coleco provided an option that allowed the Adam to use all Atari 2600 cartridges as well. Adam SmartBASIC is partly compatible with Apple Basic. Adams that you find today are often incomplete or not working. The printer in particular was troublesome; it was designed for the Adam and cost-cutting efforts resulted in a weak print mechanism.

Complete working systems bring higher prices than many of the Adam's contemporary peers. The Adam needs the printer to run, because the computer shares the power supply housed in the printer. Keep in mind, however, that the Adam does not hold up well and repairs will be difficult.

Coleco Adam (June 1983, home computer)
Original Retail Price: $700
Base Configuration: Z80A CPU, three internal and one Colecovision expansion slots, Colecovision ROM cartridge slot, 80K RAM (144K max), proprietary data pack storage, TV and composite video ports, integral keyboard, Adam-Net port, SmartBASIC and SmartWriter in ROM, Buck Rogers game, two game controllers, daisy-wheel printer, setup instructions, owner's and software manuals **Video:** 256 x 192 graphics, 16 colors **Size/Weight:** 18.75 x 10.37 x 4.12 inches **Important Options:** Personal CP/M, expansion module, 5.25-inch floppydisk drive, 80-column upgrade, SuperAction controllers, modem
Value: $20 to $125

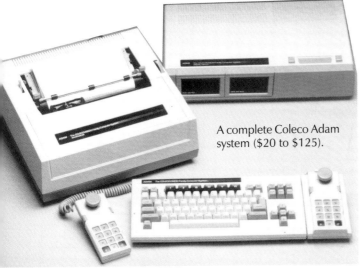

A complete Coleco Adam system ($20 to $125).

Collins International Trading Corp.
(Calabassas, California)

The Orange+Two used the EuroROM to ensure compatibility with Apple software.

Collins International Trading Orange+Two
(1983, Apple II-class desktop)
Original Retail Price: $1,095
Base Configuration: 6502 and Z80A CPUs, CP/M 3.0, six slots, 64K RAM (256K max), integral keyboard/keypad, cassette port, OrangeFORTH-83 and Z80A FORTH in ROM **Important Options:** Apple-compatible 5.25-inch floppy disk drive, 10MB hard disk drive, monochrome monitor, joysticks
Value: $15 to $50

Columbia Data Products
(Columbia, Maryland)

Columbia was an important early manufacturer of IBM PC compatibles. The MPC stands for Multi-Personal Computer, which was Columbia's way of saying that you could upgrade this XT-compatible to a multi-user system.

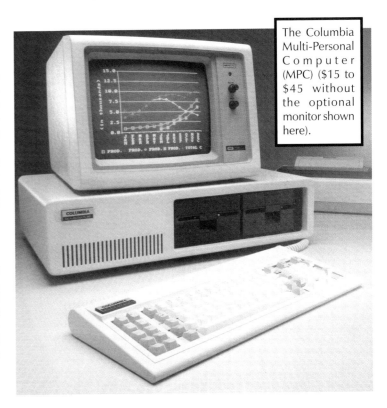

The Columbia Multi-Personal Computer (MPC) ($15 to $45 without the optional monitor shown here).

Columbia Multi-Personal Computer (MPC)
(1983, desktop PC)
Original Retail Price: $2,995 to $4,995
Base Configuration: 4.77MHz 8088 CPU, MS-DOS 2.0, eight ISA slots, 128K RAM (1MB max), two 5.25-inch floppy disk drives, keyboard/keypad, two RS-232 and one parallel port **Video:** 640 x 200 graphics **Size/Weight:** 22.5 x 15 x 5 inches, 25 lbs. **Important Options:** Z80 coprocessor; CP/M-86, MP/M, or Oasis-16; 12- to 40MB hard disk drive; color monitor
Value: $15 to $45

The Columbia VP ($10 to $35).

Columbia VP (1983, transportable PC)
Original Retail Price: $2,995
Base Configuration: 4.77MHz 8088 CPU, MS-DOS and CP/M-86, 128K RAM (256K max), 12K ROM, two 5.25-inch floppy disk drives, integral 9-inch monochrome CRT display, keyboard/keypad, RS-232 and parallel ports **Video:** 640 x 200 graphics **Size/Weight:** 18 x 16 x 8 inches, 30 lbs.
Value: $10 to $35

Commodore Business Machines Inc. (Westchester, Pennsylvania)

Parent company Commodore International was founded in 1958 as a Canadian marketer and assembler of typewriters and electromechanical business machines. In 1968, the company entered the electronic calculator market—one of the first to do so in the U.S.—and sold off its other interests. Commodore Business Machines was created with the purchase of MOS Technology, a semiconductor manufacturer that developed the 6502 CPU used in many Apple, Commodore, and other computers.

Along with Tandy/Radio Shack and Apple Computer, Commodore was one of the first mass marketers of personal computers in 1977. In fact, its PET line outsold the Apple II until sometime in 1978. Commodore considered the PET (Personal Electronic Transactor or Programmable Electronic Terminal, according to different Commodore literature) models as scientific and educational computers, and if you attended grade school in the late 1970s or early 1980s, you might have used one.

The PET's integrated design appealed to schools, although Commodore never matched Apple's educational presence. Chuck Peddle, who designed the 6502 processor in the PET, also designed the computer itself along with Leonard Tramiel, son of then-Commodore chairman Jack Tramiel. The earliest PETs had a closely spaced Chiclet-style keyboard and keypad, and they are the most prized finds by Commodore collectors. These early PETs have sold for $500 to $600 in excellent condition. The subsequent PET 2001 series came in three models: The PET 2001-8 had 8K RAM and a typewriter-style keyboard. The PET 2001-16N and 32N had 16K and 32K, respectively, and a keypad and graphics keys on its large-style keyboard.

The PET 3000 was Commodore's international designation for the PET 2000 series, although some sources indicate that there were minor differences in the two lines. By 1980, Commodore had sold 107,000 PETs. The optional floppy drives used by both the PET and CBM series had their own processors, which freed up system resources for other tasks.

The two models in the PET 4000 series were the PET 4016 with 16K of RAM and the 4032 with 32K of RAM. Based on the CBM 8032, the SuperPET was a high-end professional system. It offered dual-processing power and wide support for popular programming languages of the day. A few PET 64 systems were made with the Commodore 64 electronics in a PET housing.

The CBM 2001 was a renamed but improved PET 2001. Models 16B and 32B had 16K and 32K RAM, respectively. A CBM 8032 mode allowed it to run all 8032 software. A CBM 8096 model was identical to the 8032 but had 96K RAM.

The intended successor to the PET/CBM lines was the so-called B series starting with the B128 and B256 (called the 600 and 700 series in Europe, respectively). Enhanced versions of the B128 and B256, the BX128 and BX256, offered dual processors and more memory. The BX128 and BX256 were referred to as the 630 and 730, respectively, in Europe. Commodore positioned the BX series against the IBM PC and the Apple III. The Commodore 900 was a later attempt to break into the business market, but relatively few units were sold. The 900 was sold primarily in Europe.

The B series business systems sold poorly. Fortunately for Commodore, it was making waves in the home computer market with the VIC-20 and C64. The VIC referred to the Video Interface Chip at the heart of the VIC-20. It combined RAM, ROM, and video circuitry, reducing cost and complexity. The VIC-20 marked Commodore's entry into the home computer market, and the system offered several nice features for the price. They include a full-size keyboard with four programmable function keys, a built-in RF modulator, and lowercase character display. The VIC-20 was sold as the VIC 1001 in Japan. Commodore sold its millionth VIC-20 by January 1983. They are common today, so be patient and wait for a complete working unit in good condition.

The 64 (also referred to as the C64) was Commodore's answer to the Apple II Plus and other home computers. With the optional IEEE-488 cartridge, the 64 could use CBM peripherals. Commodore sold 50,000 64s in the first five months it was available. By the time the 64C rolled out, nearly 6 million 64s had been sold—more than any other model of microcomputer at the time and since. Total sales of all 64 models are estimated to be more than 17 million worldwide.

The 64C features a new physical design similar to the 128, which was introduced earlier, with the same light beige color. The Graphics Environment Operating System (GEOS) provided a graphical, easier-to-use interface with the computer. GEOS also included a paint program and a word processing application.

One of the rarest 64-based systems, The UltiMax, was aimed at the video game player and based on the C64 design. It had a custom graphics chip and nine-octave sound. Few UltiMax systems were sold, and they are among the most sought-after models by Commodore collectors. The system was introduced simultaneously with the C64 in Japan as the Max Machine. It was advertised in Germany as the VIC-10 and announced in the U.S., but apparently sold only in Japan.

In 1990 and 1991, Commodore developed a successor to the C64 called the C65. The company never sold it, but examples surfaced after 1994, the year Commodore went out of business. Apparently, another company acquired an unknown number of functioning beta or prototype units and resold them. C65s are rare and comparable in value to the UltiMax.

Originally introduced as the SX-64, the Executive 64 could run all C64 software, and the optional Z80 cartridge allowed it to use CP/M. The PET Emulator made the PET software library available. Far fewer of the C64-compatible Commodore portables were produced than their desktop counterparts, but they are not rare today. Nonetheless, clean working examples command over $100 as they are favorites among Commodore and portable enthusiasts.

Most 64, VIC-20, and other Commodore models share common peripherals such as the C1541, C1571, and C1581 floppy drives; Datasette cassette recorder; and various printer and monitor models. The model descriptions below provide details.

In 1984, Commodore announced a confusing array of new systems. All were similar to existing architecture, yet did not offer much more value than the 64C or VIC-20. The 264 and V364 offered more colors, but had poorer sound and no sprite capability. Consequently, many VIC-20 and C64 programs had to be adapted before they would work on them. Needless to say, this shortcoming limited the available software and the appeal of the systems. Although a small number of 264 and a smaller number of V364 systems made it into the hands of consumers, these models are best described as prototypes.

The Plus/4 gets its name from its four built-in applications, each accessible by a keystroke. The concept wasn't a hit with consumers, however, and the Plus/4 lived a short life. These systems often show up in good condition in their original boxes, which might reflect how useful their original owners considered them. The Commodore 16 fit somewhere between the VIC-20 and the Plus/4. A system similar to the 16, the Commodore 116, sold in Europe only.

The Commodore 128 introduced the following year was a different story. It was a success because it addressed a few obvious shortcomings of the 64. First, it provided twice the memory and a better BASIC. It also improved the video for 80-column display, and it could run CP/M, making a much larger software library available. More than 600,000 128s were sold worldwide in its first year. The 128D had a built-in C1571 floppy drive and higher graphics resolution thanks to 64K of video RAM.

In 1984, Commodore bought a former joystick manufacturer that had designed a new computer called the Amiga-PC. That computer was to sell for $2,000 with its own graphical operating system and exceptional sound and graphics thanks to custom chipsets. It would also optionally run CP/M and MS-DOS. That design, with some changes, became the first Commodore Amiga.

The Commodore Amiga set a new standard for graphics-based computing. Its custom graphics and sound chipsets were years ahead of what its competition offered and remained so for some time. Amiga users are extremely loyal, and many Amiga clubs still provide support for the system. Commodore renamed the original system the Amiga 1000 (A1000) in 1987 when it launched the Amiga 2000 (A2000) and 500 (A500) models.

Commodore launched the A500 in 1987 to better position itself in the home and education markets. It is a less expensive version of the A1000 in an integrated keyboard/CPU housing. An A500+ appeared in 1991 with 1MB RAM standard and an enhanced chipset, but it lasted only six months before the Amiga 600 replaced it. The A600 was smaller and lacked a keypad, but it was cheaper for Commodore to produce. The A600 was Commodore's attempt at making a game machine with the Amiga architecture.

The A2000 in 1987 represented the first major upgrade to the Amiga line. In late 1989, Commodore introduced the A2630 accelerator board for the A2000 designed to boost video performance. It had a 25MHz 68030 processor and 2MB of RAM. The Amiga 2500 series used the A2000 motherboard with either the A2620 accelerator board with a 68020 CPU and a 68881 coprocessor or the A2630.

With the A2500 and A3000, Commodore moved to much faster processors and provided more tools for users to take advantage of the Amiga's multimedia capabilities. Many of the later Amigas are still used by multimedia, animation, and video production professionals. While standard configuration Amiga 2000 and 3000 systems are priced reasonably, a heavily upgraded system with desirable third-party options such as the Newtek Video Toaster editing system could add $1,000 to $2,000 to its value. In fact, upgrades such as video editing hardware or accelerator boards often sell for more than the computers themselves. Note that although the A3000 claims VGA and RGB video compatibility, it does not support all modes.

The last Amiga that Commodore produced was the A4000 in 1992. It had Motorola's then-new 68040 processor, but Commodore introduced a 68030 version of the A4000 in the following year.

Like every other surviving computer maker, Commodore sold several PC-compatible models, including the PC10 in 1986 and the Commodore Colt in 1988. Both were undistinguished, me-too PC XT clones. If it weren't for the Commodore name, the PC10 and Colt would have little collector interest. Commodore collectors might pay as much as $65 for excellent examples, however.

The original version of the Commodore PET 2001 series ($150 to $400) with the calculator-style keyboard. *Reused with permission CMP Media LLC, Byte.com (Byte Magazine), Manhasset NY. All rights reserved.*

Commodore PET 2001 Series (Oct. 1977, desktop)
Original Retail Price: $595
Base Configuration: 1MHz 6502 CPU, 4K RAM (32K max), 14K ROM, integral cassette recorder, integral 9-inch monochrome CRT, integral keyboard or keyboard/keypad, IEEE-488 port **Video:** 25-line x 40-column text **Size/Weight:** 17.5 x 19 x 15.5 inches, 37 lbs. **Important Options:** CBM 2040 dual 5.25-inch floppy disk drives, CBM 2022 or 2023 printer
Value: $150 to $400 (early calculator-style keyboard); $25 to $150 (later typewriter-style keyboard)

Commodore PET 4000 Series (1978, desktop)
Base Configuration: 6502 CPU, 16K RAM (32K max), 18K ROM, integral 12-inch monochrome CRT, integral keyboard/keypad, RS-232C and IEEE-488 ports, BASIC 4.0 **Video:** 25-line x 40-column text **Important Options:** CBM 2031, 4040, 8050, or 8250 floppy disk drive; Datasette; CBM 4022, 8023P, or 8300P printer; CBM 8010 modem
Value: $20 to $95

The last two digits of the Commodore PET 4000 series indicate how much memory it has. This PET 4016 ($20 to $95), for example, has 16K of RAM. *Photo courtesy of Sellam Ismail, Vintage Computer Festival.*

Commodore SuperPET 9000 Series (1981, desktop)
Original Retail Price: $1,995
Base Configuration: 6502 and 6809 CPUs; CP/M; 96K RAM, 36K ROM; integral 12-inch monochrome CRT; integral keyboard/keypad; RS-232C, IEEE-488, and user ports; BASIC 4.0; Waterloo language set; 6809 assembler **Video:** 25-line x 80-column text **Important Options:** external CBM 2031, 4040, 8050, or 8250 floppy disk drive; CBM 4022, 8023P, or 8300P printer; CBM 8010 modem
Value: $65 to $225

Commodore CBM 2001 Series (1978, desktop)
Base Configuration: 6502 CPU, 16K RAM (32K max), integral 12-inch monochrome CRT, integral keyboard/keypad **Video:** 25-line x 80-column text
Value: $25 to $75

The Commodore CBM 2001 Model 32B ($25 to $75).

Commodore B128/B256 (June 1982, desktop)
Base Configuration: 6509 CPU; ROM cartridge slot; 128K RAM (256K max); 40K ROM; monochrome monitor (B128)/integral monochrome CRT (B256); keyboard/keypad; RS-232, IEEE-488, user, and cassette ports; BASIC 4.0, three-voice sound **Video:** 25-line x 80-column text, 640 x 400 graphics **Important Options:** Z80 coprocessor, CP/M or CP/M-86, UCSD Pascal
Value: $75 to $150

Commodore BX128/BX256 (June 1982, desktop)
Original Retail Price: $2,995
Base Configuration: 6509 and 8088 CPUs; 128K (BX128)/256K (BX256) RAM (960K max), 40K ROM; two 5.25-inch floppy disk drives; integral monochrome CRT; keyboard/keypad; RS-232, IEEE-488, and user ports; BASIC 4.0, three-voice sound **Video:** 25-line x 80-column text **Important Options:** Z80 coprocessor; UCSD Pascal; CBM 4022, 4023, 6400, 8023, or 8300 printer
Value: $100 to $300

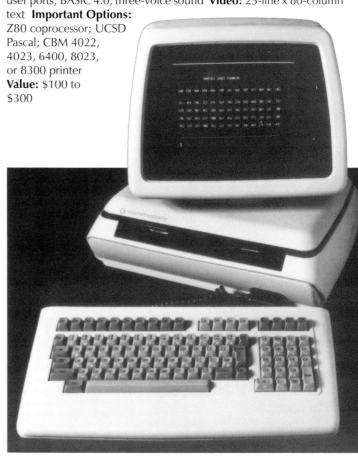

The Commodore BX128 ($100 to $300).

Commodore CBM 8000 Series (1980, desktop)
Base Configuration: 6502 CPU, 32K RAM (96K max), 18K ROM, integral keyboard/keypad, RS-232C and IEEE-488 ports, BASIC 4.0 **Video:** 25-line x 80-column text **Important Options:** external CBM 8062 3.2MB hard disk drive; external CBM 2031, 4040, 8050, or 8250 floppy disk drive; Datasette; CBM 4022, 8023P, or 8300P printer; CBM 8010 modem
Value: $20 to $85

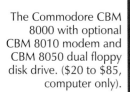

The Commodore CBM 8000 with optional CBM 8010 modem and CBM 8050 dual floppy disk drive. ($20 to $85, computer only).

The Commodore 900 is one of the rarest Commodores and was sold only in Europe ($300 to $600).

Commodore 64 (Sept. 1982, home computer)
Original Retail Price: $595
Base Configuration: 6510 CPU, ROM cartridge slot, 64K RAM, 20K ROM, TV video and monitor ports, integral keyboard, RS-232 port, BASIC in ROM, three-channel synthesizer **Video:** 25-line x 40-column text, 320 x 200 graphics, 16 colors **Important Options:** Z80 coprocessor, CP/M, VIC or 1541 external 5.25-inch floppy disk drive, Datasette, IEEE-488 interface, VIC printer, joysticks, VICModem, game controller, light pen
Value: $3 to $35

Probably the best-selling computer of all time, the Commodore 64 ($3 to $35).

Commodore 64C (1986, home computer)
Base Configuration: 8500 CPU; GEOS; expansion and ROM cartridge ports; 64K RAM, 20K ROM; TV video and monitor ports; integral keyboard; serial, user, and two game ports; BASIC 2.0 in ROM; sound synthesizer **Video:** 25-line x 40-column text, 320 x 200 graphics, 16 colors **Size/Weight:** 3 x 8 x 16 inches, 4.4 lbs. **Important Options:** C1541, C1571, or C1581 external 5.25-inch floppy disk drive; C1530 Datasette; C1702 or C1802 monitor; C1350 or C1351 mouse; MPS 801, MPS 802, MPS 803, MPS 1000, or MPS 1200 printer; C1660 or C1670 modem
Value: $5 to $40

Commodore 900 (1985, desktop)
Original Retail Price: $3,000
Base Configuration: 8MHz Z8000 CPU; Coherent; 512K RAM (2MB max); 5.25-inch floppy disk drive; 20MB hard disk drive; 14-inch monochrome monitor; keyboard/keypad; mouse; RS-232C, parallel, and IEEE-488 ports **Video:** 25-line x 80-column text **Important Options:** second 5.25-inch floppy disk drive, 40MB or 67MB hard disk drive, tape backup, 17-inch monochrome monitor
Value: $300 to $600

A restyled case and redesigned electronics distinguishes the Commodore 64C from the 64 ($5 to $40).

Commodore VIC-20
(1981, home computer)
Original Retail Price: $300
Base Configuration: 6502A CPU, expansion port, 5K RAM (32K max), 16K ROM, integral keyboard, RS-232C and game ports, BASIC in ROM, music synthesizer **Video:** 23-line x 22-column text, 176 x 184 graphics, 16 colors **Important Options:** external 1540 floppy disk drive, cassette recorder, IEEE-488 interface, 1520 printer/plotter, VIC modem
Value: $3 to $30

The Commodore VIC-20 ($3 to $30).

Commodore UltiMax (a.k.a. Max Machine, VIC-10) (1983, home computer)
Original Retail Price: $180
Base Configuration: 6510 CPU, Commodore OS, 4K RAM, integral keyboard, RS-232C port, three-voice sound **Video:** 25-line x 40-column text, 16 colors **Important Options:** Max BASIC
Value: $500 to $900

Sold only in Japan, the UltiMax ($500 to $900) is the ultimate prize for many Commodore enthusiasts.

Commodore Executive 64/SX-64 (1983, transportable)

Original Retail Price: $995

Base Configuration: 1.02MHz 6510 CPU, expansion slot, 64K RAM, 20K ROM, 5.25-inch floppy disk drive, integral 5-inch color CRT, composite video port, keyboard, RS-232C and IEEE-488 ports, BASIC 2.0 in ROM, three-channel music/voice synthesizer **Video:** 25-line x 40-column text, 320 x 200 graphics, 16 colors **Size/Weight:** 5 x 14.5 x 14.5 inches, 27.6 lbs. **Important Options:** Z80A coprocessor; CP/M; second 5.25-inch floppy disk drive; PET emulator; MCS 801, MPS 802, or DPS 1101 printer; C1520 printer/plotter; C1312 game controller; C1311 joystick

Value: $40 to $125

The ever-popular Commodore Executive 64, a.k.a. SX-64 ($40 to $125).

Commodore 264

(early 1984, home computer)

Base Configuration: 1.76MHz 7501 CPU; user expansion slot; 64K RAM; 32K ROM; integral keyboard; serial, two game, parallel, and cassette ports; BASIC 3.5 and monitor software in ROM; AC adapter **Video:** 320 x 200 graphics, 16 colors **Size/Weight:** 13.25 x 2.5 x 7.75 inches, 3.62 lbs. **Important Options:** C1551 5.25-inch floppy disk drive; C1531 Datasette; C1703 color monitor; application suite in ROM; MCS 801, MPS802, DPS 1101, or C1520 printer; joysticks

Value: $100 to $200

Commodore V364 (Jan. 1984, home computer)

Base Configuration: 1.76MHz 7501 CPU; "user" expansion slot; 64K RAM; 48K ROM; integral keyboard; serial, parallel, cassette, and two game ports; BASIC 3.5 and monitor software in ROM; AC adapter; speech synthesizer **Video:** 320 x 200 graphics, 121 colors **Size/Weight:** 16.62 x 2.62 x 9.37 inches **Important Options:** SFS 481 or C1542 5.25-inch floppy disk drive; C1531 Datasette; C1703 color monitor; MCS 801, MPS802, DPS 1101, or C1520 printer; joysticks

Value: $150 to $400

The Commodore Plus/4 was based on the 264 design ($5 to $30).

Commodore Plus/4 (1984, home computer)

Original Retail Price: $299

Base Configuration: 7501 CPU; serial bus expansion port; 64K RAM; RF modulator; composite video port; integral keyboard; RS-232, cassette ports and two game ports; Extended BASIC; application suite in ROM; two-channel sound **Video:** 25-line x 40-column text, 320 x 200 graphics, 121 colors **Important Options:** SFS 481 external 5.25-inch floppy disk drive, CM 141 color monitor, MPS 802 or DPS 1101 printer

Value: $5 to $30

The Commodore 16 ($7 to $40).

Commodore 16 (1984, home computer)

Base Configuration: 7501 CPU, RF modulator, integral keyboard **Video:** 25-line x 40-column text, 320 x 200 graphics, 121 colors **Important Options:** 1531 cassette recorder, CM 141 color monitor, MPS 802 printer

Value: $7 to $40

Very few Commodore 264s were released ($100 to $200).

Commodore 128 (1985, home computer)
Original Retail Price: $400
Base Configuration: 2MHz 8502 and Z80 CPUs; 128K RAM (512K max); TV, RGB, and NTSC video ports; integral keyboard/keypad; serial, user, and game ports **Video:** 25-line x 80-column text, 640 x 200 graphics, 16 colors **Important Options:** CP/M Plus 3.0, external 5.25-inch floppy disk drive, color monitor
Value: $7 to $50

The Commodore 128 with the optional color monitor and floppy disk drive ($7 to $50, computer only).

Commodore 128D (1985, home computer)
Base Configuration: 2MHz 8502 and 4MHz Z80A CPUs; ROM cartridge slot; 128K RAM (512K max); 64K ROM; 5.25-inch floppy disk drive; RGB video port; keyboard/keypad; serial, user, cassette, and two game ports **Video:** 25-line x 80-column text, 640 x 400 graphics **Important Options:** CP/M
Value: $20 to $100

Commodore Amiga 1000 (A1000) (Sept. 1985, desktop)
Original Retail Price: $1,295
Base Configuration: 7.16MHz 68000 CPU, AmigaDOS, Amiga System Bus slot, 256K RAM (512K max), 3.5-inch floppy disk drive, keyboard/keypad, mouse, RS-232 and parallel ports, Workbench, AmigaBASIC, four-voice sound **Video:** 640 x 400 graphics **Size/Weight:** 17.75 x 13 x 14.25 inches, 13 lbs. **Important Options:** PC-compatibility upgrade
Value: $20 to $90

Commodore Amiga 500 (A500) (1987, desktop)
Original Retail Price: $649
Base Configuration: 7.16MHz 68000 CPU, AmigaDOS 1.2, Amiga System Bus slot, 512K RAM (1MB max), 3.5-inch floppy disk drive, integral keyboard/keypad, mouse, RS-232 and parallel ports, Workbench, AmigaBASIC, four-voice sound **Video:** 640 x 400 graphics **Size/Weight:** 18.25 x 12.62 x 2.25 inches, 7.5 lbs.
Value: $17 to $47

Commodore Amiga 2000 (A2000) (1987, desktop)
Original Retail Price: $1,499
Base Configuration: 7.16MHz 68000 CPU; AmigaDOS 1.2 with Workbench; three Amiga System Bus, two ISA slots, and two Amiga/ISA slots; 1MB RAM (9MB max); 3.5-inch floppy disk drive; keyboard/keypad; mouse; RS-232 and parallel ports; AmigaBASIC; four-voice sound **Video:** 640 x 400 graphics **Size/Weight:** 17.37 x 15.27 x 6 inches, 22.5 lbs. **Important Options:** MS-DOS, A2630 accelerator, Bridgeboard PC/XT add-on
Value: $50 to $185

A trio of Commodore Amigas: the A1000 ($20 to $90), A500 ($17 to $47), and A2000 ($50 to $185).

Commodore Amiga 2500/20/2500/30 (A2500/30)
(1988, desktop)
Original Retail Price: $4,699
Base Configuration: 14.3MHz 68020 (2500/20)/25MHz 68030 (2500/30) CPU; AmigaDOS; five Amiga System Bus and four ISA slots; 2MB RAM; 3.5MB floppy disk drive; 40MB hard disk drive; SCSI, RS-232, and parallel ports **Video:** 640 x 400 graphics **Important Options:** MS-DOS, video accelerator, Unix System V Release 4
Value: $60 to $195 (2500/20)/$75 to $210 (2500/30)

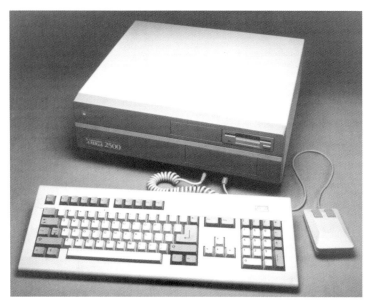

The Commodore Amiga 2500 ($60 to $195, 68020 version, or $75 to $210, 68030 version).

Commodore Amiga 3000 (A3000) (July 1990, desktop)
Original Retail Price: $3,299 to $4,499
Base Configuration: 16MHz or 25MHz 68030 CPU; AmigaDOS 2.0; Amiga System Bus; four Zorro III and two ISA slots; 1MB RAM (2MB plus16MB Fast RAM max); 512K ROM; 3.5-inch floppy disk drive; 40MB hard disk drive; keyboard/keypad; mouse; SCSI, RS-232, and parallel ports; AREXX; speech recognition **Video:** 1280 x 400 graphics, VGA **Size/Weight:** 15.5 x 14.5 x 4.75 inches, 20 lbs. **Important Options:** 100MB hard disk drive, 2024 monochrome or 1950 color monitor, AmigaVision authoring system, Amiga 10 speakers
Value: $100 to $350

The Commodore Amiga 3000 with the optional Model 1950 color monitor ($100 to $350 without monitor).

Commodore Amiga 4000 (A4000) (1992, desktop)
Base Configuration: 25MHz 68040 CPU; AmigaOS 3.0; four Zorro and three IDE slots; 2MB RAM and 4MB Fast RAM (16MB Fast RAM max); 512K ROM; 3.5-inch floppy disk drive; or 120MB hard disk drive; RGB video port; keyboard/keypad; mouse; serial, parallel, and two game ports; four-voice sound **Video:** 256,000 colors **Size/Weight:** 15.25 x 15 x 5 inches, 20 lbs.
Value: $150 to $425

Commodore Amiga 1200 (A1200) (1992, desktop)
Base Configuration: 14MHz 68020 CPU; AmigaOS 3.0; PCMCIA slot; 2MB RAM (8MB max); 3.5-inch floppy disk drive; RGB and composite video ports; keyboard/keypad; mouse; RS-232C, parallel, and game ports; AC adapter **Video:** 1280 x 512 graphics, 256 colors **Size/Weight:** 19.1 x 9.75 x 2.7 inches **Important Options:** 170MB hard disk drive
Value: $75 to $150

Commodore Amiga 600 (1992, home computer)
Base Configuration: 7.16MHz 68000 CPU; 1MB RAM (2MB plus 6MB Fast RAM max); AmigaDOS 2 in ROM; PCMCIA slot; 3.5-inch floppy disk drive; RGB and composite video ports; integral keyboard; mouse; RS-232C, parallel, and two game/mouse ports; four-voice sound **Size/Weight:** 14 x 9.5 x 3 inches, 6 lbs. **Important Options:** 40MB hard disk drive
Value: $20 to $90

Commuter Computer Corp. (Northridge, California)

The Commuter was sold with no software, as the company's strategy was to allow the customer as many options as possible. The customer could configure the system to run Apple II or CP/M software, and an optional 8088 CPU card provided MS-DOS compatibility.

Say this three times fast: the Commuter Computer Commuter ($35 to $75).

Commuter Computer Commuter (1983, transportable)
Original Retail Price: $1,995
Base Configuration: 6502 and Z80B CPUs; three expansion slots; 64K RAM (256K max); 16K ROM; two 5.25-inch floppy disk drives; integral 9-inch monochrome CRT; keyboard/keypad; two RS-232; two parallel, and one game port **Video:** 24-line x 80-column text, 280 x 192 graphics, 16 colors **Size/Weight:** 18.5 x 14.25 x 8 inches, 26 lbs. **Important Options:** 8088 coprocessor, MS-DOS
Value: $35 to $75

Companion Computers
(Apex, North Carolina)

The CP/M 2.2 Companion could serve as a standalone computer with the addition of a terminal, or as a means of expanding a CP/M-based portable computer.

Companion Computers CP/M 2.2 Companion
(1983, desktop)
Original Retail Price: $1,095
Base Configuration: Z80A CPU, CP/M 2.2, expansion slot, 256K RAM, 5.25-inch floppy disk drive, two RS-232C and one parallel port **Size/Weight:** 7 x 4 x 14 inches, 8 lbs. **Important Options:** dual external 5.25-inch floppy disk drives
Value: $15 to $35

Compaq Computer Corp.
(Houston, Texas)

Founded in February 1982, Compaq had over $111 million in sales in 1983, making it the most successful first year for any company up to that point. It did so on the strength of its Compaq Portable and Compaq Plus models.

Compaq's Portable put the company on the PC map, and the Portable series was by far the most successful luggable PC design. Compaq shipped more than 28,000 Portables in the first nine months of 1983 alone. Damaged cases, non-working drives, and faulty displays are common ailments in systems found today. Be careful taking Portables and Pluses apart. The case is held in place by tabs on the sides that snap into the chassis. You need to find these tabs and press to release them.

In 1985, Compaq introduced the TeleCompaq, a modified Portable design for use in telephone communications. It had a separate Z80 processor for communications tasks and a phone handset. Compaq thought enough of the TeleCompaq's potential to form a subsidiary to market it and other communications products, but it was short-lived and an uncommon find today.

The PC AT-compatible version of the Portable, the Portable 286, was a good seller for Compaq, at least until the Portable II became available. The Portable II was a smaller, improved version of the PC AT-class Portable 286.

A change of form factor came with the Portable III. The so-called sewing machine format was replaced by the smaller "lunchbox" shape. The Portable III came in three versions. The Model 1 had a single floppy drive, and the Model 20 and Model 40 had 20MB and 40MB hard drives, respectively. The Portable 386 used similar model designations, but offered a 100MB Model 100 and no 20MB model.

The Deskpro was Compaq's first desktop computer, and it soon established itself as one of the best made and most IBM-compatible PCs on the market. Many Deskpros saw years of business use, and examples in excellent condition are unusual. The PC AT-compatible Deskpro 286 appealed to power users in part because of its expandability. It could accommodate up to 8.2MB RAM by using expansion boards. The Deskpro 286 model was upgraded to a 12MHz 80286 in early 1987. The new model also had faster memory and more mass storage options.

The Deskpro 386 was one of the first 386 systems, and it was a hot seller. In September 1987, Compaq introduced the Deskpro 386/20 with a 20MHz 80386 CPU. The 386/20 incorporated Compaq's then-new Flex Architecture, which featured improved memory caching and a combined memory and I/O bus. Compaq assigned Deskpro model numbers according to the size of the hard drive.

Compaq Deskpro (June 1984, desktop PC)
Original Retail Price: $2,495 to $7,195
Base Configuration: 7.14MHz 8086 CPU, MS-DOS 2.11, six ISA slots, 128K RAM (640K max), 5.25-inch floppy disk drive, 12-inch monochrome Dual Mode Monitor, RF modulator, composite and RGB video ports, keyboard/keypad, parallel and serial ports **Video:** 25-line x 80-column text, 720 x 350 graphics **Size/Weight:** 5 x 19 x 16 inches, 40 lbs. **Important Options:** Unix, 10- or 30MB hard disk drive, tape backup drive
Value: $15 to $55

Compaq Deskpro 286 (April 1985, desktop PC)
Original Retail Price: $4,244
Base Configuration: 8MHz 80286 CPU, MS-DOS, seven ISA slots, 256K RAM (2.1MB max), 5.25-inch floppy disk drive, keyboard/keypad, serial and parallel ports **Video:** EGA, 16 colors **Size/Weight:** 19.8 x 6.4 x 16.5 inches **Important Options:** 20- or 40MB hard disk drive, Compaq Color or Dual Mode Monitor, Compact EGA or Video Display Controller card, technical reference
Value: $7 to $28

Compaq Deskpro 386 (Sept. 1986, desktop PC)
Original Retail Price: $6,499 to $8,799
Base Configuration: 16MHz 80386 CPU, MS-DOS 3.0, three ISA slots, 1MB RAM (10MB max), 5.25-inch floppy disk drive, keyboard/keypad, serial and parallel ports **Video:** CGA **Size/Weight:** 19.8 x 6.4 x 16.5 inches **Important Options:** Xenix System V/286, 40- or 130MB hard disk drive, Compaq Color or Dual Mode Monitor, Compaq EGA or Video Display Controller card, technical reference
Value: $7 to $25

Compaq Portable/Compaq Plus (Jan. 1983 [Portable]/Oct. 1983 [Plus], transportable PC)
Original Retail Price: $2,995 to $3,590 (Portable)/$4,995 (Plus)
Base Configuration: 4.77MHz 8088, MS-DOS 2.0, two (Plus) or three (Portable) ISA slots, 128K RAM (640K max), one (Plus) or two (Portable) 5.25-inch floppy disk drives, 10MB hard disk drive (Plus), integral 9-inch monochrome CRT display, keyboard/keypad, parallel and RGB and composite video ports, operations manual **Video:** 25-line x 80-column text **Size/Weight:** 8.5 x 20 x 16 inches, 28 lbs., off-white **Important Options:** serial port, internal modem, carrying case, technical reference
Value: $20 to $75 (Portable) $15 to $50 (Plus)

Compaq Portable 286 (April 1985, transportable PC)
Original Retail Price: $5,499 to $6,199
Base Configuration: 8MHz 80286 CPU, MS-DOS, three ISA slots, 256K RAM (2.6MB max), 5.25-inch floppy disk drive, 20MB hard disk drive, integral 9-inch monochrome CRT, RF modulator, RGB and composite video ports, keyboard/keypad, serial and parallel ports **Size/Weight:** 20 x 8.5 x 16 inches, 30.5 lbs.
Value: $7 to $45

Compaq classics, clockwise from top left: the Deskpro ($15 to $55), Deskpro 286 ($7 to $28), Portable 286 ($7 to $45), Plus ($15 to $50), and Portable ($20 to $75).

Compaq Portable II
(Feb. 1986, transportable PC)
Original Retail Price: $3,499 to $4,799
Base Configuration: 8MHz 80286 CPU, MS-DOS 3.0, two ISA slots, 256K RAM (640K max), 5.25-inch floppy disk drive, RGB and composite video ports, integral 9-inch monochrome CRT, keyboard/keypad, serial and parallel ports, BASIC **Video:** 25-line x 80-column text, 640 x 200 graphics **Size/Weight:** 17.7 x 7.5 x 13.9 inches, 23.6 lbs. **Important Options:** second 5.25-inch floppy disk drive, 10MB hard disk drive, internal modem, carrying case
Value: $10 to $50

The Compaq Portable II ($10 to $50).

Compaq Portable III (1987, transportable PC)
Base Configuration: 12MHz 80286 CPU, MS-DOS, 640K RAM (6.6MB max), 5.25-inch floppy disk drive, RGB video port, monochrome gas plasma display, keyboard/keypad, serial and parallel ports, owner's manual **Video:** 640 x 400 graphics **Size/Weight:** 9.8 x 16 x 7.8 inches, 18 lbs. **Important Options:** expansion unit, 20- or 40MB hard disk drive, internal modem, carrying case, technical reference
Value: $15 to $55

The Compaq Portable III ($15 to $55).

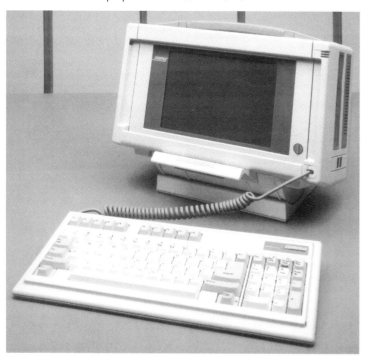

Compaq Portable 386 (transportable PC)
Original Retail Price: $7,999 to $9,999
Base Configuration: 20MHz 80386 CPU, MS-DOS, 1MB RAM (10MB max), 5.25-inch floppy disk drive, 40MB hard disk drive, RGB video port, monochrome gas plasma display, keyboard/keypad, serial and parallel ports, owner's manual **Size/Weight:** 20 lbs. **Important Options:** expansion unit, 100MB hard disk drive, internal modem, nylon or leather carrying case, technical reference
Value: $10 to $30

Compucolor Corp.
(see "Intelligent Systems Corp.")

Compucorp (Santa Monica, California)
Compucorp was a significant vendor of networking software and hardware, and the OmegaMite was designed to be compatible with the company's OmegaNet local area network. Series 700 models ranged from the diskless 745 to the 795 with a floppy disk drive and a 15MB hard disk drive.

Compucorp 600 Series (desktop)
Original Retail Price: $7,000
Base Configuration: Z80 CPU, proprietary operating system, 60K RAM, 12-inch monochrome monitor, RS-232C and parallel ports, BASIC, application suite **Video:** 24-line x 80-column text
Value: $15 to $35

The Compucorp 700, ($15 to $35).

Compucorp 700 Series (1982, desktop)
Base Configuration: CP/M, 64K RAM (256K max), 5.25-inch floppy disk drive, keyboard/keypad **Important Options:** second 5.25-inch floppy disk drive, 5- to 15MB hard disk drive
Value: $15 to $3

Compucorp OmegaMite
(1983, transportable)
Original Retail Price: $3,000
Base Configuration: 4MHz Z80, CP/M, 64K RAM (256K max), 5.25-inch floppy disk drive, integral 9-inch monochrome CRT, keyboard/keypad, RS-232C port, internal acoustic coupler, carrying case **Video:** 25-line x 80-column text **Size/Weight:** 21 x 10.35 x 9.4 inches, 25 lbs. **Value:** $17 to $40

The Compucorp OmegaMite with its carrying case ($17 to $40).

CompuPro (Hayward, California)

CompuPro was founded by Bill Godbout in 1973 as CompuKit, which sold microcomputer kits to hobbyists. As CompuPro, the company became one of the top vendors of S-100 bus microcomputer products. It was one of the first companies to take advantage of the component interchangeability that the S-100 bus provided. By the early 1980s, CompuPro became a manufacturer of multi-user, multi-processor systems.

Sold primarily to system developers and technology professionals, each System 816 was built to the customer's specifications down to the choice of CPU and operating system. Like many S-100 systems, the 816 line required a terminal for data input and readout. The 816/C had both 8085 and 8088 CPUs, 512K RAM, and three operating systems: CP/M-80, CP/M-86, and MP/M 8-16. The latter enabled the 816/C as a multi-user system. The System 68K uses the same enclosure and backplane as the System 816 series.

CompuPro System 816 Series (desktop)
Base Configuration: 8085, 8088 CPU; CP/M, CP/M-86, Concurrent CP/M-86, MP/M-86, or CP/M-68K; S-100 bus; 512K RAM (1MB max) **Important Options:** M-Drive/H RAM disk, one or two 8-inch floppy disk drives, terminal, printer **Value:** $50 to $150

The CompuPro System 816 with the optional dual 5.25-inch floppy disk drive unit ($50 to $150, computer only).

CompuPro System 68K (late 1983, desktop)
Original Retail Price: $8,995
Base Configuration: 4- or 8MHz 68000 CPU, CP/M-68K, 20 S-100 slots, 512K RAM, 1.5MB RAM disk, two 8-inch floppy disk drives, C compiler, MAPFORTH **Important Options:** terminal, printer **Value:** $50 to $150

CompuSource Inc. (Minneapolis, Minnesota)

CompuSource offered a portable and a desktop with similar technical specifications that could run Apple DOS, MS-DOS, and CP/M.

Shown with its namesake, the Compusource Abacus Portable ($20 to $65).

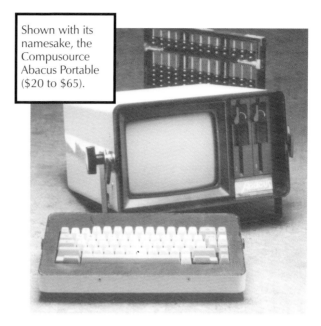

Compusource Abacus Portable (Apple II-class transportable)
Original Retail Price: $1,645 to $1,995
Base Configuration: five Apple-compatible slots, 64K RAM, 5.25-inch floppy disk drive, monitor and TV video ports, integral 9-inch monochrome CRT, keyboard, game port, application suite, games **Important Options:** second 5.25-inch floppy disk drive **Value:** $20 to $65

Compu-Sultants Inc. (Huntsville, Alabama)

Compu-Sultants' Micro-440 might have been the first 4040-based kit. An entry-level system for hobbyists, its processor had only a 4-bit word length, as opposed to the Intel 8080 8-bit length, so the system was limited even by the day's standards. Partial kits were sold, so it's possible to find Micro 440 components in other home-made systems.

Compu-Sultants Micro 440 (Dec. 1975, early micro)
Original Retail Price: $275 kit, $375 assembled
Base Configuration: 4040 CPU, 256 bytes RAM (8K max), I/O and Teletype ports, monitor software, debugger, editor, owner's manual, power supply, enclosure
Value: $100 to $250

Was this the first 4040-based computer kit? The Compu-Sultants Micro 440 ($100 to $250).

Computer Ancillaries Ltd.
(Surrey, U.K.)

Computer Ancillaries Caltext Micro Processor (desktop)
Base Configuration: 4MHz Z80A CPU, CP/M, two 5.25-inch floppy disk drives, monitor port, integral 12-inch monochrome CRT, keyboard/keypad, RS-232C and parallel ports **Video:** 24-line x 80-column text **Important Options:** 5- to 15MB hard disk drive
Value: $17 to $45

Computer Data Systems
(Newark, Delaware)

Some sources indicate that the Versatile 2 had an Intel 8080 CPU.

Computer Data Systems Versatile 2 (1977, early micro)
Original Retail Price: $996 kit
Base Configuration: Z80 CPU, CP/M, 10 S-100 slots, 16K RAM, integral 9-inch monochrome CRT, integral keyboard, RS-232 and parallel ports **Video:** 16-line x 64-column text **Important Options:** 5.25-inch floppy disk drive, keypad
Value: $100 to $300

Computer Designed Systems Inc.
(Minneapolis, Minnesota)

The Adviser Micro Plus was a multiprocessor system that could accommodate either or both an Intel 8086 and a Motorola 68000 CPU in addition to its standard Zilog Z80. Its unusual configuration with a built-in printer makes it stand out from other CP/M systems. The system appears to be a relabeled Oki-made if800.

Computer Designed Systems Adviser Micro Plus (Nov. 1983, desktop)
Original Retail Price: $1,995 to $4,995
Base Configuration: Z80 CPU, CP/M, 64K RAM (256K max), 5.25-inch floppy disk drive, integral 12-inch monochrome CRT, keyboard/keypad, integral printer **Video:** 24-line x 80-column text
Important Options: 8086 or 68000 coprocessor, 20MB hard disk drive, integral color CRT
Value: $20 to $60

Computer Ancillaries' Caltext Micro Processor ($17 to $45, sans bulldog).

Computer Devices Inc.
(Burlington, Massachusetts)

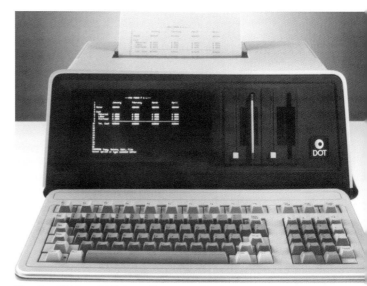

The Dot ($15 to $40) from Computer Devices.

Computer Devices The Dot (1983, transportable PC)
Original Retail Price: $3,295 to $3,995
Base Configuration: 8088 CPU, MS-DOS, two expansion slots, 128K RAM (256K max), 24K ROM, 3.5-inch floppy disk drive, integral 9-inch monochrome CRT, video port, keyboard/keypad, two RS-232 ports, carrying case **Video:** 1056 x 256 graphics **Size/Weight:** 8.5 x 18 x 15 inches, 31 lbs. **Important Options:** Z80 coprocessor, CP/M, integral printer
Value: $15 to $40

Computer Designed Systems Advisor Micro Plus ($20 to $60).

Computer Power & Light (Studio City, California)

Computer Power & Light was a computer store that put together its own system to sell.

Computer Power & Light COMPAL-80 (1977, early micro)
Original Retail Price: $1,863
Base Configuration: 8080A CPU, 12K RAM, cassette interface, 9-inch monochrome monitor, keyboard, Teletype or RS-232 port, BASIC **Video:** 16-line x 64-column text
Value: $85 to $250

Computer Technology International (CTI) (East Rutherford, New Jersey)

Sold as a complete package including printer, the Eve system needed only a copy of Apple DOS to run Apple II software. The Eve II Portable was a reconfigured Eve II Personal Computer.

Computer Technology International Eve II Personal Computer (1984, Apple II-class desktop)
Original Retail Price: $2,195
Base Configuration: 6502 and Z80 CPUs; CP/M; eight Apple-compatible slots; 64K RAM; external 5.25-inch floppy disk drive; 12-inch CTI-83X monochrome monitor; video port; integral keyboard/keypad; parallel, game, and cassette ports; application suite, CT-80 printer, software and CP/M manuals, Apple II user's guide **Video:** 24-line x 80-column text, 16 colors
Value: $25 to $65

Everything shown here came standard with the Computer Technology International Eve II Personal Computer ($25 to $65).

Computer Technology International Eve II Portable Computer (1984, Apple II-class transportable)
Original Retail Price: $1,595
Base Configuration: 6502 and Z80 CPUs; CP/M; three Apple II-compatible slots; 64K RAM; two 5.25-inch floppy disk drives; integral 5-inch monochrome CRT; video port; keyboard/keypad; RS-232, parallel, and game ports **Video:** 24-line x 80-column text **Size/Weight:** 5 x 15 x 14.5 inches, 17 lbs.
Value: $20 to $55

Computer Transceiver Systems Inc. (Paramus, New Jersey)

A reddish-brown and beige color scheme was the most distinguishing feature of the Execuport. Also unusual was the aspect ratio of the built-in monitor—132 characters wide when most of its competitors were 80 characters. The 16-bit version of the system—with either the 8086 or 80186 CPU—was called the Execuport XL+.

Sporting a reddish-brown enclosure, the Execuport XL ($20 to $50) from Computer Transceiver Systems.

Computer Transceiver Systems Execuport XL (1983, transportable)
Original Retail Price: $2,495 to $3,195
Base Configuration: 4MHz Z80A CPU, CP/M 2.2, 80K RAM (512K max), two 5.25-inch floppy disk drives, monitor port, integral monochrome CRT, keyboard/keypad, two RS-232 and one parallel port **Video:** 25-line x 132-column text, 960 x 288 graphics **Size/Weight:** 18.12 x 15.62 x 6.5 inches, 28 lbs. **Important Options:** 8MHz 8086 or 6MHz 80186 coprocessor, MS-DOS 2.11, 10MB hard disk drive, modem, portable printer
Value: $20 to $50

The Eve II Portable Computer ($20 to $55) from Computer Technology International.

COMX World Operations Ltd. (Hong Kong)

The COMX 35 was sold around the world but not in large numbers. It is unusual in that it was probably the only home computer of the era to use the RCA CDP 1802 processor.

COMX 35 (1983, home computer)
Original Retail Price: £120
Base Configuration: CDP 1802 CPU, expansion port, 35K RAM (67K max), TV video port, integral keyboard and joystick, cassette port, COMX BASIC **Video:** 24-line x 40-column text, 320 x 200 graphics, four colors
Value: $35 to $125

Convergent Technologies Inc. (Sunnyvale, California)

Although the Workslate wasn't the first notebook computer of its type, it was ahead of its time. It was thinner than its contemporaries such as the Tandy/Radio Shack Model 100, ran on AA or NiCad batteries, and had the biggest LCD in its class. The Taskware software library functioned within a spreadsheet-like template—no games for this computer. Workslates are popular today and are easily found with a bit of patience.

Corona Data Systems (Westlake Village, California)

Corona shipped 5,000 desktop and portable PCs in December 1983 and January 1984. Docutel/Olivetti sold the Corona PC as the Olivetti PC M18. Docutel/Olivetti sold the Portable PC as the Olivetti PC M18 P-1. A PC AT-compatible, the Corona AT Transportable (ATP) was introduced in 1985.

Corona PC (1983, desktop PC)
Original Retail Price: $2,595
Base Configuration: 8088 CPU, MS-DOS, four ISA slots, 128K RAM (512K max), 5.25-inch floppy disk drive, 12-inch monochrome monitor, keyboard/keypad, RS-232C and parallel ports, GW-BASIC, spreadsheet software **Video:** 640 x 325 graphics **Important Options:** CP/M-86, 10MB hard disk drive
Value: $10 to $35

Corona Personal Best PB400 (June 1984, desktop PC)
Original Retail Price: $5,995
Base Configuration: 4.77MHz 8088, MS-DOS 2.0, four ISA slots, 512K RAM (1MB max), two 5.25-inch floppy disk drives, 10MB hard disk drive, 12-inch monochrome monitor, keyboard/keypad, RS-232C and parallel ports, MultiMate word processor, tutorial software **Video:** 640 x 400 graphics **Size/Weight:** 6.3 x 19.5 x 17 inches
Value: $8 to $25

Convergent Technologies WorkSlate
(1983, notebook)
Original Retail Price: $895
Base Configuration: 6303 CPU, 16K RAM, 64K ROM, integral microcassette drive, monochrome LCD, integral keyboard/keypad, two serial ports, Scheduler software in ROM, internal modem, AC adapter **Video:** 16-line x 46-column text **Size/Weight:** 8.5 x 11 x 1 inches, 4 lbs. **Important Options:** Taskware applications, MicroPrinter, NiCad battery pack
Value: $45 to $100

Ahead of its time, the WorkSlate ($45 to $100) from Convergent Technologies.

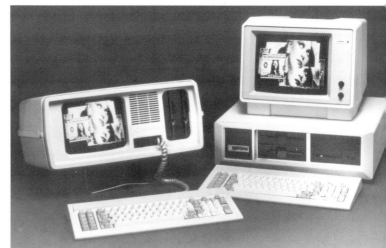

From Corona Data Systems, an important early PC-compatible maker, the Corona Portable PC ($15 to $45) and the Corona PC ($10 to $35).

Corona Portable PC (1983, transportable PC)
Original Retail Price: $2,395
Base Configuration: 8088 CPU, MS-DOS, four ISA slots, 5.25-inch floppy disk drive, integral 9-inch monochrome CRT display, keyboard/keypad, RS-232C and parallel ports, spreadsheet software **Video:** 640 x 325 graphics **Size/Weight:** 9.6 x 18.6 x 19.8, 28 lbs. **Important Options:** 10MB hard disk drive, carrying case
Value: $15 to $45

Corvus Systems (San Jose, California)

The Corvus Concept was an interesting design. It was optimized for networked business applications with a page-length, high resolution display. The display could be rotated for a portrait or landscape view. A separate 6801 processor was dedicated to networking tasks. A pull-out drawer made the expansion slots easily accessible. Versions ranged from a diskless workstation to a high-end networking system. The Concept could run CP/M software through emulation.

Shown with the display in the portrait position, the Corvus Concept ($75 to $200).

Corvus Concept (1982, desktop)
Original Retail Price: $4,995 to $8,000
Base Configuration: 8MHz 68000, proprietary operating system, four expansion slots, 256K RAM (512K max), 15-inch monochrome monitor, keyboard/keypad, two RS-232 ports and one IEEE-488 port, UCSD Pascal, FORTRAN 77, Constellation II and Omninet network, application suite, sound generator **Video:** 72-line x 80-column text, 720 x 560 graphics **Size/Weight:** 4.5 x 15 x 17 inches, 24.5 lbs. **Important Options:** 5.25- or 8-inch floppy disk drive, 6- to 20MB hard disk drive, videotape backup drive
Value: $75 to $200

Cromemco (Mountain View, California)

Cromemco got its name from Crothers Memorial Hall at Stanford University, where Roger Melen and Harry Garland founded the company as students. The company still exists in Europe selling massively parallel and multiprocessor systems.

The Z-1 was the first system that Cromemco produced, and it used an IMSAI I-8080 chassis to house the Z-1 CPU and other Cromemco boards.

The Z-2 series was the first commercial microcomputer that the U.S. Navy allowed for use aboard ship as is. The system was overbuilt with an industrial-strength 30-watt power supply and a heavy card cage. Early units had no bays in the front panel for mounting storage devices. Cromemco sold the Z-2 for dedicated computing tasks, which is why its front panel has no switches or keys. Users could let the Z-2 run its tasks without fear of someone interfering with its operation. In late 1977, Cromemco introduced the Z-2D, which had an RS-232C interface and could accommodate up to four internal 5.25-inch floppy drives.

Cromemco used custom LSI gate arrays to reduce the overall chip count for the C-10 SP to 45. Without this technology, the count would have been 105. The company might have been the first to use this technology for a personal computer. The main system is built into the monitor, which sold alone as the C-10 model.

The CS1 became a dual-processor system with the addition of the 68000 CPU capable of running both CP/M and CROMIX. CROMIX is a multi-user operating system and a variant of Unix that is capable of running CP/M software. The company shipped 1,000 68000-based systems a month in late 1982. Cromemco also offered a System Two (CS2) series that was configured similarly to the CS1, but designed for industrial applications.

Cromemco Z-1 (1976, early micro)
Original Retail Price: $2,495
Base Configuration: 4MHz Z80 CPU, 22 S-100 slots, 8K RAM, up to 8K ROM, RS-232 port, monitor in ROM, PROM programmer, power supply **Important Options:** color terminal interface, joystick interface, BASIC in ROM, Cyclops data digitizer
Value: $85 to $225

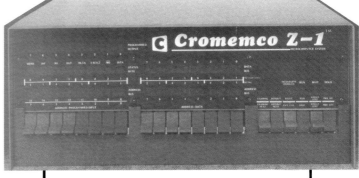

The Cromemco Z-1 ($85 to $225).

Cromemco Z-2 Computer System (1977, early micro)
Original Retail Price: $595 kit, $995 assembled
Base Configuration: 4MHz Z80 CPU, 21 S-100 slots, power supply, rack-mount enclosure **Important Options:** color graphics card, DAC converter, BASIC, bench cabinet
Value: $65 to $155

Cromemco System Zero (desktop)
Original Retail Price: $1,295
Base Configuration: Z80A CPU, CDOS or CROMIX, 128K RAM, RS-232C and parallel ports, BASIC **Video:** 24-line x 80-column text
Value: $20 to $75

Cromemco C-10 SP (1982, desktop)
Original Retail Price: $1,785 to $2,895
Base Configuration: 4MHz Z80A CPU, CP/M or CDOS, 64K RAM, 24K ROM, external 5.25-inch floppy disk drive, integral 12-inch monochrome monitor, keyboard, two RS-232 and one parallel port, application suite
Video: 25-line x 80-column text, 720 x 384 graphics
Important Options: CLQ printer
Value: $15 to $75

Shown with its documentation, the Cromemco C-10 SP ($15 to $75).

Cromemco System One (a.k.a. CS1) (1982, desktop)
Original Retail Price: $4,995 to $9,995 **Base Configuration:** Z80A CPU; CROMIX, CP/M emulator, or CDOS; eight S-100 slots; 64K RAM (2MB max); two 5.25-inch floppy disk drives **Important Options:** 68000 CPU, 5- or 20MB hard disk drive, dual 8-inch floppy disk drives
Value: $15 to $75

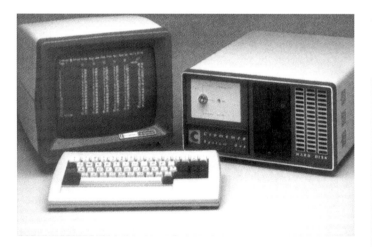

The Cromemco System One ($15 to $75).

Cromemco A1000 (1985, desktop)
Base Configuration: 68000 CPU, 256K RAM (8MB max), 256K ROM, floppy disk drive, NTSC and PAL video ports, RS-232 port **Video:** 640 x 512 graphics
Value: $15 to $5

Data General (Westboro, Massachusetts)

At one time, Data General was mentioned in the same breath as Digital Equipment Corp. as a premier provider of mid-range systems. In the early 1980s, the company started producing high-end, business-oriented microcomputers such as the Model 10.

The Data General/One created a stir when it was release in 1984. It offered a level of power and PC compatibility never before available in an under 10-pound package. Because of Data General's corporate customer base, many DG/Ones were used by sales or field personnel. In 1986, DG introduced a bigger, heavier DG/One Model 2 that had an ELD and a 10MB hard drive standard. Hobbyists recognize the DG/One's historical significance, making it a sought-after system. DG/Ones are not rare, but they aren't common, either.

Data General Model 10 (1983, desktop)
Original Retail Price: $9,660
Base Configuration: 8086 CPU, CP/M-86, 128K RAM (768K max), 5.25-inch floppy disk drive, keyboard/keypad, serial and parallel ports **Video:** 25-line x 80-column text **Important Options:** MS-DOS, AOS, RDOS, or MP/AOS-SU; 15- or 30MB hard disk drive
Value: $17 to $45

Data General/One (Sept. 1984, laptop PC)
Original Retail Price: $2,895 to $5,595
Base Configuration: 4MHz 80C88 CPU, MS-DOS or CP/M-86, 128K RAM (512K max), 32K ROM, 3.5-inch floppy disk drive, 10.75-inch monochrome LCD, integral keyboard, two RS-232C ports, AC adapter, battery pack **Video:** 25-line x 80-column text, 640 x 256 graphics **Size/Weight:** 13.7 x 11.7 x 2.8 inches, 9.1 lbs. **Important Options:** expansion chassis, internal or external modem, battery pack and charger, hard or soft carrying case, printer
Value: $12 to $50

A laptop classic, the Data General/One ($12 to $50).

Datapoint Corp. (San Antonio, Texas)

Datapoint was primarily a networking company whose main product was the ARCNET local area network. The base 1560 model was a diskless network workstation, but high end models were standalone systems aimed at a small business or professional market.

Datapoint 1560 Processor (1982, desktop)
Base Configuration: Z80A CPU, Datapoint DOS or CP/M, 64K RAM (128K max), 12K ROM, integral 10-inch monochrome CRT, keyboard/keypad, RS-232C port **Video:** 24-line x 80-column text **Size/Weight:** 12.4 x 20 x 22.7 inches, 54 lbs. **Important Options:** 8-inch floppy disk drive, 10MB hard disk drive, 9621 or 9627 printer, ARCNET interface
Value: $15 to $65

The Datapoint 1560 Processor ($15 to $65).

Data Technology Industries (DTI) (San Leandro, California)

DTI and Gnat Computers jointly developed the System 10 computer in 1979, selling about 2,000 units through 1980. The System 10 then became The Associate, and DTI bought out Gnat in 1983. In that year, DTI introduced the Assistant CP, a dual-processor system that was both Apple II and CP/M compatible.

By adding Apple compatibility to a CP/M system, DTI hoped to have a machine that appealed to both the business and home markets. This strategy almost never worked, and few Assistant CPs were sold.

DTI The Associate Series (1979, desktop)
Base Configuration: Z80 CPU, CP/M, 64K RAM (256K max), 5.25-inch floppy disk drive **Important Options:** 6502 coprocessor, second 5.25-inch floppy disk drive, 6MB hard disk drive, enhanced video board
Value: $20 to $50

DTI Assistant CP (Oct. 1983, Apple II-class desktop)
Base Configuration: Z80A and 6502 CPUs, CP/M, 10 expansion slots, TV adapter, keyboard/keypad, game port **Size/Weight:** 14 lbs. **Important Options:** printer
Value: $15 to $35

Digital Electronics Corp. (Oakland, California)

Two models were available from Digital Electronics: the DE68C without a floppy drive in a smaller enclosure and the floppy-based DE68DT.

Digital Electronics DE68 (1977, early micro)
Original Retail Price: $2,200
Base Configuration: 6800 CPU, nine expansion slots, up to 65K RAM, cassette recorder, 5.25-inch floppy disk drive, integral 20-character LED, integral keyboard, RS-232C port, BASIC, FORTRAN, integral printer **Important Options:** second cassette recorder, operating system in ROM
Value: $50 to $175

An early keyboard unit, the Digital Electronics DE68 ($50 to $175).

Digital Equipment Corp. (DEC) (Maynard, Massachusetts)

In the 1970s, it looked as if DEC might supplant IBM as the world's leading computer company. Its PDP and VAX minicomputers were selling well all over the world, and the mainframe's status as the primary business computing platform appeared threatened. It's a great irony, then, that DEC would eventually succumb in part because it failed to appreciate how important microcomputers would become to business.

The company's first microcomputer, in fact, was really a small minicomputer. The low-cost 16-bit PDP-11/03 used DEC's four-chip LSI-11 microprocessor to emulate the PDP-11 instruction set. It can run the full line of PDP-11 software. The LSI-11 was also available as a standalone CPU board, some of which were sold to hobbyists. These systems were also used as front-end processors for the DEC VAX 11-780. They are reasonably easy to find for systems of this era.

The Rainbow series was DEC's first serious attempt to enter the microcomputer market. Although the Rainbow runs both MS-DOS and CP/M, it recognizes only software recorded in its own disk format. The Rainbow 100+ model, introduced in September 1983, will read IBM PC-format disks, but cannot write to that format. The Rainbow 100+ had a 10MB hard disk drive, two floppy drives, and 128K RAM standard. A Rainbow 100B followed with a configuration similar to the 100+, but with a lower base price.

DEC's other micro-class systems were compatible with its minicomputer lines and were designed to work within a network of DEC systems. The DECmate series was sold primarily for word processing applications, although it was a capable general-purpose personal computer. All, including the more limited DECmate I, were compatible with DEC's PDP-8 minicomputers. The DECmate III (also known as the PC23X) was introduced in 1984. It was an enhanced version of the DECmate II in a smaller enclosure.

DEC referred to the Professional series as the Personal PDP-11, as it could run software for the PDP-11 minicomputer line. In fact, most were sold as workstations to run on PDP-11- and VAX-based networks. The 350 and 380 ran a wide range of operating systems, including RT-11, CTS-300, MS-DOS, CP/M-80, IDRIS, and Xenix.

DEC claimed that the VAXmate was the first networked personal computer, meaning that it was designed from the ground up to work as part of a network. That network could include all DEC systems or any PC-compatible computer.

DEC PDP-11/03
(June 1975, early micro)
Original Retail Price: $1,000
Base Configuration: LSI-11 chipset; Unix; LSI bus (Qbus); 4K RAM (32K max); serial, parallel, and cassette ports; power supply; mounting box **Size/Weight:** 3.5 x 19 x 13.5 inches
Value: $50 to $175

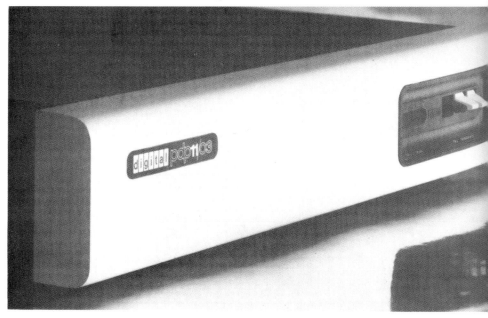

Digital Equipment Corp.'s first micro, the PDP-11/03 ($50 to $175).

DEC Rainbow (1983, desktop)
Original Retail Price:
$3,495 to $6,295
Base Configuration: 4MHz Z80A and 4.8MHz 8088 CPUs, CP/M-86/80, three slots, 64K RAM (896K max), 24K ROM, two 5.25-inch floppy disk drives, 12-inch monochrome monitor, keyboard/keypad, two RS-232/423 ports, tutorial software, user manuals **Video:** 24-line x 132-column text, 800 x 240 graphics, 16 colors **Size/Weight:** 6.5 x 22 x 14.3 inches, 35 lbs. **Important Options:** MS-DOS, Concurrent CP/M, or UCSD p-System; 5- or 10MB hard disk drive; 13-inch color monitor; graphics card; LA50, LA100, or LQP02 printer; technical reference
Value: $20 to $70

The DEC Rainbow 100+ ($20 to $70) with optional monitor.

DEC DECmate II (May 1982, desktop)
Base Configuration: 8MHz 6120 CPU, COS 310, three expansion slots, 96K RAM, two 5.25-inch floppy disk drives, monochrome monitor, keyboard/keypad, RS-232 and RS-232C/423-A ports, WPS word processor, tutorial software **Video:** 24-line x 132-column text **Size/Weight:** 6.5 x 19 x 14.3 inches, 30 lbs. **Important Options:** CP/M-80; 8-inch floppy disk drive; 10MB hard disk drive; LA50, LA100, or LQP02 printer
Value: $17 to $45

DEC DECmate Office Workstation (Oct. 1983, desktop)
Original Retail Price: $4,735
Base Configuration: Z80A CPU, CP/M 2.2, monochrome monitor, keyboard/keypad, WPS word processor, EasyCom **Important Options:** 10MB hard disk drive
Value: $15 to $40

DEC Professional 325 (desktop)
Base Configuration: J-11 chipset, P/OS, expansion slot, 512K RAM, two 5.25-inch floppy disk drives, monochrome monitor, keyboard/keypad, two RS-232/423 ports, PROSE editor, tutorial software **Video:** 24-line x 132-column text **Important Options:** 13-inch color monitor; LA50, LA100, or LQP02 printer
Value: $15 to $40

DEC Professional 350 (desktop)

Base Configuration: J-11 chipset, P/OS, three expansion slots, 512K RAM (1MB max), two 5.25-inch floppy disk drives, 5MB hard disk drive, monochrome monitor, keyboard/keypad, two RS-232/423 ports, PROSE editor, tutorial software **Video:** 24-line x 132-column text **Important Options:** CP/M-80; 10MB hard disk drive; 13-inch color monitor; LA50, LA100, or LQP02 printer
Value: $15 to $40

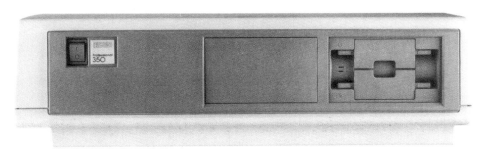

The DEC Professional 350 ($15 to $40).

DEC Professional 380 (desktop)

Original Retail Price: $8,995
Base Configuration: J-11 chipset, 512K RAM (1MB max), 10MB hard disk drive, monochrome monitor, keyboard/keypad **Video:** 960 x 480 graphics, eight colors **Important Options:** 33MB hard disk drive, color monitor
Value: $15 to $40

DEC's famous VAX architecture in micro form: the VAXmate ($17 to $45).

DEC VAXmate

(Sept. 1986, desktop PC)
Original Retail Price: $4,045
Base Configuration: 8MHz 80286 CPU, MS-DOS 3.1 and Windows, 1MB RAM (3MB max), 5.25-inch floppy disk drive, integral monochrome CRT, keyboard/keypad, mouse, VT220 and VT240 terminal emulators, DECnet/Thinwire Ethernet **Important Options:** 20MB hard disk drive, modem, LN03 or LA75 printer
Value: $17 to $45

The Digital Group
(Denver, Colorado)

Talk about giving your customer choices. The Digital Group offered many of the most popular CPU cards and operating systems of the day, along with a healthy selection of interfaces and peripherals. All of the company's models had three different system buses: one each for CPU, memory, and I/O. The Digital Group built about 4,000 systems before closing in 1979.

The Bytemaster series was the last model The Digital Group produced. It was a compact design for the era, with the main CPU unit mounted in a swiveling cradle. Some company literature indicates that it was available in kit form, but other sources show only assembled models. There might have been a model without cassette or disk storage as well.

Digital Group Series 1 (1975, early micro)
Original Retail Price: $375 kit
Base Configuration: Z80 CPU, nine expansion slots, 2K RAM (10K max), video interface, I/O card **Video:** 16-line x 64-column text **Important Options:** 8080, 6800, or 6502 CPU; PHIMON, DISKMON, CP/M, OASIS, or MCOS; Phideck tape drive, 5.25- or 8-inch floppy disk drive, 9-inch monochrome monitor, keyboard/keypad, printer, power supply
Value: $50 to $275

Digital Group Series 2 (1975, early micro)
Original Retail Price: $1,095 to $2,245 kit,
$1,475 to $2,695 assembled
Base Configuration: Z80A CPU, nine expansion slots, 10K RAM (64K max), video interface, keyboard/keypad, I/O card **Video:** 16-line x 64-column text **Important Options:** 8080, 6800, or 6502 CPU; PHIMON, DISKMON, CP/M, OASIS, or MCOS; Phideck tape drive, 5.25- or 8-inch floppy disk drive, 9-inch monochrome monitor, printer, power supply, enclosure
Value: $50 to $250

Digital Group Series 3 (1975, early micro)
Original Retail Price: $1,695 to $3,875 kit,
$1,995 to $5,795 assembled
Base Configuration: Z80A CPU, CP/M, nine expansion slots, 18K RAM (64K max), PROM, video interface, I/O card **Video:** 16-line x 64-column text **Important Options:** 8080, 6800, or 6502 CPU; PHIMON, DISKMON, OASIS, or MCOS; Phideck tape drive, 5.25- or 8-inch floppy disk drive, 9-inch monochrome monitor, keyboard/keypad, printer, power supply, enclosure
Value: $60 to $275

Shown with the optional 5.25-inch dual floppy drives, monitor, and keyboard, the Digital Group Series 3 ($60 to $275, computer only).

An advanced design for its time, the Digital Group Series 4 Bytemaster ($100 to $325).

Digital Group Series 4: Bytemaster
(1978, desktop)
Original Retail Price: $1,995 kit
Base Configuration: Z80A CPU, PHIMON or DISKMON, 18K RAM (64K max), Phideck tape drive or 5.25-inch floppy disk drive, integral 9-inch CRT, keyboard/keypad, I/O card **Video:** 16-line x 64-column text **Important Options:** CP/M, OASIS, or MCOS; printer
Value: $100 to $325

Digital Microsystems
(Oakland, California)

The System 5000 had a swivel display that could be positioned in a page-length portrait mode or in a landscape mode.

Digital Microsystems The Fox (1982, desktop)
Original Retail Price: $3,995
Base Configuration: Z80A CPU, CP/M, 64K RAM, 5.25-inch floppy disk drive, 9-inch monochrome monitor, keyboard/keypad, four RS-232C and two parallel ports, network connector, application suite
Value: $15 to $45

Digital Microsystems System 5000 (1982, desktop)
Original Retail Price: $3,295 to $4,195
Base Configuration: Z80 8086 CPU, 64K RAM (Z80) or 256K RAM (512K max; 8086), monochrome monitor, integral keyboard **Video:** 66-line x 80-column text (portrait mode)
Value: $17 to $50

Digital Systems (Oakland, California)

An earlier, unnamed system was advertised with features similar to the Micro-2. Its value would be the same as the Micro-2.

Digital Systems Micro-2 (1978, early micro)
Original Retail Price: $4,995
Base Configuration: Z80 CPU, CP/M, 32K RAM (64K max), two 5.25-inch floppy disk drives, four RS-232 and one parallel port, Disk BASIC
Value: $50 to $125

Dimension Electronics
(see "Micro Craft Corp.")

Diser Corp. (Orem, Utah)

Originally designed and sold in Europe as the Lilith in 1980, the Modula Computer took advantage of Niklaus Wirth's Modula-2 programming language. Wirth created the Pascal language, and Modula-2 was an evolutionary step above Pascal. However, Diser stopped production of the computer within a year of its launch to concentrate on software. Modula Computer Systems continued to sell Lilith computers in the U.S.

Diser Modula Computer (1983, desktop)
Base Configuration: Am2901 CPU, Modula-2, 128K RAM, 2K ROM, 10MB hard disk drive, page-length monochrome monitor, keyboard/keypad, mouse, RS-232 port **Video:** 832 x 640 graphics **Size/Weight:** 30 x 15 x 30 inches
Value: $125 to $300

For Modula-2 programmers only, the Diser Modula Computer ($125 to $300).

Docutel/Olivetti Corp. (see "Olivetti Corp.")

Dragon Data Ltd. (West Glamorgan, U.K.)

The Dragon 32/64 enjoyed success in Europe, and eventually the company sold the system in the U.S. Although the Dragon 32 and 64 (labeled according to the amount of RAM) were by far the best-selling TRS-80 Color Computer compatibles, their run in the U.S. was short. The market for 8-bit home computers had peaked, and Tandy had begun to offer more powerful systems at a similar price point. Dragon 32/64 systems will run most CoCo software.

Dragon Data Dragon 32/Dragon 64 (home computer)
Base Configuration: 6809E CPU, expansion slot, 32K RAM (64K max), 16K ROM, TV adapter, integral keyboard, parallel and two game ports, Microsoft Extended Colour BASIC, BASIC manual **Video:** 256 x 192 graphics **Important Options:** cassette recorder, joysticks
Value: $15 to $60

Dulmont Electronic Systems (New South Wales, Australia)

The Dulmont Magnum was unusually small for an MS-DOS portable when new. It achieved this by sacrificing on screen size and storage. It had a dinky eight-line display (a U.S. version had a 16-line display) and no disk drive, relying instead on ROM packs. The system was later sold by Time Office Computers as the Kookaburra.

Dulmont Magnum (Nov. 1983, laptop PC)
Original Retail Price: $2,995
Base Configuration: 80186 CPU, MS-DOS 2.0, expansion slot, 96K RAM (256K max), 128K ROM (384K max), 256K ROM pack storage, integral monochrome LCD, integral keyboard, two serial and one parallel port, application suite in ROM, battery pack, AC adapter **Video:** 8-line x 80-column text **Size/Weight:** 12 x 11 x 1 inches, 8.6 lbs. **Important Options:** dual external 5.25-inch floppy disk drives, modem, BASIC 86
Value: $75 to $125

An early laptop from Australia, the Dulmont Magnum, a.k.a. the Kookaburra ($75 to $125).

A popular home computer in Europe, the Dragon 32 ($15 to $60).

Durango Systems Inc. (San Jose, California)

The Durango Poppy was available as a standalone MS-DOS system. The Poppy II was the multi-user version that used both 80186 and 80286 CPUs and either Xenix or a CP/M-based operating system.

Durango Poppy (April 1983, desktop PC)
Original Retail Price: $4,395
Base Configuration: 8MHz 80186 CPU, MS-DOS, 128K RAM (1.125MB max), two 5.25-inch floppy disk drives, 14-inch monochrome monitor, keyboard/keypad, two RS-232/422 and one parallel port, Star BASIC **Size/Weight:** 6 x 19 x 18 inches **Important Options:** 80286 coprocessor; Concurrent CP/M-86, MP/M-86, or Xenix; 20MB hard disk drive; Poppywriter printer
Value: $15 to $45

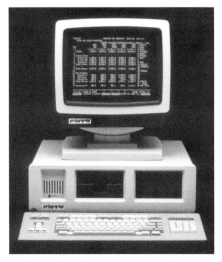

The Durango Poppy ($15 to $45).

Dynalogic Info-Tech, Bytec, Bytec-Comterm, Bytec/ Dynalogic (Ottawa, Canada)

This company changed names more often than some people change socks. At least the Hyperion portable kept its name through it all. The system changed cosmetically during its production run; some have beige cases and others are gray with minor differences on the front panels. The Hyperion was one of the first luggable PC-compatible systems, beating the Compaq Portable to market, and Bytec-Comterm was one of the first system vendors to endorse Microsoft Windows in 1983.

Dynalogic Info-Tech Hyperion
(1983, transportable PC)
Original Retail Price: $3,195 to $3,690
Base Configuration: 4.77MHz 8088 CPU, MS-DOS, 256K RAM, 8K ROM, 5.25-inch floppy disk drive, integral 7-inch monochrome CRT, keyboard/keypad, RS-232C and parallel ports, BASIC, Aladin database software, internal modem **Video:** 25-line x 80-column text, 640 x 250 graphics **Size/Weight:** 8.8 x 18.3 x 11.3 inches, 18 lbs. **Important Options:** expansion chassis, 10MB hard disk drive, phone-management system, carrying case
Value: $35 to $100

Dynasty Computer Corp. (Dallas, Texas)

Dynasty was the Amway of computer companies. It enlisted more than 3,000 "independent distributors"—individuals who sold the computers door-to-door. However, the company stopped signing new distributors in November 1983, citing competition from the pending launch of the IBM PCjr.

The smart-Alec II was an Exidy Sorcerer-compatible system introduced in the late 1970s. Some sources indicate that later models could accommodate 64K RAM and an 80-column display. Examples of the smart-Alec Jr. have labels indicating that they were made by Video Technology. The system might be a relabeled VZ200.

Dynasty smart-Alec II (home computer)
Base Configuration: 2.1MHz Z80 CPU, CP/M, S-100 bus, 8K RAM (48K max), 4K ROM (16K max), keyboard/keypad **Video:** 30-line x 65-column text, 512 x 240 graphics **Important Options:** 5.25- or 8-inch floppy disk drive, printer, joysticks
Value: $25 to $75

Compatible with the Exidy Sorcerer, the Dynasty smart-Alec II ($25 to $75).

One of the earliest PC-compatible transportables, the Dynalogic Info-Tech Hyperion ($35 to $100).

Made by Video Technology but sold by Dynasty, the smart-Alec Jr. ($10 to $30).

Dynasty smart-Alec Jr. (1982, home computer)
Original Retail Price: $389
Base Configuration: 20K RAM (64K max), keyboard, Microsoft BASIC **Important Options:** cassette recorder, printer, joysticks
Value: $10 to $30

Eaca International Ltd. (Kowloon, Hong Kong)

The Genie I was hardware- and software-compatible with the TRS-80 Model I, but not as reliable. The Genie I was sold in Europe as the Video Genie, in the U.S. by Personal Micro Computers Inc. as the PMC-80, in South Africa as the TRZ-80, and in Australia as the Dick Smith System 80. A Genie II was also TRS-80 Model I-compatible, but did not have a built-in cassette recorder or RF modulator. The systems were poorly shielded for RF interference. In the U.S., the PMC-80 Expander allowed up to four floppy drives to be connected to the system and provided an S-100 expansion slot.

Tandy sued Personal Microcomputers and Eaca International for patent infringement in early 1981. That didn't stop PMC from introducing the PMC-81 that year. It was similar to the PMC-80, but with a keypad and an optional EXP-100 Expander. The EXP-100 provided an S-100 bus and interfaces for a disk drive, printer, and RS-232C. A Genie II EG3008 model had an integrated keyboard/keypad combination.

Primarily a CP/M system, the Genie III's BASIC was same used in Tandy TRS-80 systems. A multi-user version of the Genie III was available with 192K RAM and the MPM/II operating system. The Colour Genie was sold primarily in Europe, Asia, and Australia.

The poor man's TRS-80 Model I, the Eaca Genie I Model EG3003 ($15 to $50).

Eaca International Genie I EG3003 (1980, desktop)
Original Retail Price: $645
Base Configuration: 1.79MHz Z80, 16K RAM (48K max), 13.5K ROM, TV video and monitor ports, integral keyboard, RS-232 port, Level II BASIC in ROM, user's guide, beginner's programming manual, BASIC reference manual **Video:** 16-line x 64-column uppercase text, 128 x 48 graphics **Size/Weight:** 21.26 x 4.33 x 14.57 inches, beige **Important Options:** internal or external cassette recorder, floppy disk drive, monochrome monitor, uppercase character modification, Expander box, Communicator (modem and parallel ports)
Value: $15 to $50

Eaca International Genie III (1982, desktop)
Base Configuration: 3.2MHz Z80A CPU, CP/M 2.2 or GDOS 2.0, 64K RAM, 2K ROM, two 5.25-inch floppy disk drives, integral 12-inch monochrome CRT, keyboard/keypad, RS-232C and parallel ports, Microsoft Level II BASIC, owner's and programming manuals **Video:** 24-line x 80-column text **Size/Weight:** 21 x 4.3 x 14.4 inches **Important Options:** MPM/II, 5MB hard disk drive, cassette recorder, hi-res graphics card, technical reference
Value: $17 to $40

The Eaca Genie III ($17 to $40).

Eaca International EG2000 Colour Genie (1982, desktop)
Base Configuration: 2.2MHz Z80 CPU; expansion port; 16K RAM (32K max); 16K ROM; monitor port; TV adapter; keyboard; RS-232C, parallel, and light-pen ports; Extended Microsoft BASIC, two BASIC manuals; setup cassettes **Video:** 24-line x 40-column text, 160 x 96 graphics, eight colors **Size/Weight:** 17.3 x 3.3 x 10.9 inches **Important Options:** expansion unit, EG2016 cassette recorder, 5.25-inch floppy disk drive, EG2013 joysticks, light pen, EG602 printer
Value: $20 to $50

The Eaca EG2000 Colour Genie ($20 to $50) shown with a TV monitor, optional EG2013 joysticks, and optional EG602 printer.

Eagle Computer Inc. (Los Gatos, California)

The story of Eagle Computer is a sad one. The company launched a line of popular CP/M systems in 1980/1981. By 1983, it was considered one of the premier manufacturers of IBM-compatibles—on par with the likes of Compaq. The company went public that year, but on the day of the initial public offering, company founder and CEO Dennis Barnhart was killed in a car crash. Eagle was forced to rescind the stock issue and re-issue it the following week. Eagle was out of business within a few years. Today its IBM-compatibles are among the most collectible in their class.

Eagle renamed its Eagle Model I, II, III, and IV systems the Eagle IIE Series in April 1983. The only difference among the models was in storage capability. For example, the Model I was a single-floppy system and the Model IV had both floppy and hard disk drives. The change occurred as Eagle was switching product emphasis to its PC-compatible lines. The E in IIE stood for "economy," as the company repositioned its CP/M systems to the low end. At least 7,500 IIE systems were sold.

The Eagle PC was more compatible with IBM software than many of its competitors. An Eagle Plus XL, introduced at about the same time as the Eagle Plus, had a 10MB hard disk drive as standard equipment. A Spirit XL portable with only one floppy drive and a 10MB hard disk drive was also available

A leading early PC-compatible, the Eagle 1600 ($15 to $45).

Eagle Computer Eagle IIE Series (a.k.a. Eagle Model I, Model II, Model III, Model IV)

(Sept. 1981, desktop)
Original Retail Price: $1,595 to $3,995
Base Configuration: 4MHz Z80A CPU, CP/M, 64K RAM, 5.25-inch floppy disk drive, integral monochrome CRT, integral keyboard/keypad, two RS-232 and two parallel ports, CBASIC, application suite **Video:** 24-line x 80-column text **Important Options:** second 5.25-inch floppy disk drive, 10MB hard disk drive, daisy-wheel printer
Value: $15 to $45

The Eagle IIE ($15 to $45).

Eagle Computer Eagle 1600 Series (July 1983, desktop PC)
Original Retail Price: $4,495 to $8,995
Base Configuration: 8MHz 8086 CPU, MS-DOS and CP/M-86, eight ISA slots, 128K RAM (512K max), 5.25-inch floppy disk drive, 10MB hard disk drive, 12-inch monochrome monitor, keyboard/keypad, two RS-232C and one parallel port, application suite **Important Options:** 32MB hard disk drive, videotape backup drive, CGA card
Value: $15 to $45

Eagle Computer Eagle PC Series (Aug. 1983, desktop PC)
Original Retail Price: $1,995 to $4,495
Base Configuration: 4.77MHz 8088 CPU, MS-DOS and CP/M-86, three ISA slots, 64K RAM (512K max), 5.25-inch floppy disk drove, 12-inch monochrome monitor, keyboard/keypad, two serial and one parallel port, owner's manual **Video:** 720 x 352 graphics **Size/Weight:** 20.5 x 5.75 x 13 inches, 30 lbs. **Important Options:** 10- or 32MB hard disk drive, CGA card, GW-BASIC, application suite
Value: $15 to $50

Eagle Computer Eagle Plus (Dec. 1983, desktop PC)
Original Retail Price: $2,395 to $2,795
Base Configuration: 4.77MHz 8088 CPU, MS-DOS 2.0 and CP/M-86, four ISA slots, 128K RAM (640K max), 5.25-inch floppy disk drive, keyboard/keypad, two serial and parallel ports **Size/Weight:** 20.5 x 5.75 x 13 inches **Important Options:** second 5.25-inch floppy disk drive, videotape backup drive, 12-inch monochrome or 14-inch color monitor, CGA or hi-res monochrome card
Value: $12 to $35

Eagle Computer Eagle Turbo XL (1984, desktop PC)
Original Retail Price: $4,995
Base Configuration: 8MHz 8086 CPU, five ISA slots, 256K RAM (512K max), 5.25-inch floppy disk drive, 10MB hard disk drive, keyboard/keypad, parallel port **Video:** 25-line x 80-column text, 720 x 352 graphics **Important Options:** 12-inch monochrome or 13-inch color monitor, CGA or hi-res monochrome card, serial interface, EagleNet I LAN software
Value: $12 to $30

Eagle Computer Eagle Spirit (Dec. 1983, transportable PC)
Original Retail Price: $3,295
Base Configuration: 4.77MHz 8088 CPU, MS-DOS and CP/M-86, four ISA slots, 128K RAM (640K max), two 5.25-inch floppy disk drives, integral 9-inch monochrome CRT, keyboard/keypad, two serial and one parallel port **Video:** 640 x 200 graphics **Size/Weight:** 19.37 x 8.37 x 15.5 inches, 32.5 lbs. **Important Options:** CGA or hi-res monochrome card, FlexMenu and FlexKey software
Value: $12 to $37

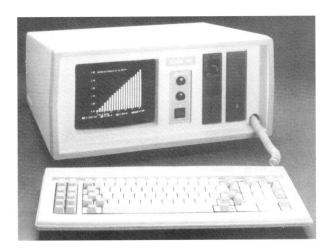

The Eagle Spirit transportable ($12 to $37).

Ebnek Inc (Wichita, Kansas)

Ebnek 77 (1977, early micro)
Original Retail Price: $2,770 kit, $3,800 assembled
Base Configuration: TMS9900 CPU, 16K RAM (64K max), 8K ROM, Phideck tape transport, monochrome TV monitor, keyboard, serial and parallel ports, enclosure, power supply **Video:** 15-line x 64-column text, 256 x 240 graphics
Value: $45 to $110

A complete Ebnek 77 ($45 to $110).

ECD Corp. (Cambridge, Massachusetts)

The Micromind was ahead of its time. It had an interconnect bus that allowed the use of up to 15 processors working in parallel on the same system. A separate display processor handled graphics and text, and memory was expandable to 64MB at a time when 64K was considered more than most people would ever need. Some sources indicate that a Micromind II was built, but little information exists on it.

ECD MicroMind (1977, early micro)
Original Retail Price: $988
Base Configuration: 6500A CPU, 8K RAM (64MB max), cassette interface, keyboard, notsoBASIC, two games, word processor, assembler, debugger, power supply, enclosure
Value: $65 to $200

Educational Microcomputer Systems (Irvine, California)

Although promoted as a portable system, the Micro-One was not a true portable because it did not have its own display or keyboard. It was a small system, and unusual for an American computer in that it used the 3.25-inch microdrive floppy disks.

Educational Micro Systems Micro-One (1983, desktop)
Original Retail Price: $1,295
Base Configuration: 4MHz or 6MHz Z80 CPU, CP/M 2.2, 64K RAM, 2K ROM, 3.25-inch floppy disk drive, two RS-232C and one parallel port, Perfect Software application suite **Size/Weight:** 3 x 8 x 12 inches
Important Options: second 3.25-inch floppy disk drive
Value: $15 to $35

Elan Computers Ltd. (London, U.K.)

The Elan Enterprise had a futuristic design with a colorful keyboard and a built-in joystick. Modular add-ons plugged into a side port in either a stacked or side-by-side fashion. A custom video chip called Nick provided outstanding graphics, and a custom chip called Dave produced superior sound output. The company produced its own line of software for the machine—mostly games and programming tools. The Elan Enterprise apparently was not sold in the U.S., but in Europe it matched up favorably against other machines in its class such as the Dragon 32 and Acorn Electron. Today, good examples are in demand by collectors, especially in Europe.

Elan Enterprise 64/Enterprise 128
(early 1984, home computer)
Base Configuration: 4MHz Z80A CPU; EROS; external expansion slot; 64K RAM (128K max), 32K ROM; TV and RGB video ports; integral keyboard; RS-423, parallel, two game, and two cassette ports; BASIC; word processor in ROM; integral joystick; two manuals; stereo sound output, AC adapter **Video:** 56-line x 84-character text, 672 x 512 graphics, 256 colors **Important Options:** dual external 3.5-inch floppy disk drives
Value: $50 to $275

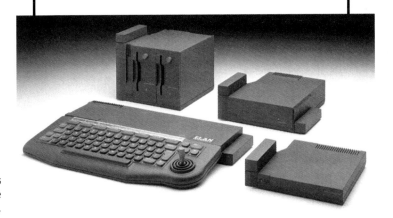

A sought-after collectible in Europe, the Elan Enterprise 64 ($50 to $275) with optional add-on modules and dual floppy drives.

Electronic Product Associates Inc. (San Diego, California)

EPA introduced a Micro68b in 1977 with an RS-232 interface and either single or dual floppy disk drives.

Electronic Product Associates Micro68 (1976, early micro)
Original Retail Price: $430 **Base Configuration:** 6800 CPU, 8K RAM (64K max), 512 bytes ROM, status readout, integral hex keypad, I/O card, enclosure, power supply **Important Options:** TTY/RS-232 interface, carrying case
Value: $65 to $200

Electronic Tool Co. (Hawthorne, California)

An early multi-processor computer, the Etcetera System could support up to five different CPUs, each with its own memory, yet sharing other resources such as power supply and I/O. The ETC-1000 was actually the central control unit of the Etcetera System configured as a standalone computer. The company claimed that a "ruggedized" version of the ETC-1000 could "go almost anywhere: under water, out in nature, or up in space." Like the Etcetera System, it was a multi-processor computer. Production of both systems ended in 1977.

Electronic Tool Etcetera System (1975, early micro)
Base Configuration: 8080A, 6800, 6502, or F8 CPU; 16 expansion slots, 1K RAM (64K max), 256 bytes ROM (4K max), 8-digit LED, integral hex keypad, RS-232C and 20-mA DC current loop ports, enclosure, power supply
Value: $65 to $250

The Electronic Tool ETC-1000 ($50 to $150) had an interesting front panel.

Electronic Tool ETC-1000
(1976, early micro)
Original Retail Price: $830 to $7,197 **Base Configuration:** 6502 CPU; Monitor Control System (MCS); 1K RAM (64K max); 256 bytes ROM (4K max); eight-digit LED; integral hex keypad; RS-232C, cassette, and 20-mA DC current loop ports, debugger, enclosure, power supply **Important Options:** 8080A, 6800, or F8 coprocessor, floppy disk drive, ADM-3 terminal
Value: $50 to $150

Epson America Inc. (Torrance, California)

In the early 1980s, Epson tried to leverage its success in the printer business with a line of business microcomputers. Unfortunately, it made the mistake of creating a new operating system for the computers just as MS-DOS was becoming established.

Valdocs (Valuable Documents)—used only on the QX-10 and QX-16—was part operating system, part application suite. Epson's goal was to create an easy-to-use business computer with the menu structure of Valdocs and special keyboard commands for common functions. Valdocs, which was similar to CP/M, won over many users, but not enough. Also, the Z80A did not deliver the processing power that Valdocs demanded.

The QX-16 added a 16-bit 8088 processor to go with the Z80A used in the QX-10 and bundled three operating systems with the computer.

Epson wisely followed the QX-16 with a line of PC-compatible desktop systems called the Equity I. In March 1987, Epson introduced an enhanced version of the Equity I, the Equity I+, which used a faster (10MHz) version of the 8088 CPU and provided five expansion slots. An Equity II+ followed in 1988 with a 12MHz 80286 CPU. Equity systems sold reasonably well and are relatively common finds today.

The company also had some success with portable computers, starting with the HX-20 notebook in 1982. The HX-20 played a key role in an infamous prank during the 1984 Rose Bowl game. Two CalTech students used an HX-20 and an RF modem to take control of the electronic scoreboard and write their own messages during the game. They also changed the team names for the final score from UCLA and Illinois to CalTech and MIT. An HX-40 followed that was faster, more expandable, and larger, but it was sold only to value-added resellers—middlemen who would configure and develop specialized applications for the system for resale to businesses.

The Geneva PX-8 took advantage of the Tandy TRS-80 Model 100's success with a somewhat improved design, including more memory. In the late 1980s and into the 1990s, Epson sold a series of PC-compatible laptops and notebooks that as of yet have little or no collector value.

Epson QX-10 (1983, desktop)
Original Retail Price: $2,995
Base Configuration: 4MHz Z80A; Valdocs; five slots; 256K RAM (512K max); two 5.25-inch floppy disk drives; 12-inch monochrome monitor; keyboard/keypad; RS-232C, parallel, and light-pen ports; word processor and e-mail software **Video:** 25-line x 80-column text, 640 x 400 graphics **Size/Weight:** 20.3 x 13.6 x 4.1 inches, 20.6 lbs. **Important Options:** MS-DOS
Value: $20 to $75

The innovative but underpowered Epson QX-10 ($20 to $75).

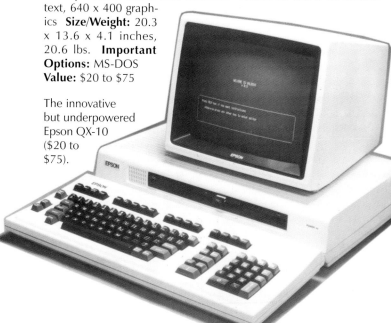

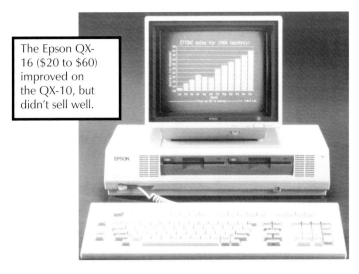

The Epson QX-16 ($20 to $60) improved on the QX-10, but didn't sell well.

Epson QX-16 (1984, desktop)
Original Retail Price: $3,000
Base Configuration: 8088 and Z80A CPUs, Valdocs 2, CP/M, and MS-DOS; 256K RAM (512K max); two 5.25-inch floppy disk drives, RS-232C and parallel ports **Video:** 640 x 400 graphics **Important Options:** hard disk drive
Value: $20 to $60

Epson Equity I (1986, desktop PC)
Original Retail Price: $1,295
Base Configuration: 4.77MHz 80C88 CPU, MS-DOS 2.11, three ISA slots, 256K RAM (640K max), 16K ROM, 5.25-inch floppy disk drive, keyboard/keypad, RS-232C and parallel ports **Video:** CGA **Size/Weight:** 14.5 x 15 x 5.75 inches, 24.3 lbs. **Important Options:** second 5.25-inch floppy disk drive, 20MB hard disk drive, 12-inch monochrome or 13-inch color monitor, mouse
Value: $5 to $30

Epson's first PC-compatible, the Equity I ($5 to $30).

Epson Equity II (desktop PC)
Base Configuration: 7.16MHz V-30 CPU, MS-DOS 3.1, five ISA slots, 640K RAM, 16K ROM (64K max), 5.25-inch floppy disk drive, keyboard/keypad, RS-232C and parallel ports **Video:** CGA **Size/Weight:** 14.5 x 15 x 5.75 inches, 25 lbs. **Important Options:** second 5.25-inch floppy disk drive, 20MB hard disk drive, 12-inch monochrome or 13-inch color monitor, mouse
Value: $5 to $25

Epson Equity LT (Sept. 1987, laptop PC)
Original Retail Price: $1,899 to $2,999
Base Configuration: 10MHz V-30 CPU, MS-DOS 3.2, two proprietary expansion slots, 640K RAM, 16K ROM, 3.5-inch floppy disk drive, RGB video port, monochrome LCD, integral keyboard, RS-232C and parallel ports, LapLink, NiCad battery pack, AC adapter **Video:** 25-line x 80-column text, 640 x 200 graphics **Size/Weight:** 12.2 x 13.6 x 3.2 inches, 12 lbs. **Important Options:** second 3.5-inch floppy disk drive, 20MB hard disk drive, external 5.25-inch floppy disk drive, 13-inch color monitor, internal modem, carrying case
Value: $7 to $30

The Epson Equity LT ($7 to $30) was one of the better laptop PCs.

Epson HX-20 (1982, notebook)
Original Retail Price: $795
Base Configuration: 6301 CPU, proprietary expansion slot, 16K RAM (32K max), 32K ROM (64K max), integral microcassette drive, monochrome LCD, integral keyboard, RS-232C and serial ports, SkiWriter word processor in ROM, integral printer, tutorial and reference manuals, NiCad battery pack, AC adapter **Video:** 4-line x 20-column text **Size/Weight:** 11.38 x 8.5 x 1.75 inches, 3.75 lbs. **Important Options:** expansion unit, CX-20 acoustic coupler
Value: $15 to $75

An early notebook system, the Epson HX-20 ($15 to $75) is a popular and still reasonably priced collectible.

Epson HX-40 (1984, notebook)

Base Configuration: 3.68MHz Z80 CPU; CP/M 2.2; 64K RAM (128K max), 96K ROM; monochrome LCD; integral keyboard; RS-232C, serial, parallel, and bar-code ports; NiCad battery pack; AC adapter **Video:** 8-line x 40-column text **Size/Weight:** 8.37 x 11.62 x 1.37 inches, 3.5 lbs. **Important Options:** microcassette drive, 5.25-inch floppy disk drive, modem, printer, bar-code reader
Value: $15 to $75

The big brother to the HX-20, the Epson HX-40 ($15 to $75) is harder to find today.

Epson Geneva PX-8 (1984, notebook)

Original Retail Price: $995
Base Configuration: 2.45MHz Z80 CPU, CP/M 2.2, 64K RAM (184K max), 32K ROM, integral microcassette drive, monochrome LCD, integral keyboard/keypad, RS-232C and parallel ports, application suite in ROM, NiCad battery, AC adapter **Video:** 8-line x 80-column text **Size/Weight:** 8.5 x 11.5 x 1.75 inches, 4 lbs. **Important Options:** 3.5-inch floppy disk drive, modem, thermal printer
Value: $25 to $100

Another popular Epson notebook, the Geneva PX-8 ($25 to $100) shown with its optional printer, floppy drive, and add-on modules.

Ericsson Inc. (Greenwich, Connecticut)

The Portable PC's detachable keyboard stowed under the gas plasma display, which folded up.

Ericsson Portable PC (1985, laptop PC)
Original Retail Price: $2,995
Base Configuration: 8088 CPU, MS-DOS, 256K RAM (512K max), monochrome gas plasma display, keyboard/keypad **Video:** 25-line x 80-column text, 640 x 400 graphics **Size/Weight:** 12.2 x 15.4 x 4.5 inches, 15 lbs. **Important Options:** expansion box, 512K RAM disk, internal modem, integral printer
Value: $8 to $30

ET Computer Systems (Lemon Grove, California)

The ET-2010 was upgradeable to multi-user capability.

ET Computer Systems ET-2010 (1984, desktop)
Original Retail Price: $1,225
Base Configuration: 4MHz Z80A CPU, CP/M 2.2-compatible operating system, 64K RAM, 5.25-inch floppy disk drive, integral 9-inch monochrome CRT, keyboard/keypad, serial and parallel ports, BASIC, application suite **Video:** 24-line x 80-column text **Important Options:** 6MHz Z80B CPU, 10MB hard disk drive, second 5.25-inch floppy disk drive
Value: $15 to $45

Exidy Systems Inc. (Sunnyvale, California)

The Sorcerer might have been the first computer to use plug-in ROM cartridges (which Exidy called ROM-PACs) as a software medium. Users had to supply their own video monitor and cassette recorder. Sorcerers are prized and uncommon collectibles today. Personal Systems Consulting made the Sorcerer-compatible PS-80.

Exidy Sorcerer (June 1978, desktop)
Original Retail Price: $895
Base Configuration: 2MHz Z80 CPU; CP/M; ROM cartridge slot 8K RAM (48K max), 12K ROM; integral keyboard; RS-232, parallel, and two cassette ports **Video:** 30-line x 64-column text, 512 x 240 graphics **Important Options:** S-100 bus expansion chassis
Value: $100 to $200

The Exidy Sorcerer ($100 to $200) might have been the first micro to use a ROM cartridge (on the right). The cassette recorder and TV were user-supplied.

Extec Corp. (Carmel, Ind.)

With its hinged keyboard folded up and latched, the Extec 1000 looked much like a piece of luggage.

Extec 1000 (1983, transportable)
Original Retail Price: $4,995
Base Configuration: CP/M, 64K RAM (512K max), two 5.25-inch floppy disk drives, integral 9-inch monochrome CRT, keyboard/keypad, BASIC, spreadsheet, integral printer
Value: $15 to $40

Extra Computer Corp. (San Francisco, California)

One unusual feature of the System One is that it had a metal enclosure rather than plastic. Perhaps this was a convenient way to shield for RFI, which the government was cracking down on at the time.

Extra Computer System One
(June 1983, Apple II-class desktop)
Original Retail Price: $795
Base Configuration: Z80A and 6502 CPUs, CP/M 2.2 and AppleDOS, seven Apple-compatible slots, 64K RAM, 24K ROM, NTSC and RF video ports, integral keyboard/keypad, game port, Perfect Writer and Perfect Calc, CP/M manuals **Video:** 80-column text, 280 x 192 graphics
Value: $12 to $40

Facit Inc. (Nashua, New Hampshire)

Facit was known primarily as a manufacturer of printers for business. The Facit DTC had a few small ergonomic innovations, such as an anti-glare screen and a wrist rest on the keyboard. Facit's Swedish parent company, Facit AB, sold different configurations of the DTC in Europe for business and technical applications.

Facit DTC Series (Jan. 1983, desktop)
Base Configuration: Z80A CPU, CP/M 2.2 and Facit DOS, 64K RAM, 32K ROM, two external 5.25-inch floppy disk drives, 15-inch monochrome monitor, keyboard/keypad, two RS-232C ports, BASIC **Video:** 80-column text
Value: $15 to $40

The Facit DTC ($15 to $40) was the only micro offered by this manufacturer of printers and storage devices.

Findex (Torrance, California)

A System 100 replaced the bubble memory storage of the System 128 with a 5.25-inch floppy drive.

The Findex Portable Computer ($100 to $250) featured bubble memory storage and a built-in keyboard and printer.

Findex System 128
(1979, early micro)
Original Retail Price: $5,000
Base Configuration: five S-100 slots, 128K bubble memory, 48K RAM (2MB max), 8K ROM (32K max), floppy disk drive, integral monochrome gas plasma display, integral keyboard/keypad, serial and parallel ports, BASIC, integral printer
Video: 6-line x 40-column text
Value: $75 to $200

Findex Portable Computer (transportable)
Original Retail Price: $6,980
Base Configuration: Z80 CPU; CP/M; 48K RAM; bubble memory storage, integral monochrome display; RS-232C, parallel, and IEEE-488 ports; BASIC; integral printer **Video:** 6-line x 40-column text
Value: $100 to $250

Fortune Systems (San Carlos, California)

Fortune designed the Unix-based 32:16 to be used as either a multi- or single-user system. It was network ready and offered many upgrade options. The stylish white enclosure, keyboard, and monitor were a welcome departure from the boxy utilitarian look that many of the 32:16's competitors displayed.

Fortune 32:16 (March 1982, desktop)
Original Retail Price: $4,995
Base Configuration: 68000 CPU, Fortune Operating System, five expansion slots, 128K RAM (1MB max), 4K ROM (16K max), 5.25-inch floppy disk drive, 12-inch monochrome monitor, keyboard/keypad, RS-232C port **Video:** 80-column text **Size/Weight:** 5.8 x 13.9 x 22.3 inches, 30 lbs. **Important Options:** second 5.25-inch floppy disk drive, 5- to 20MB hard disk drive, tape backup drive, parallel interface, printer
Value: $15 to $40

The sharp-looking, Unix-based Fortune 32:16 ($15 to $40).

Franklin Computer Corp. (Pennsauken, New Jersey)

Franklin was considered the second largest manufacturer of Apple II clones behind Video Technology. By mid-1984, it had sold more than 100,000 Ace 100, Ace 1000, and Ace 1200 systems. A long legal battle with Apple Computer over the use of Apple system ROMs eventually forced the company to abandon the Apple line and turn to building specialized handheld computing devices. The company also briefly produced a line of unremarkable PC compatible systems.

An Ace 1000 Plus model used the same housing as the Ace 1200 to offer an internal floppy disk drive. Franklin sold the 1000 series with several different option and software bundles under different model names, but the base 1000 or 1000 Plus units were unchanged.

The Ace 1200 was a hybrid Apple-CP/M system aimed at a more professional user. It had a larger enclosure with room above the keyboard for up to two disk drives. The Ace 2200 was the last Apple II-compatible that Franklin produced.

The portable CX line could accommodate either a Z80 or Intel 8086 CPU in addition to its standard 6502 processor. Fully configured, a CX could run Apple DOS plus CP/M or MS-DOS software. The CX system had a short production run and is an unusual find today.

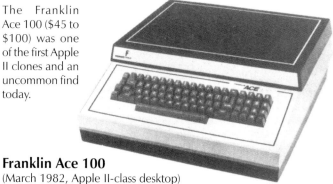

The Franklin Ace 100 ($45 to $100) was one of the first Apple II clones and an uncommon find today.

Franklin Ace 100

(March 1982, Apple II-class desktop)
Original Retail Price: $1,495
Base Configuration: 6502 CPU, Apple DOS-compatible, Apple-compatible expansion slots, integral keyboard/keypad, BASIC **Video:** 24-line x 40-column text, 280 x 160 graphics, 15 colors **Size/Weight:** 19 x 5.5 x 21.12 inches
Value: $45 to $100

Franklin Ace 1000 (June 1982, Apple II-class desktop)

Original Retail Price: $1,595
Base Configuration: 1.02MHz 6502 CPU, eight Apple-compatible slots, 64K RAM, integral keyboard/keypad, game port, BASIC manual **Video:** 40-column text, 260 x 192 graphics **Size/Weight:** 17.75 x 4.5 x 19.75 inches, 15 lbs. **Important Options:** 5.25-inch floppy disk drive, 10MB hard disk drive, monochrome Video Monitor, AceWriter
Value: $10 to $42

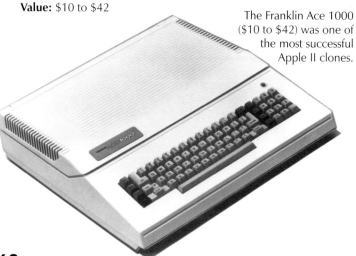

The Franklin Ace 1000 ($10 to $42) was one of the most successful Apple II clones.

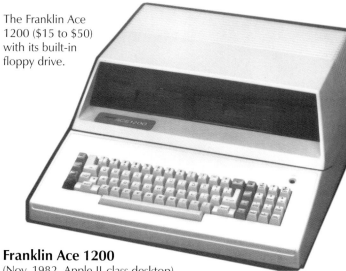

The Franklin Ace 1200 ($15 to $50) with its built-in floppy drive.

Franklin Ace 1200

(Nov. 1982, Apple II-class desktop)
Original Retail Price: $1,995
Base Configuration: 1.02MHz 6502 and 6MHz Z80 CPUs; CP/M; three Apple-compatible slots; 128K RAM; 5.25-inch floppy disk drive; integral keyboard/keypad; serial, parallel, and game ports **Video:** 80-column text, 280 x 192 graphics **Size/Weight:** 17.75 x 8 x 19.75 inches, 22.25 lbs. **Important Options:** second 5.25-inch floppy disk drive, external 10MB hard disk drive, monochrome Video Monitor
Value: $15 to $50

Franklin Ace 2200 (Apple II-class desktop)

Original Retail Price: $999
Base Configuration: 1.02MHz 65SC02 CPU, Franklin DOS 2, two Apple-compatible slots, 128K RAM, 24K ROM, two 5.25-inch floppy disk drives, composite video port, keyboard/keypad, serial and game ports, Franklin BASIC, owner's manual **Video:** 24-line x 80-column text **Size/Weight:** 15.75 x 13.5 x 4 inches **Important Options:** expansion chassis, monochrome monitor
Value: $12 to $45

Franklin CX Series (May 1984, Apple II-class transportable)

Original Retail Price: $1,395 to $2,295
Base Configuration: 1MHz 6502 CPU, Franklin DOS, 64K RAM (128K max), 5.25-inch floppy disk drive, integral 7-inch monochrome CRT, composite video port, keyboard/keypad, RS-232C and parallel ports, application suite **Video:** 80-column text, 280 x 192 graphics **Size/Weight:** 15.7 x 16.9 x 6.5 inches, 27 lbs. **Important Options:** 5MHz 8086 or 6MHz Z80 coprocessor, CP/M or MS-DOS, second 5.25-inch floppy disk drive, modem, carrying case, technical reference manual
Value: $20 to $50

Fujitsu Microelectronics Professional Microsystem Division (Santa Clara, California)

Japan's Fujitsu Ltd. was the largest computer manufacturer outside of the U.S. when the Micro 16s was introduced. The Micro 16s was Fujitsu's first attempt to enter the American microcomputer market. The system featured an early graphical user interface called GSX-86, developed by CP/M vendor Digital Research Inc. (DRI). DRI would later create the GEOS GUI and operating system used on some Commodore, Atari, and other computers. Interestingly, in 1983 DRI and Microsoft cooperated in adapting GSX-86 for MS-DOS. This was before Microsoft introduced Windows. An optional 68000 CPU was promised. In 1984, Fujitsu rolled out the Micro 16sx, which came standard with a hard drive.

APCS-II used with the 9450-II computer is Fujitsu's proprietary multitasking operating system.

The FM (Fujitsu Micro) 7 was the first of the FM line. It sold well in Japan, but is hard to find in North America. Fujitsu also sold an FM 8 with similar specifications but a different case. The FM 11 BS was a well-regarded CP/M and MS-DOS system. An FM AD 2 system used the same housing but was based on the Motorola 6809 CPU and the OS-9 operating system. The FM 77 bears a little similarity to the Tandy TRS-80 Color Computer in that it uses a 6809-based CPU and runs OS-9.

The Fujitsu Micro 16s ($15 to $50) looks like a PC, but came standard with CP/M.

Fujitsu Micro 16s (Feb. 1983, desktop)
Original Retail Price: $3,995
Base Configuration: 8MHz 8086-2 and 4MHz Z80A CPUs; CP/M-86 with GSX-86; five slots; 128K RAM (1MB max); two 5.25-inch floppy disk drives; 12-inch monochrome monitor; keyboard/keypad; RS-232C, parallel, and light-pen ports; application suite **Video:** 25-line x 80-column text, 640 x 200 graphics, eight colors **Size/Weight:** 19.25 x 14.5 x 5.75 inches, 33 lbs. **Important Options:** MS-DOS or Concurrent CP/M, 10- or 20MB hard disk drive, color monitor, printer
Value: $15 to $50

Fujitsu 9450-II (1983, desktop)
Base Configuration: two MN1613 CPUs, APCS-III, 256K RAM (384K max), two 5.25- or 8-inch floppy disk drives, application suite **Video:** 640 x 480 graphics **Important Options:** 8086 coprocessor, CP/M-86, 10MB hard disk drive
Value: $20 to $55

Fujitsu FM 11 BS (1984, desktop)
Original Retail Price: $1,775
Base Configuration: 8MHz MBL8088-2 CPU, CP/M-86, 256K RAM (1MB max), two 5.25-inch floppy disk drives, serial and parallel ports, FBASIC, word processor **Important Options:** MS-DOS, 20MB hard disk drive, mouse
Value: $12 to $45

Fujitsu FM 7 (1982, home computer)
Base Configuration: 6809 CPU; RAM/ROM cartridge slot; 64K RAM; RGB video port; integral keyboard/keypad; RS-232, cassette, and two game ports **Video:** 25-line x 80-column text, 640 x 200 graphics, eight colors **Size/Weight:** 16.8 x 11.2 x 3.9 inches, 9.9 lbs. **Important Options:** external 5.25-inch floppy disk drive
Value: $20 to $65

Fujitsu FM 77 (1984, home computer)
Original Retail Price: $850 to $980
Base Configuration: 2MHz MBL68B09 CPU, OS-9, 64K RAM (256K max), 3.5-inch floppy disk drive, keyboard, Logo and BASIC **Important Options:** 4MHz Z80A coprocessor, second 3.5-inch floppy disk drive, hi-res graphics card, mouse, voice-input card
Value: $15 to $40

Fujitsu FM-X (1984, MSX-based home computer)
Original Retail Price: $205
Base Configuration: Z80 CPU, ROM cartridge slot, 16K RAM, composite video port, integral keyboard, MSX BASIC **Video:** 24-line x 40-column text, 256 x 192 graphics
Value: $7 to $35

Fujitsu FM 16Pi (1985, laptop)
Base Configuration: 5MHz MBL8086L CPU, CP/M-86, ROM cartridge slot, 128K RAM (448K max), monochrome LCD, RS-232C port, BASIC, battery pack, AC adapter **Video:** 25-line x 80-column text, 640 x 200 graphics **Size/Weight:** 6 lbs. **Important Options:** external 3.5-inch floppy disk drive
Value: $15 to $35

Gavilan Computer Corp. (Campbell, California)

The Gavilan was one of the first true laptop computers. It offered PC compatibility, expansion capabilities, and a full keyboard and keypad in an under-10-pound package. It might have been the first computer to use a docking station that locked onto the back of the unit holding a printer and/or another floppy disk drive. A touchpad—Gavilan called it a solid-state mouse—above the keyboard served as a pointing device. The first Gavilan had an eight-line screen, but the company soon upgraded it to a 16-line LCD and introduced a second, less expensive Gavilan SC model, which used an eight-line display and came with no software.

Company founder Manny Fernandez had been the CEO of semiconductor manufacturer Zilog. Interestingly, he chose to use the Intel 8088 CPU instead of Zilog's Z80, probably to ensure the ability to run MS-DOS. Gavilans are rare today, and as milestone systems command higher prices than most other portables.

Gavilan/Gavilan SC
(1983 [Gavilan]/March 1984 [Gavilan SC], laptop)
Original Retail Price: $3,995 (Gavilan)/$2,995 (Gavilan SC)
Base Configuration: 8088 CPU, MS-DOS, 64K RAM (288K max), 8K ROM, 3-inch floppy disk drive, monochrome LCD, monitor port, integral keyboard/keypad and touchpad, RS-232C port, MS-BASIC (Gavilan), application suite (Gavilan), internal modem, battery pack, AC adapter **Video:** 8-line x 80-column text **Size/Weight:** 2.75 x 11.4 x 11.4 inches, 9.8 lbs. (9.6 lbs. for the Gavilan SC) **Important Options:** docking module, external 3- or 5.25-inch floppy disk drive, MS-BASIC (Gavilan SC), printer
Value: $45 to $125

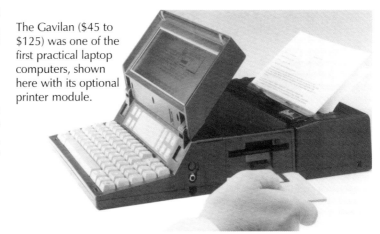

The Gavilan ($45 to $125) was one of the first practical laptop computers, shown here with its optional printer module.

Gnat Computers (San Diego, California)

Gnat merged with Data Technology Industries in 1983. The floppy-drive version of the Gnat Pac was called the Extended System 8.

A brutish-looking computer, the Gnat-Pac System 8 ($65 to $175) shown with optional 5.25-inch floppy drives.

Gnat Computers Gnat-Pac System 8
(1977, early micro)
Original Retail Price: $3,690
Base Configuration: 16K RAM, 2K ROM (16K max), front panel switches, serial and parallel ports
Important Options: dual 5.25-inch floppy disk drives with DOS, PL/M, BASIC, FORTRAN
Value: $65 to $17

GRiD Systems Corp. (Mountain View, California)

The GRiD Compass is a milestone system, as it was probably the first true laptop sold. It featured several unusual features, including a magnesium case (lightweight and durable), bubble memory, and ROM packs in place of a floppy disk drive. All Compass models are among the more desirable laptop collectibles. In late 1983, GRiD introduced a Compass Model 1107 at more than $14,000. It was expensive because it was built to meet Department of Defense Tempest standards designed to block the emission of radio signals from the computer. GRiD billed the 1107 as an espionage-proof portable. The Compass II offered several incremental improvements over the Compass, including the Model 1131 that offered a 128-column ELD.

The three GRiDCase models were defined by their video displays. The GRiDCase I had an LCD, the GRiDCase II had an enhanced LCD, and the GRiDCase II had a gas plasma display.

The GRiDCase EXP was a GRiDCase Plus with a bigger enclosure to house two PC XT-compatible expansion slots. The EXP model was aimed at the field automation market. The GRiDCase 1500 series represented several industry firsts. GRiD claimed that the GRiDCase 1500 was the first battery-powered laptop to use the low-power 80C286 and 80C386 CPUs. Several months after its introduction, the GRiDCase 1500 became the first laptop to use a high resolution 640 x 400 LCD. In early 1988, the 80C386 version became the first laptop to offer a Unix-based operating system.

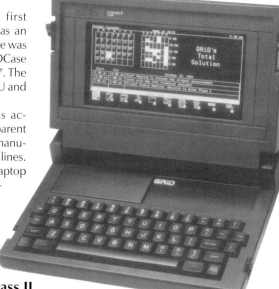

The GRiDLite was the first laptop to offer EMS memory as an option—up to 1MB. This feature was extended to the existing GRiDCase Plus line introduced in late 1987. The GRiDCase Plus had a faster CPU and an optional 10MB hard drive.

In June 1988, GRiD was acquired by Tandy Corp., the parent company of Radio Shack and manufacturer of TRS-80 computer lines. Tandy maintained the GRiD laptop and desktop brands as its high-end offering. GRiD produced several interesting pen-based portables while part of Tandy.

GRiD Compass/Compass II
(April 1982 [Compass]/June 1984 [Compass II], laptop PC)
Original Retail Price: $3,450 to $6,195
Base Configuration: 8086 CPU, MS-DOS 2.0 and GRiD/OS, 256K RAM (512K max), up to 512K ROM, 384K bubble memory storage, 6-inch monochrome LCD, integral keyboard, RS-232C and IEEE-488 ports, lithium battery, AC adapter **Video:** 25-line x 80-column text, 320 x 240 graphics
Size/Weight: 11 x 15 x 2 inches, 10 lbs. **Important Options:** 5.25-inch floppy disk drive, 10MB hard disk drive, internal modem
Value: $50 to $125 [Compass]; $20 to $55 [Compass II]

This GRiD Compass II Model 1139 ($20 t0 $55) was lightweight but tough.

GRiD GRiDCase (April 1985, laptop PC)
Original Retail Price: $3,000 to $4,500
Base Configuration: 4.77MHz 80C86 CPU, MS-DOS 2.11, external expansion bus, 128K RAM (640K max), up to 512K ROM, 3.5-inch floppy disk drive, 9.5-inch LCD, integral keyboard, RS-232C and parallel ports, carrying case, NiCad battery pack, AC adapter **Video:** 25-line x 80-column text, 640 x 200 graphics **Size/Weight:** 2.25 x 11.5 x 15 inches, 12 lbs. **Important Options:** expansion chassis, external 5.25-inch floppy disk drive, gas plasma display, RGB video interface, keypad, internal modem, battery pack
Value: $10 to $35

GRiD GRiDCase Plus (Sept. 1986, laptop PC)
Base Configuration: 4.77 MHz 80C86 CPU, MS-DOS 2.11 and GRiD OS, external expansion bus, 128K RAM (640K max), 3.5-inch floppy disk drive, 9.5-inch monochrome LCD, RGB video port, integral keyboard, RS-232C and parallel ports, AC adapter, NiCad battery pack **Video:** 25-line text, 640 x 200 graphics **Size/Weight:** 2.25 x 11.5 x 15 inches, 11.5 lbs. **Important Options:** expansion chassis, 10- or 20MB hard disk drive, external 5.25-inch floppy disk drive, CGA card, keypad, internal modem **Value:** $10 to $40

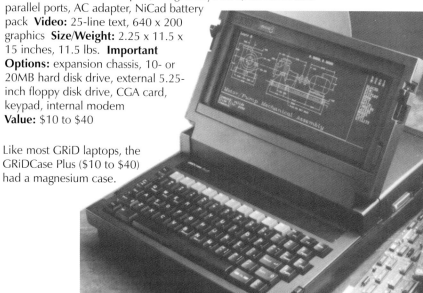

Like most GRiD laptops, the GRiDCase Plus ($10 to $40) had a magnesium case.

GRiD GRiDCase EXP (Sept. 1986, laptop PC)
Original Retail Price: $4,640
Base Configuration: 4.77MHz 80C86 CPU, MS-DOS 3.2 or 2.11, GRiD OS, two ISA slots, external expansion bus, 128K RAM (640K max), 3.5-inch floppy disk drive, RGB video port, 9.5-inch monochrome LCD, integral keyboard, RS-232C and parallel ports, NiCad battery pack, AC adapter **Video:** 25-line x 80-column text, 640 x 200 graphics **Size/Weight:** 3.5 x 11.5 x 15 inches, 15 lbs. **Important Options:** expansion chassis, 10- or 20MB hard disk drive, external floppy disk drive, 9.5-inch monochrome gas plasma display, CGA board, internal modem
Value: $10 to $40

GRiD GRiDCase 1500 Series (Oct. 1987, laptop PC)
Original Retail Price: $3,495 to $4,695
Base Configuration: 10MHz 80C286 or 12.5MHz 80386 CPU, MS-DOS 3.2 Extended, external expansion bus, 1MB RAM (8MB max), two 3.5-inch floppy disk drives, RGB video port, 10-inch monochrome LCD, integral keyboard, RS-232C and parallel ports, InteGRiD Application Environment, NiCad battery pack, AC adapter **Video:** 640 x 400 graphics **Size/Weight:** 2.3 x 11.5 x 15 inches, 11.5 lbs. **Important Options:** Xenix System V, 10- to 40MB hard disk drive, 10-inch monochrome gas plasma display, internal modem, carrying case
Value: $10 to $40

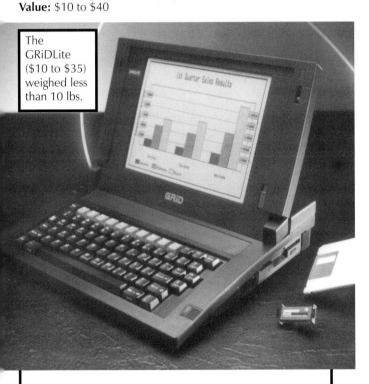

The GRiDLite ($10 to $35) weighed less than 10 lbs.

GRiD GRiDLite (Jan. 1987, laptop PC)
Original Retail Price: $1,750
Base Configuration: 4.77MHz 80C86 CPU, MS-DOS 3.2, 128K RAM (640K max), up to 1MB ROM, 3.5-inch floppy disk drive, 10-inch monochrome LCD, RGB video port, integral keyboard, RS-232C and parallel ports, NiCad battery pack, AC adapter **Video:** 25-line x 80-column text, 640 x 200 graphics **Size/Weight:** 11 x 13 x 2.8 inches, 9.3 lbs. **Important Options:** external floppy disk drive, keypad, internal modem
Value: $10 to $35

Popular with engineers when new, the Heathkit H8 ($85 to $400) is prized by vintage computer enthusiasts today.

Grundy Business Systems (U.K.)
Grundy sold three models of the NewBrain. The Model AD had a one-line by 16-character LCD built in. The less expensive Model A lacked the LCD as well as a reset and on/off buttons. A Model M was an AD with battery power, making the NewBrain a portable. The New Brain is popular among collectors of British micros.

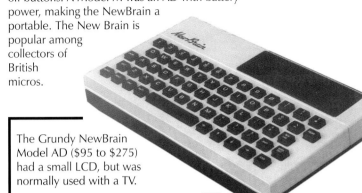

The Grundy NewBrain Model AD ($95 to $275) had a small LCD, but was normally used with a TV.

Grundy Business Systems NewBrain (1983, desktop)
Base Configuration: 4MHz Z80A CPU, external expansion bus, 32K RAM (2MB max), 29K ROM, TV and composite video ports, 14-digit LED, integral Chiclet-style keyboard, two RS-232 ports, Enhanced BASIC **Video:** 25-line x 80-column text, 640 x 220 graphics **Important Options:** CP/M
Value: $95 to $275

Heath Co. (Benton Harbor, Michigan)
Many early hobbyists cut their teeth on building an H8 from a kit, and it's not unusual to meet engineers with fond memories of the system. An H8 alone has limited functionality; you want to find one with the H9 or later H19 terminal. Working floppy drives enhance the value of this system, too. The H11 was introduced simultaneously with the H8 and is internally identical to the DEC PDP-11/03.

The H-89 was also sold in assembled form only by Zenith Data Systems as the Z-90. (Zenith purchased Heath from Schlumberger in 1979.) One CPU handled system operation, and the other video operation. The main difference between the two models is that the H-89 came with a floppy drive standard.

The H-100 was similar to the Zenith Z-100, and was sold in both kit and assembled form. The HS-151 was similar to the Zenith Z-150. The HS-161 was similar to the Zenith Z-160.

Heath Heathkit H8 Digital Computer (1977, early micro)
Original Retail Price: $375 kit
Base Configuration: 8080A CPU, nine slots, 8K RAM (64K max), 1K ROM, 9-digit LED, integral keypad, Benton Harbor BASIC, HASL-8 assembler, TED-8 text editor, power supply, enclosure **Video:** 24-line x 80-column text **Size/Weight:** 16.25 x 6.5 x 17 inches **Important Options:** HDOS, cassette interface, external 5.25- or 8-inch floppy disk drive, paper tape reader, cassette recorder, H9 terminal, serial and parallel interfaces, H14 printer
Value: $85 to $400

The Heathkit H11 ($65 to $175) was electronically the same as the DEC PDP-11/03.

Heath Heathkit H11 Digital Computer
(1977, early micro)
Original Retail Price: $1,295 kit
Base Configuration: DEC LSI-11/2 CPU, seven LSI bus (Qbus) slots, 4K RAM (32K max), cassette port, power supply, enclosure **Size/Weight:** 6.5 x 19 x 17 inches **Important Options:** HT-11 operating system, 5.25- or 8-inch floppy disk drive, paper tape reader, cassette recorder, H9 terminal, serial and parallel interfaces, H14 printer
Value: $65 to $175

Heath Heathkit H-88/H-89 All-in-One Computer
(desktop)
Original Retail Price: $1,295 (H-88)/$1,695 kit, $2,895 assembled (H-89)
Base Configuration: two 2.048MHz Z80 CPUs, 16K RAM (64K max), integral 12-inch monochrome CRT, integral keyboard/keypad, RS-232C port, BASIC **Video:** 24-line x 80-column text **Important Options:** CP/M 2.2 or HDOS 2.0, 5.25-inch floppy disk drive, external dual 5.25- or 8-inch floppy disk drives, H14 or H24 printer
Value: $25 to $125

Heath H-100 (1983, desktop)
Base Configuration: 8085 and 8088 CPUs, CP/M-85 and Z-DOS, five S-100 slots (four open), 128K RAM (768K max), 5.25-inch floppy disk drive, integral monochrome CRT, integral keyboard/keypad, two RS-232C and one parallel port, Z-BASIC **Video:** 25-line x 80-column text, 640 x 225 graphics, eight colors
Value: $15 to $45

Heath HS-151 Personal Desktop Computer
(1984, desktop PC)
Original Retail Price: $1,899 to $2,199 kit, $2,699 to $4,799 assembled
Base Configuration: 4.77MHz 8088 CPU, MS-DOS, four ISA slots, 128K RAM (640K max), 5.25-inch floppy disk drive, RGB and composite ports, keyboard/keypad, two RS-232 and one parallel port **Video:** 640 x 200 graphics **Size/Weight:** 16 x 6.25 x 16.5 inches, 42 lbs. **Important Options:** second 5.25-inch floppy disk drive, 10MB hard disk drive
Value: $10 to $40

Heath HS-161 Personal Portable Computer
(1984, transportable PC)
Original Retail Price: $2,799 to $3,199
Base Configuration: 4.77MHz 8088 CPU, MS-DOS, four ISA slots, 128K RAM (640K max), 5.25-inch floppy disk drive, integral 9-inch monochrome CRT, RGB and composite video ports, keyboard/keypad, two RS-232 and one parallel port **Video:** 640 x 200 graphics **Size/Weight:** 19.5 x 8.37 x 19.12 inches, 39 lbs. **Important Options:** second 5.25-inch floppy disk drive, 10MB hard disk drive
Value: $17 to $50

Hewlett-Packard Co. (Cupertino, California)

HP is one of the world's leading producers of microcomputers, but it missed its first opportunity. Steve Wozniak was an HP employee when he and Steve Jobs developed the Apple I. Wozniak asked HP if it would like to sell the Apple I. The company declined and did not produce its own micro until 1979 with the 80 series. (HP produced the 9800 series of desktop calculators starting in 1971 that had micro-like features, but were not true micros.)

The 80 series systems were favorites of engineers. In mid-1983, B versions of the HP-85 and HP-86 were introduced. The HP-85B had an improved operating system, more memory, solid state storage (HP called it an "electronic disk"), and integrated ROMs. The HP-86B also offered an "electronic disk," plus a 12-inch monitor and 3.5-inch floppy disk drive as standard. In terms of value, look for systems with working tape drives and printers, and the more working ROM cartridges, the better.

The HP-87XM replaced the HP-87 shortly after the latter was introduced. It added an IEEE-488 port and greater memory capacity.

The HP-125 is a larger version of the HP-120. Both could be configured as data terminals. One of the Z80As serves as the CPU, and the other handles video functions. HP later offered a 12-inch monitor option.

The Series 200 Model 16 was the first 16-bit microcomputer that HP produced. CP/M-68K did not become available for the Model 16 until July 1983.

HP received a great deal of attention for the HP 150, which was the first microcomputer to use a touchscreen. To make this possible, HP engineers had to develop innovative ways to reduce the cost and size of the technology. The touchscreen had ease-of-use advantages, but required software to be adapted for it. Relatively few applications were, which limited the appeal of the HP 150.

A PC-compatible offering from HP was inevitable, and the company's Vectra line was above average in terms of quality and performance. HP eventually offered the Vectra with a 12MHz 80286.

HP made a couple of interesting portable computers. The Integral Personal Computer had a built-in Thinkjet printer and was often used for instrument control and data acquisition applications. Its operating system was a Unix variant—an uncommon choice for a portable computer. HP's code-name for the Integral during development was 'Pisces.'

Although HP's earlier portables were well-received by engineers and other technical users, the company did not have broad success with portables until it introduced the HP 110 laptop. It offered good performance in a small but practical package. Some Hewlett-Packard literature referred to the 110 as simply The Portable. In 1985, a Plus version of the 110 was introduced with greater RAM and ROM capacity and improved graphics resolution.

Hewlett-Packard HP-83 (1979, desktop)
Original Retail Price: $2,250
Base Configuration: custom CPU, 16K RAM (32K max), integral 5-inch monochrome CRT, integral keyboard/keypad **Video:** 16-line x 32-column text, 256 x 192 graphics
Value: $25 to $85

Hewlett-Packard HP-85/HP-85A (desktop)
Original Retail Price: $3,250 (HP-85)
Base Configuration: custom CPU, four ROM drawers, 16K RAM (80K max), 32K ROM, magnetic tape drive, integral 5-inch monochrome CRT, integral keyboard/keypad, integral printer **Video:** 16-line x 32-column text, 256 x 192 graphics **Size/Weight:** 6.3 x 16.5 x 17.8 inches, 37 lbs. **Important Options:** RS-232C, parallel, GPIO, HP-IL, BCD, and HP-IB interfaces
Value: $20 to $70

The HP-85 ($20 to $70) is a popular collectible and reasonably easy to find at a good price.

Hewlett-Packard HP-86/HP86A (July 1982, desktop)
Original Retail Price: $1,795
Base Configuration: custom CPU, four ROM drawers, 64K RAM (576K max), 48K ROM, integral keyboard/keypad, HP BASIC **Video:** 24-line x 80-column text, 544 x 240 graphics **Size/Weight:** 5 x 16.5 x 17.8 inches, 31 lbs. **Important Options:** CP/M; 5.25-inch floppy disk drive; 9-inch HP 82912A or 12-inch HP 82913A monochrome monitor; RS-232C, parallel, GP-IO, and BCD interfaces; HP 82905B printer; HP 7470 plotter, modem
Value: $20 to $75

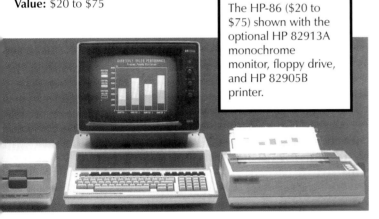

The HP-86 ($20 to $75) shown with the optional HP 82913A monochrome monitor, floppy drive, and HP 82905B printer.

Hewlett-Packard HP-87 (March 1982, desktop)
Original Retail Price: $2,995
Base Configuration: custom CPU, four ROM drawers, 32K RAM (640K max), 48K ROM, integral monochrome CRT, integral keyboard/keypad, HP-IB port, HP BASIC **Video:** 24-line x 80-column text, 544 x 240 graphics **Size/Weight:** 7.7 x 16.5 x 17.8 inches, 39 lbs. **Important Options:** CP/M; external dual 5.25-inch floppy disk drives; HP 9135 hard/floppy disk drive subsystem; 9- or 13-inch monochrome monitor; RS-232C, parallel, GP-IO, and BCD interfaces; HP 82905B printer; HP 7470 plotter, modem
Value: $25 to $100

Hewlett-Packard HP 120/HP 125
(Nov. 1982 [HP 120]/1981 [HP 125], desktop)
Original Retail Price: $2,775 (HP 120)/$2,790 (HP 125)
Base Configuration: two 3.68MHz Z80A CPUs, CP/M, 64K RAM, 32K ROM, 3.5-inch floppy disk drive, 9-inch monochrome monitor, keyboard/keypad, two RS-232C and one IEEE-488 port, three-volume manual set **Video:** 24-line x 80-column text **Size/Weight:** 15 x 18.7 x 17.3 inches, 39 lbs. (HP 125) **Important Options:** second 3.5-inch floppy disk drive, 5.25- or 8-inch floppy disk drive, 5MB hard disk drive, HP 2602A or HP 7470A plotter, integral thermal printer (HP 125)
Value: $20 to $85

The HP Series 200 Model 16 ($25 to $95).

Hewlett-Packard Series 200 Model 16
(Nov. 1982, desktop)
Original Retail Price: $3,650
Base Configuration: 8MHz 68000 CPU, 128K RAM (768K max), 3.5-inch floppy disk drive, 9-inch monochrome monitor, keyboard with integral trackball, RS-232C and HP-IB ports, HP Enhanced BASIC **Video:** 25-line x 80-column text, 400 x 300 graphics **Important Options:** Unix or CP/M-68K; second 3.5-inch floppy disk drive; 4.6MB hard disk drive; BASIC, Pascal, or HPL
Value: $25 to $95

Another of HP's 80 series, the HP-87 ($25 to $100) with its optional HP 7470 plotter, HP 82905B printer, and dual floppy drives.

Hewlett-Packard pioneered the use of touch-screen technology with the HP 150 ($20 to $55).

Hewlett-Packard HP 150 (1983, desktop PC)
Original Retail Price: $3,995
Base Configuration: 8MHz 8088 CPU, MS-DOS 2.0, 256K RAM (640K max), 160K ROM, two 3.5-inch floppy disk drives, 9-inch HPTouch monochrome monitor, keyboard/keypad, two RS-232C and one HP-IB port, Personal Application Manager, BASIC86 **Video:** 27-line x 80-column text, 512 x 390 graphics **Important Options:** 5.25-inch floppy disk drive, 5- or 15MB hard disk drive, integral thermal printer, external printer, plotter, 3270 terminal emulator
Value: $20 to $55

Hewlett-Packard Touchscreen II Personal Computer (1985, desktop PC)
Original Retail Price: $3,545 to $5,570
Base Configuration: 8MHz 8088 CPU; MS-DOS 2.11 with Personal Applications Manager; 256K RAM (640K max); 160K ROM; two 3.5-inch floppy disk drives; 12-inch monochrome monitor; RS-232C, RS-232C/422, parallel, and HP-HIL ports; HP 2623 terminal emulation **Video:** 27-line x 80-column text **Important Options:** 10- or 20MB hard disk drive, touchscreen monitor, mouse, graphics tablet, VT100 or 3276/3278 terminal emulation
Value: $10 to $40

Hewlett-Packard Vectra PC (1985, desktop PC)
Original Retail Price: $3,199 to $3,599
Base Configuration: 8MHz 80286 CPU; MS-DOS 3.1; seven ISA slots; 256K RAM (640K max); 5.25-inch floppy disk drive; keyboard/keypad; serial, parallel, and HP-IL slots **Video:** CGA **Size/Weight:** 16.7 x 15.4 x 6.3 inches **Important Options:** second 5.25-inch floppy disk drive, 3.5-inch floppy disk drive, 20- or 40MB hard disk drive, monochrome or color monitor, composite or EGA card
Value: $5 to $25

Hewlett-Packard HP Portable Vectra CS Personal Computer (transportable PC)
Base Configuration: 7.16MHz 8086 CPU, MS-DOS 3.2, four expansion slots, 640K RAM (6MB max), 3.5-inch floppy disk drive, monitor port, 12-inch monochrome LCD, integral keyboard/keypad, Personal Application Manager, battery pack, AC adapter, charger **Video:** 80-column text **Size/Weight:** 16.5 x 13.9 x 3.5 inches, 17.6 lbs. **Important Options:** second 3.5-inch floppy disk drive, 20MB hard disk drive
Value: $10 to $35

HP stuffed a Thinkjet printer into the Integral Personal Computer ($15 to $40).

Hewlett-Packard Integral Personal Computer (March 1985, transportable)
Original Retail Price: $4,995
Base Configuration: 8MHz 68000 CPU, HP-UX/RO in ROM, 512K RAM (1.5MB max), 256K ROM, 3.5-inch floppy disk drive, 9-inch monochrome ELD, keyboard/keypad, two HP-IB and two HP-HIL ports, integral Thinkjet printer **Video:** 80-column text, 512 x 255 graphics **Size/Weight:** 7 x 13 x 16, 25 lbs. **Important Options:** 55MB hard disk drive; mouse; RS-232C, BCD, and GPIO interfaces; carrying case, modem
Value: $15 to $40

A well-built PC-compatible, the HP Vectra PC ($5 to $25) shown with the optional monitor.

Hewlett-Packard HP 110 "The Portable"
(May 1984, laptop PC)
Original Retail Price: $2,995
Base Configuration: 5.44MHz 80C86, MS-DOS 2.01, 272K RAM, 384K ROM, monochrome LCD, integral keyboard, RS-232C and HP-IL ports, Lotus 1-2-3 and MemoMaker in ROM, carrying case, internal modem, owner's and software manuals, AC adapter, lead-acid batteries, battery charger **Video:** 16-line x 80-column text, 480 x 128 graphics **Size/Weight:** 13 x 10 x 3 inches, 9 lbs. **Important Options:** HP 911A 3.5-inch external floppy disk drive, HP 2225B printer, leather carrying case **Value:** $12 to $45

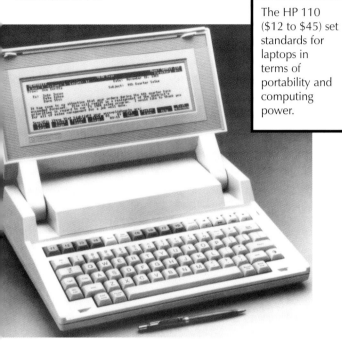

The HP 110 ($12 to $45) set standards for laptops in terms of portability and computing power.

Hitachi, Ltd. (Tokyo, Japan)

Hitachi offered a relatively refined microcomputer as early as 1978 in the MB-6880 Basic Master (upgraded to the Basic Master Level 2 in 1979). It used the same processor, the 6800, found in some popular American systems like the Altair 680 and SWTPC 6800, but in a small enclosure with a keyboard.

It's uncertain if Hitachi sold the MB-6890 in the U.S. If it did, several shortcomings would have put it at a disadvantage. For example, it had no disk operating system; the optional floppy drives were controlled by the BASIC interpreter. The drives themselves were single-density at a time when double-density was becoming popular.

At the system level, the MBE16000 was a typical PC XT-compatible design. The computer broke convention with the main enclosure. Instead of using a flat box like everyone else, Hitachi used an upright breadbox-shaped cabinet. Although attractive, the MBE16000 did not have enough room for a monitor to sit on top, so users consequently lost desk space to the design. This model was sold in Japan as the Personal Computer Basic Master 16000 series.

Like many Japanese computer makers, Hitachi had several MSX offerings. A Model MB-H1 had 32K RAM standard, and a smaller Model HB-H1E had 16K RAM and no RF video output.

Hitachi MB-6880 Basic Master/Basic Master Level 2
(1978 [Basic Master]/1979 [Basic Master Level 2], desktop)
Base Configuration: 6800 CPU, 4K RAM (Basic Master)/8K RAM (Basic Master Level 2), 16K ROM, integral keyboard, cassette port, BASIC in ROM **Video:** 24-line x 32-column text **Size/Weight:** 16.6 x 11.1 x 3.1 inches, 8.8 lbs. **Important Options:** monochrome monitor, cassette recorder, printer **Value:** $25 to $100

The Hitachi MB-6890 Basic Master Level 3 ($17 to $65) with the optional dual floppy drives.

Hitachi MB-6890 Basic Master Level 3 (1980, desktop)
Original Retail Price: $1,050
Base Configuration: 1MHz 6809 CPU; six expansion slots; 32K RAM, 24K ROM; monochrome and RGB video ports, integral keyboard/keypad; RS-232C, parallel, cassette, and light-pen ports, BASIC **Video:** 25-line x 80-column text, 640 x 200 graphics **Size/Weight:** 17.7 x 4.9 x 20.3 inches, 15.4 lbs. **Important Options:** external 5.25-inch floppy disk drive, printer, modem, light pen **Value:** $17 to $65

Hitachi MB-6885 Basic Master Jr. (1982, home computer)
Base Configuration: 6800 CPU, 16K RAM (64K max), 18K ROM, integral keyboard **Video:** 24-line x 32-column text, 256 x 192 graphics, eight colors **Size/Weight:** 15.6 x 3.8 x 12.9 inches, 9.9 lbs. **Value:** $12 to $35

Hitachi MBE16000 (1983, desktop PC)
Original Retail Price: $3,000
Base Configuration: 8088 CPU; MS-DOS; four ISA slots; 128K RAM (384K max); one 5.25-inch floppy disk drive; video port; keyboard/keypad; RS-232C, parallel, and light-pen ports; BASIC **Video:** 80-column text, 640 x 400 graphics **Important Options:** CP/M-86, second 5.25-inch floppy disk drive, 8-inch floppy disk drive, 14-inch monochrome or color monitor **Value:** $12 to $40

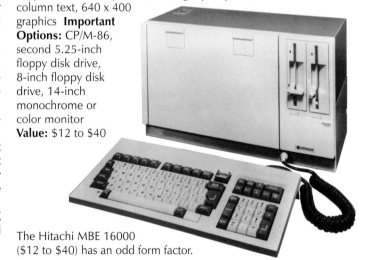

The Hitachi MBE 16000 ($12 to $40) has an odd form factor.

Hitachi MB-H1 (1984, MSX home computer)
Original Retail Price: $225 to $260
Base Configuration: 3.6MHz Z80 CPU, two ROM cartridge slots, 32K RAM, composite video port, integral keyboard, parallel port, AC adapter **Video:** 24-line x 40-column text, 256 x 192 graphics **Important Options:** RF video interface **Value:** $7 to $35

ICL (U.K.)

ICL formed in 1968 with the merger of Electric Computers and International Computers and Tabulators. It became a leading British manufacturer of large computing systems. Fujitsu bought a controlling stake in the company in 1990, and in 2001 rolled all remaining ICL operations into Fujitsu.

The ICL Professional Computer was one of several attempts the company made at selling microcomputers. It was a fairly typical CP/M system.

ICL Professional Computer (1983, desktop)
Base Configuration: 4MHz Z80 CPU, CP/M, ICL bus, 64K RAM (512K max), 5.25-inch floppy disk drive, keyboard/keypad, four RS-232 ports
Video: 25-line x 80-column text **Important Options:** monochrome monitor
Value: $15 to $40

iCOM Microperipherals (Chatsworth, California)

iCOM was a division of Pertec Computer, the company that purchased MITS in 1977. The Attache was based on Altair designs, but housed in a more user-friendly enclosure with a keyboard. Pertec discontinued all Altair lines in July 1978, so the Attache had a short production run.

You might call the iCom Attache ($400 to $850) the last Altair, as its internals were based on the MITS design.

iCOM Attache (Jan. 1978, early micro)
Base Configuration: 8080 CPU, FDOS III, 10 S-100 slots, integral keyboard, DEBBI (Disk Extended BASIC) **Important Options:** external 5.25-inch floppy disk drive
Value: $400 to $850

IMS Associates Inc. (IMSAI) (San Leandro, California); Fischer-Freitas Co. (1979 to 1986)

The IMSAI I-8080 was borne out of necessity. IMS Associates (usually referred to as simply IMSAI) was a consulting company that found it had underbid on a contract to design and build a system for a specialized application. To avoid disaster, founder Bill Millard changed his plans from using minicomputer components to the then-new microcomputer. In fact, he might have simply bought Altair 8800s for the project, but MITS needed 90 days to deliver and wanted cash up front. IMSAI was forced to build its own system from scratch, with the hope that it could recoup some of its costs by selling the Altair-compatible units to hobbyists.

IMSAI took advantage of the Altair 8800's popularity by using the same S-100 bus. Any expansion card that worked in the Altair would also work in the IMSAI, and the computer entered the market with a great deal of third-party vendor support. In fact, the company advertised that you could install an Altair CPU board in an IMSAI and run them in parallel, each sharing system resources such as memory.

Despite a relatively long production run (until May 1986) and several internal revisions, all IMSAI 8080s look the same. IMSAI introduced the Megabyte Micro in 1977, which was based on the 8080 and had 1MB of RAM. However, it is not known if IMSAI ever sold a system configured as a Megabyte Micro. Around 1978, the IMSAI 8080/1 series appeared with 32K RAM, a single S-100 slot, and either two serial ports or two parallel and one serial port. The optional 50MB hard drive was absurdly large for a microcomputer of the era.

IMSAI had designed high-end computers and disk storage systems, and its know-how was obvious to hobbyists then and to collectors today. IMSAI systems, when they come on the market, command Altair-like prices.

Support, parts, and service are still available for IMSAI systems through the Fischer-Freitas Company, run by two former IMSAI employees through the Web at www.imsai.net. If you can't find a classic IMSAI to restore, Fischer-Freitas will sell you an IMSAI Series Two, an S-100-based, modernized look-alike to the 8080 based on the Zilog Z8S180 CPU.

With the optional CRT display unit, both PCS series could be housed in big blue square enclosure that made the tiny screen look even smaller than it was. IMSAI updated the motherboard shortly after introducing the PCS-80 adding three slots. The PCS-80 was sold in France under the Data Soft brand. IMDOS was IMSAI's CP/M-compatible operating system.

VDP stood for Video Data Processor, and refers to the built-on monitors on both VDP series. The VDP-80 was sold in France under the Data Soft name.

IMSAI I-8080 Microcomputer
(Dec. 1975, early micro)
Original Retail Price: $439 kit, $621 assembled
Base Configuration: 2MHz 8080A CPU, TCOS, six S-100 slots, 4K RAM (64K max), status LEDs, front panel switches, assembler, monitor, text editor, BASIC, aluminum enclosure, expansion board, front panel control board **Size/Weight:** 19.5 x 17 x 7 inches **Important Options:** 10- or 50MB hard disk drive, floppy disk drive, video adapter, keyboard, serial and parallel interfaces, line printer, printer/plotter, clock board, rack mount enclosure
Value: $300 to $1,500

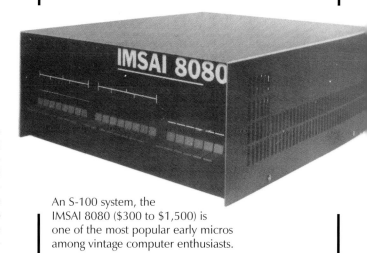

An S-100 system, the IMSAI 8080 ($300 to $1,500) is one of the most popular early micros among vintage computer enthusiasts.

IMSAI PCS-40 Series/PCS-80 Series (1977, early micro)
Original Retail Price: $1,499
Base Configuration: 3MHz 8085 CPU, IMDOS, seven S-100 slots, 2.25K RAM (64K max), 3K ROM, two 5.25-inch floppy disk drives (PCS-40), keyboard, two RS-232 and one parallel ports, BASIC-E, monitor in ROM **Video:** 24-line x 80-column text **Size/Weight:** 17 x 20 x 7 inches **Important Options:** monochrome CRT unit, dual 8-inch floppy disk drives (PCS-80), 10MB hard disk drive, printer **Value:** $100 to $375

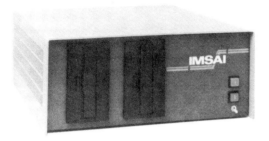

The IMSAI PCS-40 ($100 to $375).

IMSAI VDP-40 Series/VDP-80 Series (1977, early micro)
Original Retail Price: $5,995 (VDP-80)
Base Configuration: 3MHz 8085 CPU, IMDOS, six (VDP-40)/two (VDP-80) S-100 slots, 32K RAM (196K max), 2K ROM, two 5.25-inch (VDP-40)/8-inch (VDP-80) floppy disk drives, integral 9-inch (VDP-40)/12-inch (VDP-80) monochrome CRT, integral keyboard/keypad, RS-232 and parallel ports, BASIC-E **Video:** 24-line x 80-column text **Size/Weight:** 18 x 27 x 12 inches, 65 lbs. (VDP-40)/24.62 x 15.25 x 25 inches, 103 lbs. (VDP/80) **Value:** $100 to $375 (VDP-40)/$125 to $400 (VDP-80)

The IMSAI VDP-80 ($125 to $400) was an all-in-one unit.

Intel Corp. (Santa Clara, California)

Some say the Intellec 4 was the first complete commercial American microcomputer. The Intellec came out shortly after Intel released the 4004 microprocessor, so Intel was certainly the first vendor to produce a microcomputer using its own chips. Both were designed as development systems for their respective CPUs. In other words, it was a computer used to design and build other computers using the same CPU.

Intel gave an Intellec 8 to a young programmer named Gary Kildall as partial payment for writing the PL/M language used with the system. Kildall then used the Intellec to write CP/M in 1974, which until MS-DOS appeared became the most popular operating system for microcomputers.

Intel actually sold five versions of the Intellec: the Intellec 4 Mod 4 for the 4004 chipset, the Intellec 4 Mod 40 for the 4040 chipset, the Intellect 8 Mod 8 for the 8008 chipset, the Intellec 8 Mod 80 for the 8080 chipset, and the Intellec MDS-800 for the 8080 chipset. Intel has no records for the number sold, but the Computer History Association of California located five of the Intellect 8 Mod 8s in 1994. Chances are good that more are waiting to be found in storage closets and warehouses.

The single-board SIM-4 microcomputer was a development system for the Intel 4004. It was based on MCS-4 (Micro Computer Set) chip set. Intel eventually produced an 8008 version called the SIM-8. The system came in two versions. The SIM-4-01 had sockets for four Intel 1702 ROM and four Intel 4002 RAM chips, and the SIM-4-02 had sockets for 16 PROM chips and 16 4002 RAM chips.

Intel SIM-4 (1972, single-board trainer)
Base Configuration: 4004 CPU, PROM storage
Value: $150 to $375

Intel Intellec 4/Intellec 8 (1973, early micro)
Original Retail Price: $2,398 (8)
Base Configuration: 4004 or 4040 (4)/8008 or 8080 (8) CPU, MDS-DOS (8), 12 expansion slots, 16K RAM (8), PROM, front panel switches, I/O interface, PL/M compiler, FORTRAN IV, cross assembler, debugger, manual **Size/Weight:** 7 x 17 x 14, 30 lbs. **Important Options:** paper tape reader, 8-inch floppy disk drive **Value:** $300 to $1,200

Intelligent Systems Corp. (Duluth, Georgia)

The Intecolor caused a stir when it was announced—a microcomputer kit that offered an eight-color video display! That's a far cry from the millions of colors that today's typical PC can generate, but the Intecolor brought color to the low end of computing. Intelligent Systems sold assembled versions of the Intecolor 8001 to other vendors for resale, so it is possible for this machine to turn up with a different brand name. For example, the Compucolor 8001 is the same system as the Intecolor 8001.

Intelligent Systems is still in business today as Intecolor, a vendor of industrial monitors and computers.

Intelligent Systems Intecolor 8001
(1976, early micro)
Original Retail Price: $1,395 kit
Base Configuration: 8080 CPU, 4K RAM (32K max), 19-inch color monitor, keyboard, RS-232 port, EPROM sockets, manual **Video:** 25-line x 80-column text **Important Options:** graphics upgrade, light pen **Value:** $100 to $650

The Intelligent Systems Intecolor 8001 ($100 to $650) offered a color display in 1976.

The Compucolor II ($100 to $600) from Intelligent Systems broke with its earlier all-in-one design.

Intelligent Systems Compucolor II
(1977, early desktop)
Original Retail Price: $2,400
Base Configuration: DOS, 16K RAM (32K max), 17K ROM, floppy disk drive, color monitor, keyboard, RS-232 port, BASIC **Video:** 32-line x 64-column text, 128 x 128 graphics **Important Options:** keyboard/keypad, lowercase modification **Value:** $100 to $600

Intelligent Systems Intecolor 8051 (1978, early micro)
Base Configuration: 8-track tape storage, integral 19-inch color CRT, keyboard/keypad, BASIC **Video:** 48-line x 80-column text, 192 x 160 graphics, eight colors **Important Options:** floppy disk drive
Value: $150 to $550

Intelligent Systems Intecolor 8963 (1980, desktop)
Base Configuration: CP/M, two 8-inch floppy disk drives, integral 19-inch color CRT, integral keyboard/keypad, Microsoft BASIC
Value: $35 to $100

Intelligent Systems Intecolor 8000/8000 CP/M (desktop)
Original Retail Price: $4,265 (8000)/$6,845 (8000 CP/M) **Base Configuration:** 8080A CPU, FCS (8000)/CP/M (8000 CP/M), 32K RAM (8000)/64K RAM (8000 CP/M), integral 19-inch color CRT, RS-232C and parallel ports **Video:** 48-line x 80-column text, 192 x 160 graphics, eight colors
Value: $20 to $65

Intelligent Systems Intecolor 3600 (desktop)
Original Retail Price: $2,945
Base Configuration: 8080A CPU, FCS, 32K RAM, integral 13-inch color CRT, RS-232C and parallel ports, BASIC **Video:** 32-line x 64-column text, 128 x 128 graphics, eight colors
Value: $20 to $65

Interact Electronics (Ann Arbor, Michigan)

Before Interact could release its completed home computer system, the company was forced to file bankruptcy. Liquidater Protecto Industries sold some of the existing stock, and a company called MicroVideo sold the rest. The computer was produced in either 1979 or 1980.

Interact (home computer)
Base Configuration: 2MHz 8080A CPU, 8K RAM (16K max), 2K ROM, integral cassette recorder and Chiclet-style keyboard, RF modulator, BASIC, two joysticks **Size/Weight:** 4 x 10.5 x 18.25 inches, 12 lbs. **Video:** 17-column text, 112 x 78 graphics, eight colors
Value: $35 to $100

Interface Data Systems (Anaheim, California)

The Micro186 was one of a few CP/M systems to use the 80186 CPU. Interface Data Systems also produced a line of multi-user systems based on DEC PDP technology.

Interface Data Interface Micro186 (desktop)
Base Configuration: 80186 CPU, Concurrent CP/M-86 3.1, S-100 bus, 256K RAM, 64K ROM, two 5.25- or 8-inch floppy disk drives, two RS-232 and one parallel port **Important Options:** MS-DOS, CP/M-86, 10- to 368MB hard disk drive, tape backup drive, monochrome monitor
Value: $15 to $40

International Business Machines (IBM) (Boca Raton, Florida)

To many people, the terms "IBM" and "computer" are synonymous. Before micros appeared, IBM owned the mainframe market, but was feeling competitive pressure from companies like Digital Equipment and Data General. Their minicomputers were stealing sales away from IBM. By the late 1970s, it was clear that IBM would have to expand its product line into small systems.

IBM sold systems that could be considered microcomputers as early as 1975 with the 5100. Definitely not a hobbyist machine at the price, the 5100 was aimed at industrial, commercial, and professional markets. Although sold as a transportable, it was anything but at 50 pounds. IBM did not sell the Problem Solver Library for the 5100, but rented it at $500. Later versions used floppy drives in place of the tape storage unit. The IBM 5100 is a rare and desirable collectible today. The 5120 and Datamaster systems followed the 5100.

The company didn't put its full weight behind a microcomputer product until it launched the IBM PC in August 1981. Some computer industry watchers of the time thought that the new IBM PC was doomed to failure. After all, it didn't run the leading microcomputer business operating system of the day, CP/M. IBM later offered CP/M as an option, but it hardly mattered. The IBM PC changed the microcomputer world by establishing a standard that almost every manufacturer eventually would adopt. IBM briefly offered a version of the PC Model 5150 that came standard with only 16K of RAM, expandable to 64K. These examples are rare and command a 20 to 50 percent premium over later PC values, depending on condition and completeness.

More expansion bus slots and greater mass storage capabilities were the most significant improvements that the PC XT (for Extended Technology) made over the PC. IBM offered a version of the PC XT that would run its mainframe applications. The Personal Computer XT/370 used the Virtual Machine/Personal Computer (VM/PC) control program that provided compatibility with the Virtual Machine/Conversational Monitor System (VM/CMS) mainframe program. IBM developed the Portable PC in response to the popularity of other vendors' PC-compatible transportables. Its innards were based on the PC XT.

The PC AT was at the time the most significant upgrade from the original PC. Third-party tests showed that it was 2.5 times faster than the PC, and the PC AT could be expanded to 3MB of memory by using one of its expansion slots. IBM later added a PC AT Model 339, which came with 512K of RAM, a 30MB hard disk drive, and the IBM Enhanced Personal Computer Keyboard. Eventually, an 8MHz 80286 replaced the slower 6MHz version. The PC AT sold in great numbers, but finding one today that isn't scarred from years of use is uncommon.

When word got out that IBM was about the enter the home PC market with a computer code-named Peanut, sales of many existing home systems dropped as consumers anticipated the launch. The PCjr formally launched with great fanfare. However, the PCjr was not the success IBM had hoped for. The original keyboard was a mushy Chiclet style (later replaced with a more conventional keyboard). The PCjr was not compatible with many applications written for the PC, and PCjr cartridge-based software was slow to be released. IBM designed an infrared keyboard interface (a keyboard cable was optional) so that families could use the TV as the monitor and type from anywhere in the living room, but the technology proved problematic. In a school setting, for example, kids soon learned that they could point the keyboard at and control systems other than their own. The PCjr was sold in Japan as the IBM Personal Computer JX.

IBM also missed the mark with its first laptop, the PC Convertible. It was bigger, heavier, and more expensive than some of its competitors' models. Items found standard on other systems, such as serial and parallel interfaces, were options on the Convertible. Consequently, the Convertible did not sell well. It was IBM's first laptop computer, and as such is collectible. The Convertible's LCD is detachable so that users could set a CRT display atop the computer; some surviving examples might be separated from their LCDs as a result.

In 1987, IBM introduced a new line of systems, the Personal System/2 (PS/2). Models range from the entry-level 25 to the 80 tower system for power users. The higher end models used IBM's new Micro Channel system bus for higher performance and optionally the new OS/2 operating system.

IBM sold a Personal Typing System based on the PS/2 Model 30 and IBM printer through its typewriter dealers. The Model 80 could be used as a high-end personal computer or as a network server. Its tower cabinet—the same used for the Model 60—allowed for a great deal of expandability.

IBM 5100 (Sept. 1975, early micro)
Original Retail Price: $8,975 to $19,975
Base Configuration: ROM-based proprietary operating system, 16K RAM (64K max), internal magnetic tape unit, integral monochrome CRT display, integral keyboard/keypad, BASIC or APL in ROM **Video:** 16-line x 64-column text **Size/Weight:** 50 lbs. **Important Options:** TV, communications, and I/O interfaces; Problem Solver Library software; Model 5103 printer, Model 1506 auxiliary tape unit
Value: $300 to $1,000

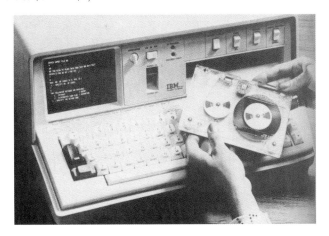

IBM's first micro was not the PC, but this 5100 ($300 to $1,000), a 50-pound "portable" computer.

IBM 5120 (1980, desktop)
Original Retail Price: $9,160
Base Configuration: 5110 Model 3 CPU, ROS, 64K RAM, integral 9-inch monochrome CRT, keyboard/keypad, BASIC, APL **Video:** 16-line x 64-column text
Value: $90 to $300

IBM System/23 Datamaster
(1981, desktop)
Original Retail Price: $3,300 to $10,000
Base Configuration: 5322 CPU, ROS, 64K RAM (128K max), two 8-inch floppy disk drives, integral 12-inch monochrome CRT, integral keyboard/keypad, RS-232C port, BASIC **Video:** 24-line x 80-column text **Important Options:** printer
Value: $75 to $250

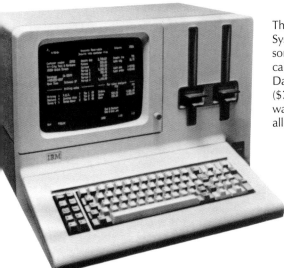

The IBM System/23, sometimes called the Datamaster ($75 to $250), was a bulky all-in-one unit.

The IBM PC ($18 to $65) established the microcomputer standard that eventually almost all manufacturers would follow.

IBM Personal Computer Model 5150
(Aug. 1981, desktop PC)
Original Retail Price: $1,565 to $4,425
Base Configuration: 4.77MHz 8088 CPU, PC-DOS 1.1, five ISA slots, 64K RAM (640K max), 40K ROM, keyboard/keypad, RS-232C and cassette ports, BASIC **Video:** 25-line x 80-column text, 640 x 200 graphics, four colors **Size/Weight:** 20 x 16 x 5.5 inches, 21 lbs. **Important Options:** CP/M-86; Model 001 Expansion Unit; one or two 5.25-inch floppy disk drives; Color Display, Enhanced Color Display, or Monochrome Display monitor; EGA or CGA card; PC Color, PC Compact, or Graphics Printer
Value: $50 to $150 (early 16K motherboard version); $18 to $65 (all later versions)

The IBM PC XT ($15 to $65) looked much like the original PC, but offered several performance enhancements.

IBM Personal Computer XT
(PC XT) Model 5160 (March 1983, desktop PC)
Original Retail Price: $4,995
Base Configuration: 4.77MHz 8088 CPU, PC-DOS 2.0, eight ISA slots, 128K RAM (640K max), 40K ROM, 5.25-inch floppy disk drive, keyboard/keypad, RS-232C port, BASIC, operations manual **Video:** 25-line x 80-column text, 640 x 200 graphics **Size/Weight:** 20 x 16 x 6 inches, 32 lbs. **Important Options:** Model 002 Expansion Unit; second 5.25-inch floppy disk drive; 10MB hard disk drive; Color Display, Enhanced Color Display, or Monochrome Display monitor; EGA or CGA card; game port; PC Color, PC Compact, or Graphics Printer; technical reference; hardware maintenance and service manual
Value: $15 to $65

IBM Personal Computer XT 286 (PC XT 286) Model 5162 (Sept. 1986, desktop PC)
Original Retail Price: $3,995
Base Configuration: 6MHz 80286 CPU, PC-DOS 3.2, eight ISA slots, 640K RAM, 5.25-inch floppy disk drive, 20MB hard disk drive, keyboard/keypad, serial and parallel ports **Video:** CGA **Size/Weight:** 19.6 x 16.1 x 5.5 inches, 28 lbs. **Important Options:** Xenix 2.0; second 5.25-inch floppy disk drive; external 3.5-inch floppy disk drive; Enhanced Color Display, Color Display, or Monochrome Display monitor; mouse; PC Color, PC Compact, or Graphics Printer
Value: $17 to $45

The IBM Portable Personal Computer ($20 to $65) was a bit larger than many of its competitors.

Still beige, the IBM PC AT ($15 to $85) was larger than the PC and PC XT.

IBM Portable Personal Computer (PC) Model 5155 (March 1984, transportable PC)
Original Retail Price: $2,795
Base Configuration: 4.77MHz 8088, PC-DOS 2.1, five ISA slots, 256K RAM (512K max), 40K ROM, 5.25-inch floppy disk drive, integral 9-inch monochrome CRT, keyboard/keypad, carrying case **Video:** 25-line x 80-column text, CGA **Size/Weight:** 20 x 17 x 8 inches, 30 lbs. **Important Options:** Model 001 Expansion Unit; second 5.25-inch floppy disk drive; Color Display or Monochrome Display monitor; EGA card; serial, parallel, and game ports; Graphics or PC Compact Printer
Value: $20 to $65

IBM Personal Computer AT (PC AT) Model 5170
(Aug. 1984, desktop PC)
Original Retail Price: $3,995 to $5,795
Base Configuration: 6MHz 80286 CPU, PC-DOS 3.0, eight ISA slots, 256K RAM (512K max), 64K ROM, 5.25-inch floppy disk drive, keyboard/keypad, technical reference manual **Video:** CGA **Size/Weight:** 21.3 x 17.3 x 6.4 inches, 37 lbs. **Important Options:** PC Xenix; second 5.25-inch floppy disk drive; 20MB hard disk drive; Enhanced Color Display, Color Display, or Monochrome Display monitor; EGA or CGA card; serial and parallel interfaces; PC Color, PC Compact, or Graphics printer
Value: $15 to $85

The IBM PC Convertible ($15 to $40), shown with its optional printer module, was considered too expensive when new.

IBM PCjr (Nov. 1983, home PC)
Original Retail Price: $669 to $1,269
Base Configuration: 4.77MHz 8088, PC-DOS 2.1, two ROM cartridge and two expansion slots, 64K RAM (640K max), 64K ROM, TV adapter, keyboard, serial port, BASIC, tutorial software **Video:** 40-column text, 640 x 200 graphics **Size/Weight:** 13.9 x 11.4 x 3.8 inches, 12 lbs. **Important Options:** 5.25-inch floppy disk drive; PCjr Color Display, Color Display, or Monochrome Display monitor; 80-column display; parallel port and two game ports; Graphics or PC Compact Printer; internal modem; joysticks; carrying case
Value: $5 to $45

IBM PC Convertible (April 1986, laptop PC)
Original Retail Price: $1,995
Base Configuration: 4.77MHz 80C86 CPU, PC-DOS 3.2, 256K RAM (512K max), 64K ROM, two 3.5-inch floppy disk drives, monochrome LCD, keyboard, battery pack, AC adapter **Video:** 80-column text, 640 x 200 graphics **Size/Weight:** 14.72 x 12.28 x 2.64 inches, 12.2 lbs. **Important Options:** nine-inch monochrome or 12-inch color CRT display, CRT display adapter, RS-232C and parallel ports, personal productivity software suite, carrying case, PC Convertible printer, internal modem
Value: $15 to $40

The IBM PCjr ($5 to $45) was aimed at the home market, and the earliest models had the ill-received Chiclet-style keyboard shown here.

IBM Personal System/2 (PS/2) Model 25

(1987, desktop PC)

Base Configuration: 8MHz 8086 CPU, PC-DOS 3.3, two ISA slots, 512K RAM (640K max), 40K ROM (64K max), 3.5-inch floppy disk drive, integrated monochrome CRT
Video: MCGA **Important Options:** 20MB hard disk drive
Value: $5 to $30

The IBM Personal System/2 Model 25 ($5 to $30), shown here missing the keyboard, was the low end of the PS/2 line. *Photo courtesy of Sellam Ismail, Vintage Computer Festival.*

IBM Personal System/2 (PS/2) Model 30

(April 1987, desktop PC)

Original Retail Price: $1,695 to $2,295
Base Configuration: 8MHz 8086 CPU, PC-DOS 3.3, three ISA slots, 640K RAM, 3.5-inch floppy disk drive, keyboard/keypad, serial and parallel ports **Video:** MCGA **Size/Weight:** 15.6 x 16 x 4, 17 lbs.
Important Options: OS/2, second 3.5-inch floppy disk drive; 20MB hard disk drive; 8503 monochrome or 8512, 8513, or 8514 color monitor; mouse; ProPrinter II
Value: $7 to $35

The IBM Personal System/2 Model 30 ($7 to $35).

One of the most popular of the IBM PS/2 line, the Model 50 ($7 to $35). The monitor was an option.

IBM Personal System/2 (PS/2) Model 50

(April 1987, desktop PC)

Original Retail Price: $3,595
Base Configuration: 10MHz 80286 CPU, PC-DOS 3.3, three MCA slots, 1MB RAM (7MB max), 128K ROM, 3.5-inch floppy disk drive, 20MB hard disk drive, keyboard/keypad **Video:** VGA **Size/Weight:** 16.5 x 14.1 x 5.5 inches, 23 lbs. **Important Options:** OS/2; 8503 monochrome or 8512, 8513, or 8514 color monitor; mouse; ProPrinter II
Value: $7 to $35

IBM Personal System/2 (PS/2) Model 60

(April 1987, desktop PC)

Original Retail Price: $5,295 to $6,295

Base Configuration: 10MHz 80286 CPU, PC-DOS 3.3, seven MCA slots, 1MB RAM (15MB max), 128K ROM, 3.5-inch floppy disk drive, 44MB hard disk drive, keyboard/keypad **Video:** VGA **Size/Weight:** 19 x 6.5 x 23.5, 52 lbs. **Important Options:** OS/2; 70- or 115MB hard disk drive; 8503 monochrome or 8512, 8513, or 8514 color monitor; mouse; ProPrinter II
Value: $10 to $40

The IBM PS/2 Model 60 ($10 to $40) shown with the optional floor stand.

IBM Personal System/2 (PS/2) Model 80

(April 1987, desktop PC)

Original Retail Price: $6,995 to $10,995
Base Configuration: 16- or 20MHz 80386 CPU, PC-DOS 3.3, seven MCA slots, 1MB RAM (4MB max), 128K ROM, 3.5-inch floppy disk drive, 44MB hard disk drive, keyboard/keypad, serial and parallel ports **Video:** VGA **Size/Weight:** 19 x 6.5 x 23.5 inches, 52 lbs. **Important Options:** OS/2; 44- to 115MB hard disk drive; 8503 monochrome or 8512, 8513, or 8514 color monitor; mouse; ProPrinter II
Value: $10 to $40

IBM PS/2 P70 (transportable PC)
Base Configuration: 16MHz 80386 CPU; two MCA slots; up to 8MB RAM; 3.5-inch floppy disk drive; 30MB hard disk drive; monochrome gas plasma display; keyboard/keypad; serial, parallel, and mouse ports
Video: VGA **Important Options:** OS/2, 60- or 120MB hard disk drive, mouse
Value: $15 to $45

IBM PS/2 L40SX (March 1991, laptop PC)
Base Configuration: 20MHz 80386SX CPU, ISA bus, 2MB RAM (16MB max), 60MB hard disk drive, monochrome LCD, integral keyboard/keypad **Video:** VGA **Important Options:** OS/2, 80MB hard disk drive
Value: $12 to $42

Intertec Data Systems (Columbia, South Carolina)

Sold as an intelligent terminal, the SuperBrain was actually a capable microcomputer. Intertec brought out the SuperBrain QD in 1980 with 64K RAM and double-sided floppy drives. A SuperBrain II introduced in 1983 came with 64K RAM and Microsoft BASIC. All units had the same all-in-one design and two-tone black and white color scheme.

The HeadStart used a RAM disk for fast data access and could be used as a standalone system or as a network server. As the latter, it could support up to 255 users.

Intertec SuperBrain Video Computer System
(1979, desktop)
Original Retail Price: $3,000
Base Configuration: two Z80 CPUs, CP/M, 32K RAM (64K max), two 5.25-inch floppy disk drives, integral 12-inch monochrome monitor, integral keyboard/keypad, RS-232 port **Important Options:** S-100 bus adapter, 10MB hard disk drive
Value: $20 to $75

Intertec HeadStart Video Processing Unit (VPU)
(Nov. 1983, desktop PC)
Original Retail Price: $1,895 to $4,495
Base Configuration: 8MHz 8086 and 4MHz Z80A CPUs; MS-DOS and CP/M-80; 128K RAM (1MB max); 3.5-inch floppy disk drive; integral 12-inch monochrome CRT display; keyboard/keypad; RS-449/RS-232, parallel, and network ports **Video:** 25-line x 132-column text **Size/Weight:** 15.75 x 12.75 x 11.3 inches, 25 lbs. **Important Options:** 10MB to 50MB hard disk drive
Value: $15 to $45

Intertek Systems Inc. (Orange, California)

Intertek System IV (1984, Apple II-class desktop)
Original Retail Price: $849
Base Configuration: 6502 and Z80A CPUs, Microsoft CP/M 2.20B, 64K RAM, integral keyboard/keypad, game and cassette ports, Integer BASIC **Video:** 16 colors **Important Options:** external 5.25-inch floppy disk drive, 12-inch monochrome or 13-inch color monitor, printer, joysticks
Value: $15 to $35

Ithaca Intersystems Inc. (Ithaca, New York)

The DPS-1 was one of the last micros designed with a switch-based front panel, but it was one of the first to have an S-100 bus that was compatible with both 8- and 16-bit hardware.

Ithaca Intersystems DPS-1 (1979, early micro)
Base Configuration: 4MHz Z80 CPU, 20 S-100 slots, status LEDs, front-panel switches
Value: $55 to $175

ITT Information Systems (San Jose, California)

ITT was a conglomerate that decided to add PC manufacturing to its portfolio. The XTRA line was considered good quality. One distinguishing feature was the optional black mouse, which had three slanted rectangular buttons. ITT-DOS is an enhanced version of MS-DOS.

The ITT Xtra Personal Computer ($5 to $25) was one of the better PC compatibles.

ITT Xtra Personal Computer
(May 1984, desktop PC)
Original Retail Price: $2,499 to $6,399
Base Configuration: 8088 CPU, ITT-DOS 2.0, five ISA slots, 128K RAM (640K max), 32K ROM, 5.25-inch floppy disk drive, keyboard/keypad, RS-232C and parallel ports, MS-DOS manuals **Video:** 25-line x 80-column text **Size/Weight:** 5.6 x 14 x 15.6 inches, 21.5 lbs. **Important Options:** MS-DOS 2.11 or CP/M-86, second 5.25-inch floppy disk drive, 10- or 20MB hard disk drive, 12-inch color or 14-inch monochrome monitor, CGA or monochrome card, mouse
Value: $5 to $25

In 1983, the Intertec Headstart Video Processing Unit ($15 to $45) must have looked futuristic in its design.

Ivy Microcomputer Corp. (Wilmington, Massachusetts)

Ivy 3000 Series (Oct. 1983, transportable PC)
Original Retail Price: $2,995 to $3,995
Base Configuration: 6MHz 80186, Ivy-DOS (PC-DOS compatible), 256K RAM (512K max), 5.25-inch floppy disk drive, composite video port, integral 9-inch monochrome CRT, keyboard/keypad, two RS-232C and one parallel port **Video:** 25-line x 80-column text **Important Options:** second 5.25-inch floppy disk drive, 10MB hard disk drive, internal modem, dot-matrix or daisy-wheel printer, carrying case
Value: $15 to $40

The Ivy 3002 ($15 to $40) transportable PC-compatible.

Jonos International Corp. (Fullerton, California)

Jonos built portables like tanks, and the military was in fact one of its customers. The company also claimed that its systems saw use on oil rigs and on submarines. The industrial look of both the C and I series is part of their appeal. The C2150, I4100, and I4300 models had floppy storage only, while the C2500, C2550, C2600, I4500, I4550, I4700, and I4750 were configured with hard disk drives.

Jonos C Series/I Series (1984, transportable)
Original Retail Price: $3,295 to $5,595 (C series)/$3,695 to $5,995 (I series)
Base Configuration: 6MHz Z80B CPU (C series)/8MHz 8088-2 CPU (I series), CP/M Plus (C series)/Concurrent DOS (I series), eight STD slots, 128K RAM (C series)/256K RAM (640K max; I series), 3.5-inch floppy disk drive, integral 9-inch monochrome CRT, composite video port, RGB video port (I series), keyboard/keypad, two RS-232C ports, parallel port (I series), owner's manual **Video:** 25-line x 80-column text **Size/Weight:** 17.25 x 7.25 x 13.25 inches, 26 lbs. **Important Options:** eight additional STD slots, 5- or 10MB hard disk drive, color video card (C series), internal modem, integral printer, ARCNet support (I series)
Value: $17 to $50

Jupiter Cantab (Cambridge, U.K.)

Designed by two former Sinclair engineers, the Jupiter Ace was much like other low-cost micros such as the ZX81. The most obvious exception is that it used FORTH as its programming language rather than the more accepted BASIC. The Jupiter Ace had a short production run, as production ceased in 1984. Examples are much sought after by collectors, especially in the U.K. Systems sold in the U.S. by agent Computer Distribution Associates were called the Jupiter Ace 4000. These models had a slightly different keyboard. Jupiter Cantab announced a Jupiter Ace 16+ model, but the company declared bankruptcy before it could be released.

Jupiter Cantab Ace
(April 1983, home computer)
Original Retail Price: $175
Base Configuration: 3.25MHz Z80A CPU, 16K RAM (51K max), monitor and TV video ports, integral Chiclet-style keyboard, cassette port, FORTH, AC adapter, owner's manual **Video:** 24-line x 32-column text, 256 x 192 graphics **Important Options:** ADC converter, parallel interface, adapter for Timex Sinclair peripherals
Value: $75 to $250

Developed by former Sinclair engineers, the Jupiter Cantab Ace ($75 to $250) is popular with enthusiasts in Europe, especially in its native U.K.

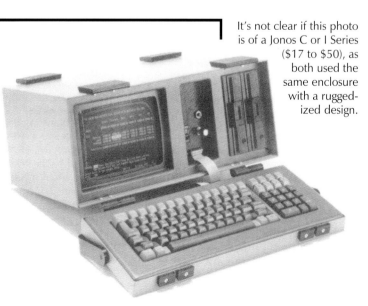

It's not clear if this photo is of a Jonos C or I Series ($17 to $50), as both used the same enclosure with a ruggedized design.

Kaypro Corp. (Formerly Non-Linear Systems) (Solana Beach, California)

People who bought Kaypro transportables often used them for a long time. They were well-built with steel enclosures, which gave an impression of ruggedness. Kaypro owners got a lot for their money, too, with standard storage and software features that most of its competitors provided only as options. Perhaps this is why you hear a lot of people say that their first computer was a Kaypro. It's no wonder that Kaypro owners were such a loyal bunch, and the company's CP/M systems are sought-after collectibles today.

Despite the desireability of Kaypro luggables, prices are still reasonable because Kaypro produced so many. Through 1983, Kaypro sold about 160,000 systems total. In 1984, Kaypro was the fourth largest manufacturer of personal business computers in the U.S., behind IBM, Apple, and Tandy/Radio Shack. Most of those systems were CP/M-based, as this was about the time the company (belatedly) made a shift to PC-compatible portables and desktop computers.

Although Kaypros are relatively common, finding one in pristine condition is tough. These systems were often well-used, and the paint on the metal cases was easily scuffed and scratched. As with all luggables, broken latches are common.

Despite the II designation, the Kaycomp II was the first portable produced by what was then Non-Linear Systems. The company quickly renamed the system the Kaypro II, upgrading the floppy drives from single- to double-density at the same time. A Kaypro 5 was introduced in late 1982, and it was a Kaypro II with a 5.5MB hard drive. The company sold 14,000 Kaypro IIs in 1982 and 42,000 in its first full year of production. The computer was eventually relabeled the Kaypro 2, because customers kept asking dealers about the "Kaypro eleven."

In late 1983, Kaypro offered dual-processor models of both the Kaypro II and Kaypro 4. Dubbed the Kaypro II Plus 88 and the Kaypro 4 Plus 88, the new models featured a 16-bit Intel 8088 CPU in addition to the standard 8-bit Z80. This gave users the option of running MS-DOS as well as CP/M software.

A portable system with a hard drive for under $3,000 was nearly unheard of in 1983, and that price allowed the Kaypro 10 to compete with more powerful PC-based portables.

The Kaypro 16 was the company's first (and only) PC-compatible transportable. It had the same solid construction as its CP/M-based kin, but at its heart was a fairly typical IBM-based architecture.

Kaypro originally planned to outsource production of the 2000 laptop to Mitsui in Japan, but in the end developed and built the system at its own U.S. facilities. It had several noteworthy features, including a detachable keyboard, a brushed aluminum case, and a floppy storage area under the keyboard. An enhanced Kaypro 2000+ model was offered later.

The strangely configured Robie was Kaypro's first desktop computer and only CP/M-based desktop. Like the portable line, the Robie had an all-steel case housing a small CRT display. In fact, it was a reconfigured Kaypro 4. The Robie's small form factor consumed only a square foot of desk space, and the unusual dual 2.6MB floppy disk drives (mounted atop the display) provided a lot of removable storage for the day. Produced by Drivetec, the high-capacity floppy drives were never popular. Few Robies sold and they are quite scarce today, and media for the Drivetec drives will be even harder to find.

Kaypro claimed that the 286i was the first AT-compatible system to market. The company later upgraded the CPU to an 8MHz version. Kaypro followed the 286i shortly with the Kaypro PC, a generic-looking IBM PC-compatible system. Although well built, the Kaypro PC compatibles were never among the top sellers. It stuck with the slower version of the 8088 CPU long after its rivals switched to the 8088-2 processor.

Kaycomp II/Kaypro II (June 1982, transportable)
Original Retail Price: $1,795
Base Configuration: 2.5MHz Z80, CP/M 2.2, 64K RAM, 2K ROM, two 5.25-inch floppy disk drives, integral 9-inch monochrome CRT, keyboard/keypad, RS-232C and parallel ports, S-BASIC, Perfect Software application suite **Video:** 24-line x 80-column text **Size/Weight:** 18 x 8 x 15.5 inches, 26 lbs. **Important Options:** 12-inch monochrome monitor, carrying case, battery pack and charger
Value: $25 to $125

The Kaypro II ($25 to $125) launched a series of popular CP/M-based transportables.

Kaypro 4 (June 1983, transportable)
Original Retail Price: $1,995
Base Configuration: 2.5MHz Z80, CP/M 2.2, two 5.25-inch floppy disk drives, integral 9-inch monochrome CRT, keyboard/keypad, RS-232C and parallel ports, application suite, owner's manuals and training guides **Video:** 24-line x 80-column text **Size/Weight:** 18 x 8 x 15.5 inches, 26 lbs. **Important Options:** vinyl or nylon carrying case
Value: $20 to $95

Kaypro 2X (transportable)
Base Configuration: CP/M, 64K RAM, integral 9-inch monochrome CRT, keyboard/keypad, two RS-232C and one parallel port, application suite **Video:** 25-line x 80-column text
Value: $20 to $95

The Kaypro 2X ($20 to $95) featured modest improvements over the original model.

Kaypro 10 (1983, transportable)
Original Retail Price: $2,795
Base Configuration: 4MHz Z80A CPU; CP/M 2.2; 64K RAM, 2K ROM; 5.25-inch floppy disk drive; 10MB hard disk drive; integral 9-inch monochrome CRT; keyboard/keypad; two RS-232C, parallel, and light-pen ports; S-BASIC; application suite; internal modem **Video:** 25-line x 80-column text, 160 x 100 graphics **Size/Weight:** 18 x 8 x 15.5 inches, 31 lbs. **Important Options:** vinyl or nylon carrying case
Value: $30 to $100

Kaypro's first and only
PC-compatible transportable, the Kaypro 16 ($20 to $50).

Kaypro 16 (Feb. 1985, transportable PC)
Original Retail Price: $3,295
Base Configuration: MS-DOS, 256K RAM (768K max), 5.25-inch floppy disk drive, 10MB hard disk drive, integral 9-inch monochrome CRT, RGB and composite video ports, keyboard/keypad, application suite, 13-volume manual set **Video:** 25-line x 80-column text, 640 x 200 graphics **Size/Weight:** 18 x 8 x 15 inches, 33.5 lbs. **Important Options:** second 5.25-inch floppy disk drive
Value: $20 to $50

Kaypro Robie
(Feb. 1984, desktop)
Original Retail Price: $2,295
Base Configuration: Z80 CPU, CP/M 2.2, 64K RAM, two 5.25-inch floppy disk drives, integral 9-inch monochrome CRT, keyboard/keypad, application suite, internal modem **Video:** 24-line x 80-column text
Value: $25 to $100

There's no mistaking the Kaypro Robie ($25 to $100) for anything else, with its top-mounted non-standard disk drives.

Kaypro 286i (Feb. 1985, desktop PC)
Original Retail Price: $4,550
Base Configuration: 6MHz 80286 CPU, eight ISA slots (five open), 512K RAM (640K max), two 5.25-inch floppy disk drives, RGB and composite video ports, keyboard/keypad, serial and two parallel ports, application suite, GW-BASIC **Video:** CGA
Value: $7 to $30

Kaypro PC (Nov. 1985, desktop PC)
Original Retail Price: $1,595
Base Configuration: 4.77MHz 8088 CPU; MS-DOS 2.11; 256K RAM (640K max); six ISA slots; two 5.25-inch floppy disk drives; 12-inch monochrome monitor; monochrome, RGB, and composite video ports; keyboard/keypad; RS-232C and parallel ports; GW-BASIC; application suite **Video:** CGA **Size/Weight:** 19.5 x 16 x 6 inches, 30 lbs. **Important Options:** 80286 upgrade, 10- or 20MB hard disk drive
Value: $7 to $30

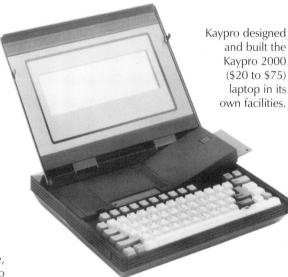

Kaypro designed and built the Kaypro 2000 ($20 to $75) laptop in its own facilities.

Kaypro 2000 (March 1985, laptop PC)
Original Retail Price: $1,995
Base Configuration: 4.77MHz 8088 CPU, MS-DOS, 256K RAM (768K max), 3.5-inch floppy disk drive, monochrome LCD, keyboard, RS-232C port, application suite, carrying case, tutorial software, AC adapter, battery pack **Video:** 25-line x 80-column text, 640 x 200 graphics **Size/Weight:** 11.5 x 13.1 x 2.6 inches, 11.5 lbs. **Important Options:** Base Unit, external 3.5- or 5.25-inch floppy disk drive
Value: $20 to $75

Kenbak
(Brentwood, California)

The Computer Museum in Boston (now the The Computer Museum History Center (TCMHC) in Mountain View, California, ran a contest to find the first commercially produced personal computer in 1986, and named the Kenbak-1 the winner. However, that title is disputed by some because the Kenbak-1 uses discrete logic ICs in place of a microprocessor. Designed by John Blankenbaker, the system was limited even by the day's standards. It had no digital I/O capability and a miniscule amount of memory. These systems are extremely rare, but TCMHC has one in its collection.

Kenbak-1 (1971, early micro)
Original Retail Price: $750
Base Configuration: two-chip discrete logic CPU, 256 bytes RAM, status LEDs, front panel switches
Value: $2,000 to $5,000

Lanier Business Products Inc.
(Atlanta, Georgia)

The Lanier Business Processor 1000 was a dual-processor system.

Lanier Business Processor 1000 (1984, desktop)
Original Retail Price: $2,995
Base Configuration: MS-DOS or CP/M, 128K RAM (256K max), two 5.25-inch floppy disk drives, integral monochrome CRT, keyboard/keypad, IBM 3270 and 3780 emulation **Important Options:** 5- or 10MB hard disk drive
Value: $12 to $35

Leading Edge Products Inc.
(Canton, Massachusetts)

Leading Edge was primarily a marketing company that started out selling other brand or rebranded peripherals. You might remember its ads for the Gorilla Banana printer or Elephant floppy disk media from the 1980s. In 1983, the company introduced a line of PCs under its own brand but manufactured in Japan by Mitsubishi (which used the same design for the Sperry PC). Its most popular system, the Model D, was made by the Daewoo Group in Korea.

Leading Edge Personal Computer System
(Nov. 1983, desktop PC)
Original Retail Price: $2,895
Base Configuration: 7.16MHz 8088-2 CPU; MS-DOS 1.25; seven ISA slots; 128K RAM; two 5.25-inch floppy disk drives; 12-inch monochrome monitor; keyboard/keypad; RS-232 and parallel ports; GW-BASIC; Leading Edge Word Processing Program; owner's, technical reference, and software manuals **Video:** 25-line x 80-column text, 640 x 200 graphics **Size/Weight:** 18 x 16.5 x 5.3 inches, 47 lbs.
Important Options: CGA
Value: $5 to $30

Leading Edge Model D Personal Computer
(1985, desktop PC)
Original Retail Price: $1,495
Base Configuration: 4.77MHz 8088, MS-DOS, four ISA slots, 256K RAM (640K max), two 5.25-inch floppy disk drives, 12-inch monochrome monitor, RGB video port, keyboard/keypad, RS-232 and parallel ports, Leading Edge Word Processing Program **Video:** Hercules **Size/Weight:** 14 x 15.5 x 5.5 inches **Important Options:** 10MB hard disk drive, 14-inch color CRT
Value: $5 to $30

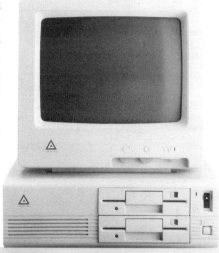

LNW Research/LNW Computers
(Costa Mesa, California)

LNW was founded in 1978 by Gene Lu, Michael Norton, and Ken Woog (the L, N, and W, respectively) as a manufacturer of expansion interfaces and disk doublers for the TRS-80 Microcomputer System (Model I). In 1980, the company introduced its first microcomputer, the LNW80 Model 1, which it sold through mail order and a few retailers. The LNW80 Model 1 was compatible with the TRS-80 Model I, while the LNW80 Model 2 was compatible with both the TRS-80 Model I and Model III. The latter could also run CP/M. LNW was considered one of the highest-quality makers of TRS-80-compatible systems, and surviving examples are treasured by TRS-80 enthusiasts.

The LNW80 was a better, color-capable TRS-80 Model I, with which it was hardware and software compatible. The company sold the LNW80 in kit form, and purchasers could buy just the system board or a complete system including enclosures. You might find some LNW80s in custom-made enclosures. The LNW80 was considered the Cadillac of TRS-80 clones, and surviving examples are treasured by TRS-80 enthusiasts. The Model II could run most TRS-80 Model I/III/4 software and offered more memory and better graphics.

The LNW80 Model II ($25 to $75) was compatible with, but improved on the TRS-80 Model I. *Reused with permission CMP Media LLC, Byte.com (Byte Magazine), Manhasset NY. All rights reserved.*

LNW Research LNW80/LNW80 Model II
(1980 [LNW80]/1983 [LNW80 Model II], desktop)
Original Retail Price: $1,200 (LNW80)/$1,195 (LNW80 Model II) **Base Configuration:** 4MHz Z80A CPU, CP/M and DOSPLUS (LNW80 Model II), 48K RAM (LNW80)/96K RAM, 16K ROM (LNW80 Model II), integral keyboard/keypad, RS 232C and parallel ports, composite video and cassette port, application suite (LNW80 Model 2), operations and technical reference manuals **Video:** 24-line x 80-column text, 384 x 192 graphics (LNW80)/480 x 192 graphics (LNW80 Model II), eight colors **Size/Weight:** 16.5 x 22 x 3.5 inches **Important Options:** LNW Expansion Interface, monochrome CRT display, floppy disk drive, parallel port
Value: $25 to $75

The Leading Edge Model D ($5 to $30) was a top-selling PC-compatible.

Lobo Systems Inc. (Goleta, California)

Lobo made a name for itself by selling floppy and hard disk units for Apple and Tandy systems. It also sold its own version of CP/M called Lobo CP/M, and later developed LDOS (Lobo DOS), a TRSDOS-compatible operating system. By late 1983, Lobo had sold about 2,000 TRS-80-compatible Max-80s.

Lobo Systems Max-80 (desktop)
Original Retail Price: $820
Base Configuration: 5MHz Z80B CPU, CP/M, 64K RAM (128K max), keyboard/keypad, two RS-232 and one parallel port **Video:** 25-line x 80-column text **Important Options:** LDOS, external dual 5.25- or 8-inch floppy disk drives, 5- or 8MB hard disk drive, 12-inch monochrome monitor
Value: $25 to $75

Known mainly as a maker of disk drives, Lobo Systems also produced the TRS-80 Model I-compatible Max-80 ($25 to $75), shown with the optional floppy and hard disk drives, and the monochrome monitor.

Logical Business Machines (Sunnyvale, California)

The L-XT was sold as a development system for custom applications. The company claimed that its bundled Diplomat natural programming language made application development accessible to programmers and non-programmers alike. Logical Business Machines shipped 175 in the first month of production.

Logical L-XT (March 1984, desktop PC)
Original Retail Price: $5,985
Base Configuration: MS-DOS 2.11, two ISA slots, 192K RAM, 5.25-inch floppy disk drive, 10MB hard disk drive, monochrome monitor, two serial and one parallel port, Diplomat natural development language **Important Options:** 60MB hard disk drive
Value: $25 to $65

Mad Computers Inc. (Santa Clara, California)

The MAD-1 (Modular Advanced Design) computer was quite different from other PC-compatibles. As the name suggests, it features a modular design with a Computing Module housing the main processor board and a Data Module housing the storage devices. An op-

tional Expansion Module provided four slots for add-on boards. However, the MAD-1 cannot use IBM-standard memory cards because of its 16-bit bus. A black and grey color scheme and its 80186 CPU further distinguish the MAD-1. These computers are collectible just because they look so cool.

Mad Computers MAD-1 (1983, desktop PC)
Original Retail Price: $4,195 to $6,295
Base Configuration: 7.2MHz 80186 CPU, MS-DOS 2.0, one ISA slot, 128K RAM (512K max), 16K ROM, 5.25-inch floppy disk drive, 12-inch monochrome monitor, RGB video port, keyboard/keypad, two RS-232 and one parallel port **Video:** 720 x 350 graphics **Size/Weight:** 12.5 x 15 x 2.4 inches, black and grey **Important Options:** Concurrent CP/M-86, Expansion Module, second 5.25-inch floppy disk drive, 5MB or 10MB hard disk drive, application suite, internal modem
Value: $15 to $45

The Mad Computers MAD-1 ($15 to $45) featured a modular design.

Magic Computer Co. (Fort Lee, New Jersey)

Magic Computer (1983, desktop)
Base Configuration: 6502 and Z80A CPUs, 64K RAM, keyboard/keypad, parallel port, CBASIC, application suite **Important Options:** one to four 5.25-inch floppy disk drives, monochrome monitor
Value: $15 to $40

Mark-8 (Jonathan Titus) (Blacksburg, Virginia)

The Mark-8 was originally a do-it-yourself project published in the July 1974 issue of Radio-Electronics magazine. Its creator, Jonathan Titus, also sold kits. The Mark-8 created a great deal of excitement among electronic hobbyists because it was a fully functional computer that was inexpensive to build. Completed systems had a reputation for being very reliable, too. It's not known how many of the 7,500 plans that Radio-Electronics sold resulted in completed Mark-8s. Titus sold about 400 kits.

Mark-8 Minicomputer (July 1974, early micro)
Original Retail Price: $350 (cost of parts to build)
Base Configuration: 8008 CPU, 256 bytes RAM, front panel switches
Value: $750 to $3,000

Martin Research (Chicago, Illinois)

The Mike 2 was a bare-bones system—just the CPU board with a 20-key keypad and a seven-digit display. The customer supplied his own cabinet and power supply. The system was upgradeable to the faster 8080-based Mike 303A. The Mike series was for hobbyists looking for an inexpensive entry-level system.

Martin Research Mike 203A (Mike 2)/Mike 303A (Mike 3)
(1975, computer trainer)
Original Retail Price: $270 kit (Mike 2)/$395 kit, $495 assembled (Mike 3)
Base Configuration: 8008 (Mike 2)/8080 (Mike 3) CPU, up to 4K RAM, PROM storage, seven-digit LED, hex keypad, monitor software, operation manual **Important Options:** I/O interface
Value: $75 to $165

Martin Research Mike 8 (1977, computer trainer)
Original Retail Price: $895
Base Configuration: Z80 CPU, 4K RAM, 1K ROM, LED readout, integral hex keypad, EPROM programmer, power supply
Value: $65 to $150

Mattel Electronics (Hawthorne, California)

Mattel enjoyed success in the electronic game console market with its Intellivision product, which sold about 3 million units. The jump to home computers, then, seemed like a good idea. Radofin Electronics manufactured the Aquarius for Mattel and sold it overseas under that brand. Problems with FCC certification delayed the release of the Aquarius, and consumer indifference to the product forced Mattel to abandon it shortly after its release.

Mattel must have produced the Aquarius in numbers, because it is not difficult to find. Some of the items that Mattel promised for the Aquarius, such as the Master Expansion Unit that added two floppy drives and CP/M capability, never got beyond the prototype stage. A number of the software titles also never made it to market. The main Aquarius unit alone is worth very little; look for complete systems.

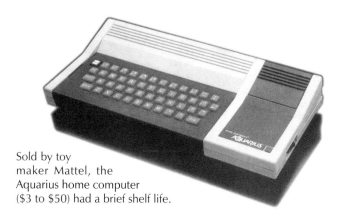

Sold by toy maker Mattel, the Aquarius home computer ($3 to $50) had a brief shelf life.

Mattel Aquarius
(1983, home computer)
Original Retail Price: $200
Base Configuration: Z80A CPU, ROM cartridge slot, Mini Expander, 4K RAM (52K max), 8K ROM, cassette recorder, integral Chiclet-style keyboard, two game controllers, Microsoft BASIC, thermal printer, instruction cards **Video:** 320 x 192 graphics, 16 colors **Size/Weight:** 13 x 6 x 2 inches, 4.25 lbs. **Important Options:** CP/M, Master Expansion Module, dual external 5.25-inch floppy disk drives, external modem
Value: $3 to $50

MCM Computers (Rexdale, Ontario, Canada)

MCM's implementation of APL was compatible with those run on larger systems.

MCM Computers System 700 Model 782 APL Computer
(1977, laptop)
Original Retail Price: $4,950
Base Configuration: 8K RAM, 32K ROM, dual integral cassette recorders, monochrome plasma display, integral keyboard, APL **Size/Weight:** 20 lbs. **Important Options:** external floppy disk drive, RS-232C interface, printer, plotter, card reader
Value: $100 to $275

The small MCM System 700 Model 782 ($100 to $275) was a development system for APL programmers.

Memotech Corp. (Needham, Massachusetts)

Memotech is a British company that started out selling expansion modules for the Sinclair ZX Spectrum and ZX81. A U.S. subsidiary began selling the MTX-512 in North America in late 1983 or early 1984. It discontinued the MTX500 in 1985.

Memotech MTX500/MTX512
(June 1983 [MTX500]/early 1984 [MTX512], desktop)
Original Retail Price: $595 (MTX512)
Base Configuration: 4MHz Z80A CPU; ROM cartridge slot; 32K (MTX500)/64K (MTX512) RAM (512K max); 24K ROM; TV and RGB video ports; integral keyboard/keypad; two parallel, two game, and cassette ports; MTX BASIC, MTX Graphics, and MTX Assembler in ROM **Video:** 256 x 192 graphics, 16 colors **Important Options:** CP/M, one or two external 5.25-inch floppy disk drives, 8-inch floppy disk drive (MTX500), external 5MB hard disk drive, dual RS-232C interface, New Word word processing software, 80-column card, DMX80 printer, Oxford Ring network
Value: $20 to $125

The Memotech MTX512 ($20 to $125) shown with the optional dual 5.25-inch floppy drive unit and DMX80 printer.

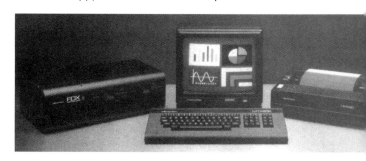

Microcomputer Associates Inc. (Sunnyvale, California)

The Jolt was a bare-bones hobbyist system. If you bought the main Jolt CPU card with the three options, the price would have been $755 kit or $998 assembled. You supplied your own case. Jolt designer Ray Holt was also responsible for the Synertek SYM-1.

Microcomputer Associates Jolt (Dec. 1975, computer trainer)
Original Retail Price: $249 kit, $348 assembled
Base Configuration: 6502 CPU, 512 bytes RAM (4K max), terminal interface, DEMON debugger/monitor in ROM, operation manual, power supply **Important Options:** I/O interface, accessory bag
Value: $100 to $250

Microcomputer Technology Inc. (MTI) (Santa Ana, California)

MTI took a stock TRS-80 Model III, added a few high-performance options, and (with later versions) painted the case white to create the Mod III Plus Series.

Microcomputer Technology Mod III Plus Series
(1982, desktop)
Original Retail Price: $2,495 to $4,999
Base Configuration: 4MHz Z80A CPU, Dosplus 4.0, 48K RAM, 5.25-inch floppy disk drive, integral monochrome CRT, integral keyboard/keypad, RS-232 port, application suite, anti-glare screen **Important Options:** CP/M 2.2, second 5.25-inch floppy disk drive, 5- or 8MB hard disk drive, printer
Value: $20 to $75

Micro Craft Corp. (Dallas, Texas)

The Dimension 68000 wasn't the only multiprocessor microcomputer, but it has taken on something of a legendary status. One of the first ads for the system placed in the December 1983 issue of *Byte* drew more than 11,000 reader responses, the most for a single-page ad to that point. Techies were intrigued by the Dimension 68000's capabilities. The original model could accommodate three processors in addition to its main Motorola 68000: Z80A, MOS Technology 6512, and Intel 8086. Each option could run CP/M, Apple II, and MS-DOS software, respectively in addition to the standard configuration's Unix. Software to emulate Tandy/Radio Shack TRSDOS was also available. The company was sold to a group in Arkansas and reformed as Dimension Electronics in 1987. The system was relaunched as the New Dimension 68000 with an Apple Macintosh emulation option.

Micro Craft Dimension 68000
(late 1983, desktop)
Original Retail Price: $3,995 to $5,895
Base Configuration: 8MHz 68000 CPU; Unix System V or CP/M-68K; six proprietary slots; 256K RAM (512K max), 16K ROM; two 5.25-inch floppy disk drives; composite video port; keyboard/keypad; RS-232, parallel, and game ports; C compiler; UniBASIC; 68000 assembler **Video:** 24-line x 80-column text **Size/Weight:** 17 x 6 inches, 27 lbs. **Important Options:** Z80A, 6512, or 8086 coprocessor; CP/M, AppleDOS, or MS-DOS; 20- to 130MB hard disk drive; tape backup drive; RGB interface
Value: $25 to $100

Microdata Systems (Woburn, Massachusetts)

Microdata Systems F800 (1977, early micro)
Original Retail Price: $499 kit, $699 assembled
Base Configuration: F8 CPU, 12 expansion slots, 8K RAM (65K max), 1K ROM, RS-232 port, BASIC, enclosure, power supply
Value: $50 to $125

MicroDyne Computer Systems Inc. (Ft. Lauderdale, Florida)

In 1983, S-100 systems were still popular, and MicroDyne claimed that the MCS-100 was the only S-100 portable available at the time, although at least one other manufacturer (MicroStandard Technologies) offered it as an option. This makes the MCS-100 an interesting find for S-100 as well as portable collectors. One of the dual Z80A CPUs controlled the video.

Microdyne MCS-100 (1983, transportable)
Base Configuration: two 4MHz Z80A CPU, CP/M Plus 3.0, four S-100 slots, 256K RAM, two 5.25-inch floppy disk drives, 46MB hard disk drive, integral 9-inch monochrome CRT, keyboard/keypad, RS-232C and parallel ports, application suite, BASIC-80, internal modem **Video:** 25-line x 80-column text
Value: $50 to $125

Microkit Inc. (Santa Monica, California)

Microkit sold the 8/16 Universal Microcomputer Development System to (you guessed it) developers.

Microkit 8/16 Universal Microcomputer Development System (1977, early micro)
Original Retail Price: $5,275
Base Configuration: 8088 or 6800 CPU, 32K RAM, two cassette recorders, Quickrun development software
Value: $75 to $150

The Micro Craft Dimension 68000 ($25 to $100) was designed to accommodate the most popular CPUs and operating systems of the day.

Micromega Corp. (Dallas, Texas)

The Micro M16 was housed in a "gunstock walnut veneer cabinet."

Micromega Micro M16 (1977, early micro)
Base Configuration: PACE 16 CPU; nine expansion slots; RS-232, two parallel, and two cassette ports; PACE BASIC; macroassembler
Value: $65 to $175

Microsci Corp. (Santa Ana, California)

Microsci was a well-known vendor of third-party floppy disk drives for Apple II and III computers. The HAVAC (Home/Academic Very Affordable Computer) was an attempt to expand its market into full systems. It was a petite unit with an unusual oblong form factor. HAVAC DOS was an AppleDOS workalike.

Microsci HAVAC (1983, Apple II-class transportable)
Original Retail Price: $850
Base Configuration: 1MHz 6502 CPU; HAVAC DOS; external expansion port; 64K RAM; 8K ROM; 5.25-inch floppy disk drive; keyboard; RS-232C, parallel, and game ports; HAVAC BASIC; application suite; tutorial software **Video:** 40-column text, 280 x 192 graphics **Size/Weight:** 5.5 x 10.75 x 13.75 inches, 12 lbs. **Important Options:** external 5.25-inch floppy disk drive
Value: $25 to $65

Shaped something like a shoebox, the Micro HAVAC ($25 to $65) was Apple II-compatible.

Micro Source Inc., MicroStandard Technologies Inc. (New Lebanon, Ohio)

Micro Source changed its name to MicroStandard Technologies sometime in 1983, and also changed the basic configuration of the M6000P at the same time, dropping the "P" designation. A 10-slot card cage became standard, and an Intel 8088 CPU became optional. A color CRT option was also made available in place of the standard monochrome display. The M6000 was sold for industrial, scientific, and military applications, while the M3000 was more business oriented.

Micro Source/MicroStandard M6000P
(1982, transportable)
Original Retail Price: $3,900 to $5,100
Base Configuration: 4MHz Z80 CPU, CP/M 2.2, eight STD slots (four open), 64K RAM (512K max), 8K ROM, two 5.25-inch floppy disk drives, integral 9-inch monochrome CRT, keyboard/keypad, C-BASIC, application suite, carrying case **Video:** 25-line x 80-column text **Size/Weight:** 17 x 20 x 7 inches, 33.75 lbs. **Important Options:** 4MHz 68000 coprocessor, Unix, 10- or 12-slot card cage, external 8-inch floppy disk drive, 10- to 40MB hard disk drive, color graphics card, color monitor, serial and parallel interfaces, modem, acoustic coupler, integral printer
Value: $17 to $45

Micro Source/MicroStandard M3000
(Jan. 1984, transportable)
Original Retail Price: $1,645 to $2,895
Base Configuration: 4MHz Z80A CPU; CP/M 2.2; four STD, two VMEbus, or two S-100 slots; 64K RAM (512K max); 8K ROM; 5.25-inch floppy disk drive, RGB video port; integral 9-inch monochrome CRT; keyboard/keypad; RS-232 and parallel ports; owner's and software manuals **Video:** 25-line x 80-column text **Size/Weight:** 7.25 x 16.3 x 14.8 inches, 30 lbs. **Important Options:** 8088 or 68000 coprocessor; Unix, MS-DOS, or CP/M-86; second 5.25-inch floppy disk drive, 8-inch floppy disk drive, 10MB hard disk drive
Value: $15 to $40

Micro Technology Unlimited (Raleigh, North Carolina)

MTU, which is still in business, was a pioneer developer of digital audio products for microcomputers. It's not surprising, then, that its first computer was optimized for recording and playing audio. It could access sound files from multiple floppy drives for continuous playback.

Micro Technology MTU-130
(Sept. 1981, desktop)
Original Retail Price: $3,599
Base Configuration: 6502 CPU, CODOS, 256K RAM, 12-inch monochrome monitor, integral keyboard/keypad, RS-232C and parallel ports, BASIC **Video:** 24-line x 80-column text, 480 x 256 graphics **Important Options:** Z80 or 68000 coprocessor
Value: $20 to $65

Two CP/M transportables from Micro Source: the more traditionally designed M3000 (left, $15 to $40) and the ruggedized M6000P (right, $17 to $45).

Microvoice Corp. (Tokyo, Japan)

Microvoice apparently sold the Formula-1 as a development system. It came standard with an EPROM (labeled "EP-ROM") programmer with an IC socket accessible on the front. Its keyboard folds up for transport. Both the Formula-1 and the Mugen below were marketed in North America.

Its name wasn't the only odd thing about the Mugen. Packed up for transport, it looks not much different from any other sewing-machine-format portable. Open it up, and you see that it is designed to sit vertically rather than horizontally, with the display beneath the floppy drives.

Microvoice Formula-1 (1984, transportable)
Base Configuration: CP/M, two 5.25-inch floppy disk drives, integral 5.5-inch monochrome CRT, integral keyboard/keypad, application suite, integral printer, EPROM programmer **Important Options:** FCP-300 acoustic coupler
Value: $15 to $40

Microvoice Mugen (1984, transportable PC)
Base Configuration: 8088 CPU, MS-DOS six expansion slots (three open), 256K RAM (512K max), 16K ROM (64K max), two 5.25-inch floppy disk drives, integral 9-inch monochrome CRT, composite and RGB video ports, keyboard/keypad, serial and parallel ports, GW-BASIC **Video:** 25-line x 80-column text, 640 x 200 graphics **Important Options:** EPROM programmer, hard disk drive, GP-IB interface
Value: $15 to $40

The strangely configured Microvoice Mugen ($15 to $40).

Midwest Scientific Instruments (Olathe, Kansas)

Midwest Scientific Instruments MSI 6800
(1977, early micro)
Original Retail Price: $595 kit, $895 assembled
Base Configuration: 2MHz 6800 CPU, 16 SS-50 slots, 8K RAM (56K max), serial interface, MIKBUG, interface adapter board **Size/Weight:** 20 x 16 x 7 inches **Important Options:** MSI FD-8 8-inch floppy disk drive
Value: $50 to $150

Mikra-D (Holliston, Massachusetts)

Mikra-D MTS-8/Basic-8 (1976, early micro)
Original Retail Price: $1,195 kit (MTS-8)/$1,695 kit (BASIC-8)
Base Configuration: 8080 CPU, 4K RAM (64K max), integral monochrome CRT, integral keyboard, serial and cassette ports, assembler, editor, debugger, BASIC-8
Value: $65 to $160

Miles Gordon Technologies (M.G.T.)

By 1989, it was a little late to be introducing an 8-bit home computer. M.G.T., however, was hoping that its Sam Coupe system would appeal to the many owners of the Sinclair ZX Spectrum, with which the Sam Coupe was compatible. The company managed to sell the system for a few years, going bankrupt once and reemerging as SamCo.

Miles Gordon Technologies (M.G.T.) Sam Coupe
(1989, home computer)
Base Configuration: 6MHz Z80B CPU; expansion port; 256K RAM (512K max); 32K ROM; RGB and composite video port; integral keyboard/keypad; mouse, light-pen, MIDI, cassette, and two game ports; BASIC; eight-voice sound **Video:** 512 x 192 graphics, four colors
Important Options: one or two 3.5-inch floppy disk drives
Value: $65 to $125

Mindset Corp. (Sunnyvale, California)

The Mindset is the computer that the PCjr should have been. It was more powerful and offered superior graphics capability thanks to a custom two-chip graphics coprocessor. The Mindset system could generate images at a 320- by 200-pixel resolution in 16 colors, or 640- by 400-pixel resolution in two colors. Although the Mindset PC could run most MS-DOS software, developers had to produce custom versions to take advantage of the enhanced graphics. Few did, and the Mindset faded not long after its introduction. The Expansion Unit adds up to 224K RAM and two floppy drives. It matches the dimensions of the main Mindset system and sits atop it. Without the Expansion Unit, the Mindset is not much more than a game system.

> ### Mindset Personal Computer
> (May 1984, desktop PC)
> **Original Retail Price:** $1,099 to $2,398
> **Base Configuration:** 6MHz 80186 CPU, MS-DOS 2.0, two ROM cartridge slots, 32K RAM (256K max), 5.25-inch floppy disk drive, TV video port, keyboard/keypad **Video:** 640 x 400 graphics, 16 colors **Size/Weight:** 16 x 12.2 x 2.8 inches, 6 lbs. **Important Options:** Expansion Unit, second 5.25-inch floppy disk drive, monochrome or color monitor, mouse, RS-232 and parallel interfaces, graphics and CAD/CAM software, Programmer's Development Library, joysticks, modem, carrying case, sound module
> **Value:** $40 to $125
>
> Providing superb graphics capability, the Mindset Personal Computer ($40 to $125), shown with its optional Expansion Unit, was a much better system than its meager sales indicated.

MiniTerm Associates Inc. (Bedford, Massachusetts)

MiniTerm Associates System 80/2 (1977, early micro)
Base Configuration: Z80 CPU, S-100 bus **Important Options:** two 5.25-inch floppy disk drives
Value: $50 to $150

MITS (Micro Instrumentation and Telemetry Systems) (Albuquerque, New Mexico)

Before 1975, MITS was a struggling calculator manufacturer when its founder, Ed Roberts, decided to develop a low-cost hobbyist computer. The Altair 8800 saved the company and generated $5 million in sales during its first year. But in 1977, Roberts sold the company to Pertec, and its fortunes soon declined. Pertec discontinued all Altair lines in July 1978. Triumph Adler bought what was left of the company from Pertec.

Future Microsoft founder Bill Gates saw an opportunity when the Altair 8800 appeared on the cover of the January 1975 issue of *Popular Electronics* magazine. In short order, he left his studies at Harvard and joined MITS, where he wrote the BASIC used in the system. The Altair 8800 is perhaps the most important early microcomputer. It was the first mass-produced micro, and with BASIC a hobbyist could program it for a wide range of tasks. Its Altair Bus was based on the IEEE 696 standard for connecting expansion boards to the main CPU board, better known as the S-100 bus.

Best of all, it was affordable with prices starting at $439. MITS offered upgrade options ranging from memory to I/O interfaces, through which hobbyists could use cassette storage devices and printers. Some 5,000 units sold in the first year, which encouraged other vendors such as Processor Technology to develop software and hardware for the Altair. In short, the Altair 8800 was the first practical, highly expandable, and affordable microcomputer. As you might guess, the Altair 8800 is a highly sought-after collectible. Although they were produced in relatively large numbers, locating a working unit in good cosmetic shape is difficult.

The early 8800s were unreliable and had weak power supplies. An 8800a version followed shortly that fixed many of the design and construction shortcomings. However, it wasn't until the Altair 8800b was released that MITS had a relatively bulletproof system. The 8800b had an updated CPU board and a ROM-driven front panel.

The 8800b Turnkey Model appeared in June 1977. It had a plain front panel with a lock and two switches. With the system locked, continuous operation for control applications was ensured. An 8800b model similar to the original 8800 was also available. Altair 8800b systems tend to sell for 10 to 15 percent less than comparable 8800 units, while the Turnkey units sell for half the amount or less.

The Altair 680 was smaller than many other systems of the day due to a design philosophy of keeping it simple. It was considered an easy-to-build kit, with most of the circuitry on one PC board. Three configurations were available: a full front panel model with all addressing, processor, and data entry controls; a turnkey model with only the control for restarting the ROM software—used in dedicated applications to minimize operator error; and a single board model that could be used as a core in other systems. The front panel had its own circuitry to control the processor—reset, halt, or start. MITS later introduced an Altair 680b, which had a serial interface and more expansion options through the 680b-MB Expander Card.

The MITS Altair 8800 ($600 to $2,500) was the first microcomputer to sell in large numbers, and this milestone system is one of the most desirable classics today.

MITS Altair 8800/8800b

(March 1975 [8800]/1976 [8800b], early micro)
Original Retail Price: $439 kit, $621 assembled
Base Configuration: 8080 CPU; 16 S-100 slots; 1K RAM (64K max); status LEDs; front-panel switches; assembly, operations, and theory manuals, expander board, aluminum enclosure, power supply **Important Options:** Altair DOS, 88-DCDD or 88-DISK floppy disk drive, cassette interface, Comter or Altair VLCT terminal, 88-2SIO serial and 88-4PIO parallel interfaces, Altair BASIC or Extended BASIC, Altair 110 Line Printer
Value: $600 to $2,500

MITS Altair 680/680b (Dec. 1975 [680]/1976 [680b], early micro)
Original Retail Price: $345 kit, $420 assembled
Base Configuration: 6800 CPU; S-100 bus; 1K RAM; front panel switches; RS-232 or Teletype interface; monitor in ROM; assembler; debugger; editor; assembly, operation, and theory manuals **Size/Weight:** 11 x 11 x 5 inches (680b) **Important Options:** PROM storage, Altair 680 BASIC
Value: $300 to $750

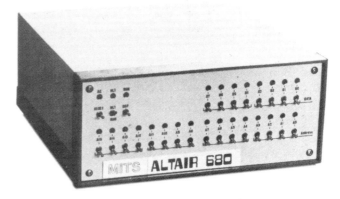

Smaller than the Altair 8800, the MITS Altair 680 ($300 to $750) used a Motorola 6800 CPU rather than the Intel 8080.

Mitsubishi Electronics America Inc. (Compton, California)

Mitsubishi sold few of its early systems in North America, but it built several popular PC-compatibles for U.S. vendors such as Sperry and Leading Edge.

The Multi16 was sold in North America and featured a two-piece design. The monitor and drives were in the top unit, while the keyboard and main circuitry were in the bottom unit.

The all-in-one Mitsubishi Multi 16 ($15 to $45).

Mitsubishi Multi 16 (1983, desktop)
Original Retail Price: $2,700
Base Configuration: 8088 CPU, CP/M-86, 128K RAM (576K max), two 5.25-inch floppy disk drives, integral 12-inch monochrome CRT, integral keyboard/keypad, RS-232C and parallel ports **Video:** 25-line x 80 column text, 640 x 400 graphics, eight colors **Important Options:** integral 12-inch color CRT, GP-IB interface, dot matrix printer
Value: $15 to $45

Mitsubishi Model 186 (1984, desktop)
Base Configuration: 8MHz 8086 CPU, Mitsubishi Operating System, six expansion slots (two open), 384K RAM (640K max), 5.25-inch floppy disk drive, 20MB hard disk drive, keyboard/keypad, RS-232 and parallel ports, BI-286 BASIC **Size/Weight:** 5.8 x 18.9 x 16.7 inches, 37.5 lbs. **Important Options:** second 5.25-inch floppy disk drive, 8-inch floppy disk drive, 50MB hard disk drive, monochrome or color monitor
Value: $13 to $40

Mitsubishi ML-F120 (1984, MSX home computer)
Original Retail Price: $270
Base Configuration: Z80 CPU, two ROM cartridge slots, 32K RAM, composite video port, integral keyboard, parallel port, MSX BASIC
Video: 24-line x 40-column text, 256 x 192 graphics
Value: $10 to $50

Modula Computer Systems (Provo, Utah)

One of the more intriguing computers ever made, the Lilith was designed around the Modula-2 programming language. Its architecture was unique and optimized for software development. The Diser Modula Computer was based on the Lilith design.

Modula Computer Systems Lilith 2.1 (1980, desktop)
Original Retail Price: $8,000
Base Configuration: Am2901 CPU, Medos-2, 256K RAM (512K max), 5.25-inch floppy disk drive, 15MB hard disk drive, 12-inch monochrome monitor, keyboard/keypad, mouse, Modula-2 compiler, debugger, editor, Lara document processor, graphics software, hardware and software manuals **Video:** 768 x 592 graphics **Size/Weight:** 15.5 x 15 x 14.5 inches **Important Options:** graphics upgrade, laser printer, hardwood cabinet
Value: $200 to $650

Modular Micros (Lawrence, Kansas)

Telcon Industries originally developed the Zorba, but sold the rights to the system to minicomputer manufacturer Modular Computer Systems (MODCOMP) in 1983. MODCOMP then formed Modular Micros to sell the Zorba. In 1985, a company called Gemini Electronics was selling the Zorba at a heavily discounted price.

Modular Micros Zorba 2000 (1983, transportable)
Original Retail Price: $1,595 to $2,295
Base Configuration: Z80A CPU, CP/M 2.2, 64K RAM (320K max with 8088 coprocessor), 16K ROM, 5.25-inch floppy disk drive, integral 7-inch monochrome CRT, keyboard/keypad, RS-232 and parallel ports, application suite **Size/Weight:** 25 lbs. **Important Options:** 8088 coprocessor, second 5.25-inch floppy disk drive, 10MB hard disk drive, integral 9-inch monochrome CRT, IEEE-488 interface, modem, printer
Value: $25 to $75

Zorba 2000 ($25 to $75), the transportable PC, from Modular Micros.

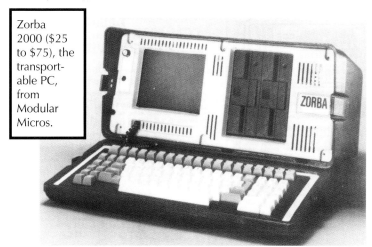

Monroe Systems for Business (Morris Plains, New Jersey)

Monroe sold the first commercially available calculator (mechanical, of course) in 1912, and is still in business today selling high-end calculators.

Monroe OC8810 Occupational Microcomputer Series (1981, desktop)
Base Configuration: 3MHz Z80A CPU, Monroe Operating System (MOS), expansion slot, 128K RAM (256K max), 2K ROM, 5.25-inch floppy disk drive, integral 9-inch monochrome CRT, integral keyboard/keypad, three RS-232 ports, BASIC, Pascal **Video:** 24-line x 80-column text **Important Options:** CP/M, second 5.25-inch floppy disk drive, 5- or 10MB hard disk drive, printer, modem
Value: $17 to $45

That's an optional hard drive unit sitting atop this Monroe OC8820 Occupational Microcomputer ($17 to $45). The optional printer is to the left.

Monroe EC 8800 (desktop)
Original Retail Price: $3,595
Base Configuration: Z80A CPU, MOS, 128K RAM, RS-232C port, BASIC, Pascal **Video:** 24-line x 80-column text, 240 x 240 graphics, eight colors **Important Options:** CP/M
Value: $15 to $40

Monroe System 2000 (Nov. 1983, desktop PC)
Original Retail Price: $3,695
Base Configuration: 8MHz 80186, MS-DOS and CP/M-86 DPX, five slots, 128K RAM (896K max), 5.25-inch floppy disk drive, 12-inch monochrome monitor, keyboard/keypad, two RS-232C and one parallel port **Video:** 25-line x 80-column text, 640 x 400 graphics **Size/Weight:** 19.5 x 15.5 x 4.37 inches, 31.5 lbs. **Important Options:** 4MHz Z80A coprocessor, 10MB hard disk drive, 14-inch color monitor, modem
Value: $10 to $40

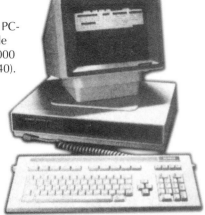

Monroe's PC-compatible System 2000 ($10 to $40).

Morrow Designs Inc. (San Leandro, California)

George Morrow's first company was Morrow's Microstuff, which sold memory boards for the MITS Altair 8800 via mail order. Morrow Designs was originally called Thinker Toys, but Playskool, the company that sells Tinker Toys, forced Morrow to change the name. Morrow was a well-regarded microcomputer designer, and the computers his company produced are popular with hobbyists today.

The Decision 1 was sold in single- and multi-user configurations. The multi-user version used Micronix, Morrow's own Unix-like multi-user, multitasking operating system that could emulate CP/M.

Morrow sold the Micro Decision—the company's first single-user-only computer—with a smart terminal (a relabeled Lear Siegler ADM 20). However, it will accept any terminal. A Micro Decision with a single double-density floppy drive was called the MD1. With two double-density drives the system is called the MD2, and a system with two double-sided, double density drives is called the MD3.

A business system with hard drive and monitor for under $3,000 was a bargain in 1983. Although Morrow was a respected brand, more and more people were looking for PC-compatible systems, and the MD11 did not sell in large numbers. The MD5-E was one of the first—if not the first—complete hard-drive systems offered for under $2,000.

The Pivot is nearly identical to the Osborne 3/Encore and the Zenith Z-171. Morrow upgraded the LCD to a 25-line backlit display in 1985 with the introduction of the Pivot 2. It was heavier but offered higher video resolution, an RGB video port, and a 272K RAM disk.

Morrow Decision 1 (1981, desktop)
Original Retail Price: $1,495 to $4,995
Base Configuration: 4MHz Z80A CPU, Micronix, 14 S-100 slots, 64K RAM (1MB max), 2K ROM, three RS-232C and one parallel port, BASIC-80, BaZic, application suite **Size/Weight:** 19 x 21 x 7.5 inches, 40 lbs. **Important Options:** 5.25-inch floppy disk drive, 10- or 16MB hard disk drive
Value: $20 to $60

The Morrow Decision 1 ($20 to $60), shown with a data terminal to the left.

Morrow Micro Decision (1982, desktop)
Original Retail Price: $1,790
Base Configuration: 4MHz Z80A CPU, CP/M 2.2, expansion port, 64K RAM, 5.25-inch floppy disk drive, 12-inch monochrome video terminal with keyboard/keypad, two RS-232C ports, BASIC-80, BaZic, application suite **Video:** 24-line x 80-column text **Size/Weight:** 16.7 x 11.3 x 5.3 inches, 14.2 lbs. **Important Options:** 8088 coprocessor, second 5.25-inch floppy disk drive
Value: $17 to $45

Morrow MD11 (Nov. 1983, desktop)
Original Retail Price: $2,745
Base Configuration: 4MHz Z80 CPU, CP/M Plus, 128K RAM, 8K ROM, 5.25-inch floppy disk drive, 11MB hard disk drive, 12-inch monochrome monitor, keyboard/keypad, three RS-232 and one parallel port, BASIC-80, application suite, nine-volume manual set **Video:** 24-line x 80-column text **Size/Weight:** 17 x 11.5 x 5.5 inches **Important Options:** 8088 coprocessor, MS-DOS, 16- or 34MB hard disk drive
Value: $20 to $55

The Morrow MD11 ($20 to $55) came standard with both floppy and hard disk drives.

Morrow MD5-E (1984, desktop)
Original Retail Price: $1,999
Base Configuration: CP/M 3.0, 128K RAM, 5.25-inch floppy disk drive, 5.4MB hard disk drive, monochrome monitor, keyboard/keypad, application suite **Important Options:** second hard disk drive
Value: $20 to $50

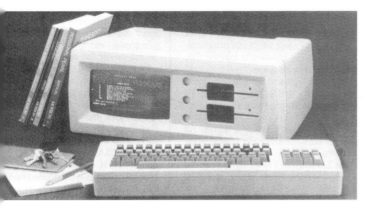

One of the smaller CP/M transportables, the Morrow Portable MD3 ($35 to $125).

Morrow Portable MD3 (early 1984, transportable)
Original Retail Price: $1,899
Base Configuration: Z80 CPU, CP/M 2.2, 64K RAM, two 5.25-inch floppy disk drives, integral 9-inch monochrome CRT, keyboard/keypad, BASIC-80 and BaZic, application suite **Video:** 24-line x 80-column text **Size/Weight:** 19 x 15.5 x 7.15 inches **Important Options:** internal modem
Value: $35 to $125

Morrow Pivot (1984, transportable PC)
Original Retail Price: $2,500
Base Configuration: 3.5MHz 80C86 CPU, MS-DOS 2.11, 128K RAM (512K max), 5.25-inch floppy disk drive, monochrome LCD, integral keyboard, RS-232C and parallel ports, internal modem, AC adapter **Video:** 16-line x 80-column text, 480 x 128 graphics **Size/Weight:** 9.5 x 13 x 5.5 inches, 9.5 lbs. **Important Options:** second 5.25-inch floppy disk drive, NiCad battery pack
Value: $25 to $65

Osborne and Zenith sold portables based on this Morrow Pivot's ($25 to $65) design.

MOS Technology (Norristown, Pennsylvania)

Several microprocessor vendors of the era sold "trainer" systems that taught users how their CPUs worked. MOS Technology, however, was one of the first to sell a full-fledged microcomputer on a single board. KIM-1 owners could buy off-the-shelf components and peripherals such as a power supply, enclosure, and a video display. The KIM-1 sold well and is among the easiest to find systems from the era. Most today are found without the optional blue or tan plastic enclosure.

MOS Technology KIM-1 Microcomputer System
(1975, computer trainer)
Original Retail Price: $245
Base Configuration: 6502 CPU; 1K RAM; six-digit LED; integral hex keypad; TTY and cassette ports; monitor in ROM; user, hardware, and programming manuals; reference card **Important Options:** enclosure
Value: $125 to $275

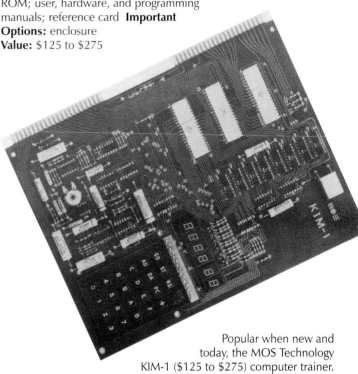

Popular when new and today, the MOS Technology KIM-1 ($125 to $275) computer trainer.

Mostek Corp. (Carrollton, Texas)

Mostek AID-80F (1978, early micro)
Original Retail Price: $5,995
Base Configuration: Z80 CPU, 16K RAM, 5.25-inch floppy disk drive, four I/O ports, text editor, assembler **Important Options:** AIM-80 in-circuit emulation board
Value: $75 to $225

Multitech Electronics Inc. (Sunnyvale, California)

Multitech later changed its name to Acer Inc., which today is a leading global manufacturer of PCs.

The MPF-III took a different form factor than its predecessors, which were single-board training units. It had a separate CPU enclosure and keyboard. It was software compatible with the Apple II.

Multitech offered two MIC-500 models: the MIC-501 had single-sided, double-density floppy drives while the MIC-504 had double-sided, double-density floppy drives. Aimed at the business market, the MIC-500 could be upgraded to a multi-user system.

Multitech Micro-Professor III (MPF-III)
(1984, Apple II-class desktop)
Original Retail Price: $995
Base Configuration: 6502 CPU; 64K RAM; 24K ROM; TV video and monitor ports; keyboard/keypad; parallel, game, and cassette ports
Video: 80-column text, 16 colors
Value: $15 to $60

Multitech MIC-500 Series (1983, desktop)
Original Retail Price: $1,310 to $1,745
Base Configuration: 5MHz Z80A CPU, CP/M 2.2, 64K RAM, two 5.25-inch floppy disk drives, keyboard/keypad, two RS-232C and one parallel port, application suite, CBASIC, owner's and software manuals **Video: Size/Weight:** 15.7 x 3.9 x 13.6 inches **Important Options:** 33MB hard disk drive, 12-inch monochrome monitor
Value: $12 to $40

Multitech would eventually change its name to Acer and become a leading global PC maker, but this MIC-500 from 1983 ($12 to $40) is CP/M-based.

Multi-Tech Systems (Brighton, Minnesota)

Multi-Tech Systems MT500 (1982, desktop)
Original Retail Price: $4,795 to $7,995
Base Configuration: Z80A CPU, CP/M, S-100 bus, 64K RAM, two 5.25-inch floppy disk drives, 5MB hard disk drive, integral monochrome CRT, keyboard/keypad **Important Options:** printer, modem
Value: $15 to $40

Nascom/Lucas Nascom (U.K.)

Before the Sinclair ZX80, there was the Nascom 1. It was an inexpensive, Z80-based computer kit sold primarily in the U.K. Unlike the ZX80, it came without an enclosure. Owners had to buy or build a case. A more capable Nascom 2 followed the original model.

Lucas bought Nascom, and in 1982 introduced the Nascom III, a more polished system with a keyboard and enclosure.

Nascom I (1978, early micro)
Base Configuration: Z80 CPU; 2K RAM; 1K ROM; TV video port; keyboard; RS-232, TTY, and parallel ports
Value: $85 to $225

Lucas Nascom III (1982, desktop)
Base Configuration: 4MHz Z80A CPU, NAS-DOS in ROM, 48K RAM, two 5.25-inch floppy disk drives, integral keyboard **Video:** 25-line x 80-column text, 640 x 256 graphics, eight colors **Important Options:** CP/M 2.2
Value: $25 to $85

National (Japan)

National was the brand under which Matsushita sold computers in Japan. The company was a leading manufacturer of MSX systems.

National Mybrain 3000 (1983, desktop)
Original Retail Price: $3,000
Base Configuration: 8088 CPU, MS-DOS or CP/M-86, 96K RAM, 16K ROM, two external 5.25-inch floppy disk drives, RS-232C and IEEE-488 ports, BASIC, printer **Video:** 640 x 400 graphics **Important Options:** external 3- or 8-inch floppy disk drive, joysticks, light pen, graphics tablet
Value: $15 to $40

National CF-2000/CF-3000 (late 1983, MSX home computer)
Original Retail Price: $230 (CF-2000)/$330 (CF-3000)
Base Configuration: Z80 CPU, two ROM cartridge slots, 16K RAM (48K max; CF-2000)/32K RAM (64K max; CF-3000), composite video port, integral keyboard (CF-2000)/keyboard (CF-3000), parallel port **Video:** 24-line x 32-column text, 256 x 192 graphics **Important Options:** video superimpose
Value: $7 to $40

NCR Corp. (Dayton, Ohio)

NCR was once a leading manufacturer of mid-range computing systems. Its 7500 model was an advanced design for 1978. It had a relatively sophisticated operating system in NCR-DOS and offered an 80-column display.

The Decision Mate series met with moderate success. NCR eventually renamed the Decision Mate V as the NCR Personal Computer. The company soon switched to producing PC-compatible systems with the PC4. NCR followed the PC4 with the PC XT-compatible PC6 and PC AT compatible PC8 in 1985.

NCR 7500 (1978, desktop)
Base Configuration: 8080 CPU, NCR OS, 48K RAM, integral 9-inch monochrome CRT, RS-232C and parallel ports, BASIC **Video:** 25-line x 80-column text **Important Options:** integral 12-inch monochrome CRT
Value: $35 to $110

NCR Decision Mate V (1983, desktop)
Original Retail Price: $3,490
Base Configuration: 4MHz Z80A CPU, CP/M-80, seven "bus station" expansion slots, 64K RAM (512K max), 4K ROM, 5.25-inch floppy disk drive, integral 12-inch monochrome CRT, keyboard/keypad, RS-232C and parallel ports, MBASIC, application suite **Video:** 24-line x 80-column text, 640 x 400 graphics **Size/Weight:** 14.9 x 18.1 x 14.6 inches, 52.9 lbs. **Important Options:** 5MHz 8088 coprocessor, CP/M-86 or MS-DOS, second 5.25-inch floppy disk drive, 10MB hard disk drive
Value: $12 to $40

The NCR Decision Mate V ($12 to $40).

NCR Personal Computer Model 4 (PC4)
(Aug. 1984, desktop PC)
Original Retail Price: $2,400
Base Configuration: 4.77MHz 8088 CPU, NCR-DOS 2.11, three ISA slots, 128K RAM (640K max), two 5.25-inch floppy disk drives, integral monochrome CRT, keyboard/keypad, RS-232C and parallel ports, GW-BASIC, tutorial software **Video:** 25-line x 80-column text, 640 x 200 graphics **Size/Weight:** 14.8 x 14.6 x 18 inches, 50 lbs. **Important Options:** dual 8-inch floppy disk drives, mouse, modem, printer **Value:** $7 to $30

The NCR Personal Computer Model 4 ($7 to $30) had an unusual design for a PC-compatible with the monitor built into the main computer unit.

NEC Home Electronics USA (Elk Grove Village, Illinois)

Japan's Nippon Electric Co., as it was originally named, sold computers in North America through two separate divisions. NEC Home Electronics sold consumer-oriented systems, and NEC Information Systems sold business computers.

NEC's first microcomputer was actually the TK-80 training system based on its 8080-workalike CPU, introduced in 1976. Two years later, the company produced a more complete system based on the TK-80 board called the Compo BS/80. That computer came in two versions, one with a built-in cassette recorder and another that required an external cassette recorder.

Introduced in Japan in 1979, the PC-8000 marked NEC's entry to the U.S. home computer market in 1981 as the PC-8001. Although it was the most popular home system in Japan, it never sold well in the U.S. By 1983, only about 100 software titles were available for the system—a far cry from the thousands of Apple, TRS-80, Atari, or Commodore titles.

NEC sold the PC-8800 as the PC-8800A series in Japan. The company introduced a PC-8801 Mk II in 1984 and a PC-8801 Mk II SR in 1985. The latter featured improved graphics performance. The PC-9801 was not exported to North America.

The NEC Trek did not sell well in North America, and the PC-6001 version of this computer was not a big seller in Japan. It was a non-MSX system competing in an increasingly MSX-dominated Japanese home computer market. The follow-on model, the PC-6001 Mk II SR, did no better.

NEC was a hold-out on the MSX standard, perhaps because its PC-6601 was so popular in Japan. It enjoyed good software support. In 1985, NEC offered an enhanced version of the PC-6601 called Mr. PC.

Notebook computers started to appear in the early 1980s, and NEC offered one of the best in the PC-8201. It was under four pounds and expandable with a built-in application suite, and in fact was the same system as the Kyocera-made Tandy Model 100. A PC-8201A model was also sold, with the most obvious difference being a light beige case. The PC-8201 was dark grey. The PC-8201A is more commonly found today.

Few CP/M notebook computers were made, and the PC-8401 was one of the best. NEC later produced the Starlet 8401A-LS, which was similar to the 8401A but with a bigger LCD.

NEC offered a MultiSpeed EL version with an electroluminescent display in mid-1987. An ELD upgrade was available for LCD-equipped MultiSpeeds. A MultiSpeed HD model was introduced in September 1987 with an internal 20MB hard disk drive.

The UltraLite lived up to its name by setting a precedent for small size with relatively few trade-offs on performance. It was the thinnest PC-compatible notebook of its time, yet offered a large screen and nearly full-size keyboard. The use of solid-state storage allowed NEC to achieve the thin profile.

NEC Compo BS/80 (1978, early micro)
Base Configuration: Z80A CPU, 7K RAM, integral cassette recorder and keyboard, NEC Level-2 BASIC **Video:** 16-line x 32-column text
Important Options: monochrome monitor, printer
Value: $75 to $225

NEC PC-8000 Series (1979, desktop)
Original Retail Price: $1,295
Base Configuration: 4MHz PD780C-1, CP/M, 32K RAM, 24K ROM, monochrome monitor, keyboard/keypad, PC-8012A I/O unit, N-BASIC **Video:** 25-line x 80-column text, 160 x 100 graphics, eight colors
Important Options: PC 8012A I/O Unit, PC 8031A external dual 5.25-inch floppy disk drives, PC-8023 printer
Value: $17 to $45

Part of the 8000 series, this NEC PC 8001A ($17 to $45) is shown with the optional PC 8012A I/O Unit and the PC 8031A dual floppy drives.

Surrounded by its most popular options, the NEC PC-6001 "NEC Trek" ($15 to $75).

NEC PC-6000 NEC Trek (1981, home computer)
Original Retail Price: $349
Base Configuration: 4MHz PD780C-1 CPU; 16K RAM (32K max), 16K ROM (32K max); TV and composite video ports; integral keyboard; RS-232C, parallel, cassette, and two game ports; Microsoft BASIC; 8-octave sound **Video:** 16-line x 32-column text, 256 x 192 graphics, nine colors **Size/Weight:** 16 x 3.5 x 11 inches, 10 lbs. **Important Options:** PC-6011A Expansion Unit, external PC-6031 floppy disk drive, PC-6082 cassette recorder, 12-inch JB-1260 monochrome or 12-inch JB-1212M color monitor, touch tablet, PC-6021 thermal printer, PC-8023A printer
Value: $15 to $75

NEC PC-6601 (1984, home computer)
Original Retail Price: $600
Base Configuration: PD780C-1 CPU, 64K RAM, 16K ROM, 3.5-inch floppy disk drive, integral keyboard, N66 BASIC, voice synthesizer/music generator **Video:** 320 x 200 graphics **Important Options:** RS-232C interface
Value: $12 to $40

NEC PC-8800 (1983, desktop)
Original Retail Price: $2,497
Base Configuration: 4MHz microPD780C-1 and 8MHz 8086; CP/M 2.2; four expansion slots; microPD780C-1: 64K RAM (128K max), 8086: 128K RAM (512K max); external 5.25-inch floppy disk drive; 12-inch monochrome monitor; RGB video port; keyboard/keypad; RS-232C, parallel, and cassette ports; N88 BASIC and N-BASIC; application suite; N88 BASIC tutorial **Video:** 640 x 400 graphics **Size/Weight:** 19.5 x 13.5 x 4.2 inches **Important Options:** CP/M-86 or MS-DOS, second external 5.25-inch floppy disk drive, external dual 8-inch floppy disk drives, 5- to 15MB hard disk drive, light pen
Value: $15 to $50

NEC PC-9800 (1983, desktop)
Original Retail Price: $2,600
Base Configuration: 8086 CPU, MS-DOS and CP/M-86, 128K RAM (640K max), 96K ROM, two 8-inch floppy disk drives, keyboard/keypad, NBASIC-86 in ROM **Video:** 640 x 400 graphics
Value: $15 to $45

This NEC-8201 ($17 to $45) is the same design as the famous Tandy TRS-80 Model 100, but often sells for less today.

NEC PC-8201 (1983, notebook)
Original Retail Price: $799
Base Configuration: 16K RAM (64K max), 32K ROM; RAM cartridge slot; monochrome LCD; integral keyboard; RS-232C, parallel, bar-code reader, and cassette ports; application suite; BASIC; NiCad battery pack; AC adapter **Video:** 8-line x 40-column text **Size/Weight:** 11.62 x 8.25 x 2.5 inches, 3.8 lbs. **Important Options:** external dual 5.25-inch floppy disk drives, video port, Authentic 300 MD external modem, PC 8826 printer/plotter
Value: $17 to $45

The NEC PC-8801A ($15 to $50) shown with the optional printer and dual eight-inch floppy drives.

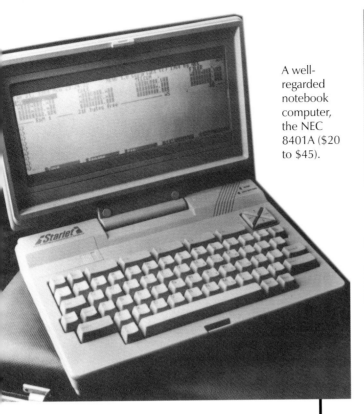

A well-regarded notebook computer, the NEC 8401A ($20 to $45).

The NEC UltraLite ($10 to $40) set a new standard for compactness in a notebook PC.

NEC UltraLite (1988, notebook PC)
Original Retail Price: $2,999
Base Configuration: 9.83MHz V-30 CPU, MS-DOS 3.3, RAM/ROM card slot, expansion pot, 640K RAM (896K max), 1- or 2MB silicon hard disk, 9.5-inch monochrome ELD, integral keyboard, serial port, LapLink, Microsoft DOS Manager, internal modem, battery pack, AC adapter **Video:** CGA **Size/Weight:** 11.75 x 8.3 x 1.4 inches, 4.4 lbs. **Important Options:** external 3.5-inch floppy disk drive, parallel interface, leather carrying case
Value: $10 to $40

NEC 8401A (Dec. 1984, notebook)
Original Retail Price: $995
Base Configuration: 3.99MHz PD7008C CPU; CP/M 2.2; expansion slot; 64K RAM (96K max), 80K ROM; monochrome LCD, integral keyboard; RS-232C, parallel, and cassette ports; application suite; internal modem; AC adapter; battery pack **Video:** 16-line x 80-column text **Size/Weight:** 8.5 x 12 x 2.25 inches, 7 lbs. **Important Options:** one or two external 3.5-inch floppy disk drives, cassette recorder, RGB and composite video interfaces, carrying case
Value: $20 to $45

NEC MultiSpeed (1986, laptop PC)
Original Retail Price: $1,995
Base Configuration: 9.64MHz V-30 CPU, MS-DOS 3.2, 640K RAM, 512K ROM, two 3.5-inch floppy disk drives, monochrome LCD, integral keyboard, RS-232C and parallel ports, application suite in ROM, NiCad battery pack, AC adapter **Video:** 25-line x 80-column text, 640 x 200 graphics **Size/Weight:** 13.6 x 12 x 3 inches, 12 lbs. **Important Options:** modem, carrying case
Value: $5 to $23

NEC made a name for itself in the 1980s with laptops like this MultiSpeed ($5 to $23).

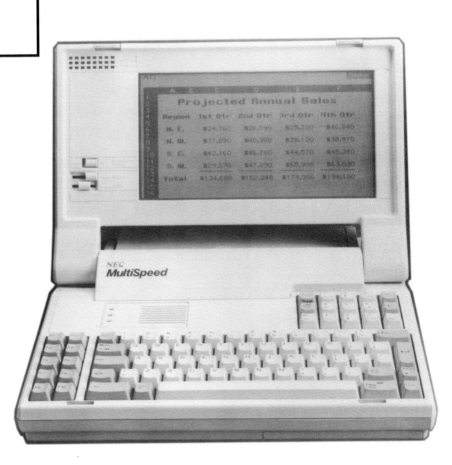

NEC Information Systems Inc. (Lexington, Massachusetts)

In 1983 and 1984, NEC was the third-largest vendor of personal computers in the world behind IBM and Apple. However, its APC line never sold as well in North America as it did in Asia (as the N5200) and Europe. As a result, the greater nostalgia factor for the APC means higher values for the system overseas.

The APC III looked more PC-compatible than the original APC, down to the generic-looking off-white case. However, it required a different software format, which meant that availability of popular software titles was limited.

The main selling point of the PC-100 was its outstanding graphics capability, which was comparable to that of the Apple Lisa. Both NEC monitors sold with the PC-100 could rotate to provide a landscape or portrait view.

The NEC Advanced Personal Computer ($20 to $55) was sold worldwide, but was especially popular in Asia.

NEC Advanced Personal Computer (APC) (May 1982, desktop)
Original Retail Price: $3,298
Base Configuration: 5MHz PD8086 CPU, CP/M-86, one expansion slot, 128K RAM (256K max), 4K ROM, 8-inch floppy disk drive, integral 12-inch monochrome CRT, keyboard/keypad, RS-232C and parallel ports **Video:** 25-line x 80-column text, 640 x 475 graphics **Size/Weight:** 19.7 x 13.8 x 18.1 inches **Important Options:** MS-DOS or Concurrent CP/M-86, second 8-inch floppy disk drive, integral 12-inch color CRT, printer
Value: $20 to $55

NEC Advanced Personal Computer (APC) III
(May 1984, desktop PC)
Original Retail Price: $1,995 to $3,995
Base Configuration: 8MHz PD8086 CPU, MS-DOS, four NEC bus slots, 128K RAM (640 max), 32K ROM, 5.25-inch floppy disk drive, 14-inch monochrome monitor, monochrome and RGB ports, keyboard/keypad, RS-232C and parallel ports, owner's manual **Video:** 25-line x 80-column text, 640 x 400 graphics, eight colors **Important Options:** Unix System III, 10MB hard disk drive, IEEE-488 interface, gameboard card, maintenance and reference manuals
Value: $10 to $35

With the Advanced Personal Computer III ($10 to $35), NEC's APC line abandoned CP/M in favor of PC compatibility.

NEC Advanced Personal Computer (APC) IV
(1986, desktop PC)
Base Configuration: 8MHz 80286 CPU, 640K RAM, 5.25-inch floppy disk drive, 20MB hard disk drive, keyboard/keypad, two RS-232C and one parallel port **Video:** 800 x 560 graphics, EGA and CGA **Important Options:** 40MB hard disk drive, MultiSync color monitor
Value: $8 to $25

NEC PC-100 (late 1983, desktop PC)
Base Configuration: 7MHz 8086 CPU, MS-DOS 2.01, 128K RAM (640K max), 5.25-inch floppy disk drive, keyboard/keypad, mouse, RS-232C port, BASIC, application suite **Video:** 750 x 512 graphics, 16 colors **Important Options:** second 5.25-inch floppy disk drive, 14-inch monochrome or color monitor, dot matrix printer
Value: $10 to $30

NeXT Computer Inc. (Palo Alto, California)

Steve Jobs founded NeXT Computer after he was forced out of Apple. The much-anticipated Cube was the first computer produced by NeXT. Sold primarily to the higher education market, the Cube lived up to its advanced billing with many innovations. The most obvious were its cube shape and the lack of a floppy drive. Its GUI-based NeXTstep operating system was based on the Mach Unix kernel, which was compatible with the BSD Unix used at many universities. A DSP chip boosted graphics and audio performance, and its removable optical disks could hold more than 200 times more data than a standard floppy.

In 1990, NeXT announced a new line-up consisting of three product lines, including an enhanced Cube confusingly called the NeXTcube. Many people refer to it as the Cube II. It used a 68040 processor, a larger hard drive, and a floppy disk drive. The NeXTdimension, commonly referred to as the Color Cube, was a color version of the Cube

II. It featured a high-performance graphics coprocessor and 4MB of video RAM. (The Cube II had only 256K.)

At the same time, Next introduced the NeXTstation. It offered Cube II-like performance at a lower cost, with the main trade-off being less expandability. A NeXTstation Color was also available. Both abandoned the cube design for a small rectangular enclosure.

Apple Computer bought NeXT in 1996 for its software, much of which was incorporated into its latest operating system (at this writing), OS X.

The innovative NeXT Cube ($50 to $250) featured optical storage, a large monochrome monitor, and a unique form factor. *Photo courtesy of Sellam Ismail, Vintage Computer Festival.*

NeXT Cube (Oct. 1988, desktop)
Original Retail Price: $6,500
Base Configuration: 25MHz 68030 CPU; NeXTstep 1.0; four NuBus slots; 8MB RAM (64MB max); 128K ROM; 40MB hard disk drive; 256MB magneto-optical drive; 17-inch MegaPixel monochrome monitor; keyboard/keypad; mouse; three serial, SCSI, and DSP ports; Ethernet; application suite **Video:** 1120 x 832 graphics **Size/Weight:** 12 x 12 x 12 inches **Important Options:** second optical drive, 670MB hard disk drive, laser printer
Value: $50 to $250

NeXTcube (Sept. 1990, desktop)
Original Retail Price: $11,495
Base Configuration: 25MHz 68040 CPU, NeXTstep 2.0, 16MB RAM (64MB max), 128K ROM, 3.5-inch floppy disk drive, 340MB hard disk drive, 17-inch MegaPixel monochrome monitor, keyboard/keypad, mouse, two RS-423 and one parallel port, Ethernet **Video:** 1120 x 832 graphics **Size/Weight:** 12 x 12 x 12 inches **Important Options:** laser printer
Value: $50 to $200

NeXTdimension (Sept. 1990, desktop)
Original Retail Price: $17,615
Base Configuration: 25MHz 68040 CPU, NeXTstep 2.0, 24MB RAM (64MB max), 128K ROM, 3.5-inch floppy disk drive, 340MB hard disk drive, 16-inch color monitor, keyboard/keypad, mouse, two RS-423 and one parallel port, Ethernet **Video:** 1120 x 832 graphics **Size/Weight:** 12 x 12 x 12 inches **Important Options:** laser printer
Value: $100 to $400

NeXTstation (Sept. 1990, desktop)
Original Retail Price: $4,995
Base Configuration: 25MHz 68040 CPU; NeXTstep 2.0; 8MB RAM (32MB max); 128K ROM; 3.5-inch floppy disk drive; 105MB hard disk drive; 17-inch MegaPixel monochrome monitor; keyboard/keypad; mouse; two RS-423, parallel, and SCSI-2 ports; Ethernet **Video:** 1120 x 832 graphics **Important Options:** 16-inch color monitor
Value: $40 to $150

Non-Linear Systems (see "Kaypro")

North Star Computers Inc. (San Leandro, California)

North Star was a well-regarded microcomputing pioneer that made a name for itself with its Horizon line of multi-user systems. Originally called Kentucky Fried Computers, the company chose a more businesslike name for itself as it grew (and likely at the prodding of a particular fast-food chain).

The Horizon was a hobbyist favorite because of its solid, reliable design. In fact, it's common to find North Star components used in other S-100 systems. Purchasers could choose either a blue metal or finished wood enclosure. The North Star terminal was a relabeled Soroc IQ 120.

North Star labeled systems sold with the 16-bit coprocessing option as Advantage 8/16s.

Metal enclosures were available for the North Star Horizon ($65 to $200), but the unit here has wooden sides.

North Star Horizon
(1977, early micro)
Original Retail Price: $1,599 to $1,999 kit, $1,899 to $2,399 assembled
Base Configuration: 4MHz Z80A CPU, North Star DOS, 12 S-100 slots, 16K RAM (64K max), 5.25-inch floppy disk drive, RS-232C and parallel ports, BASIC **Video:** 24-line x 80-column text, 480 x 250 graphics **Important Options:** CP/M, second 5.25-inch floppy disk drive, terminal, parallel interface, floating-point board
Value: $65 to $200

North Star Advantage (1982, desktop)
Original Retail Price: $3,599 to $4,999
Base Configuration: 4MHz Z80A CPU, Graphics CP/M, six S-100 slots, 64K RAM (256K max with 8088 coprocessor), 5.25-inch floppy disk drive, integral 12-inch monochrome CRT, integral keyboard/keypad, RS-232C and parallel ports **Video:** 24-line x 80-column text, 640 x 240 graphics **Important Options:** 5MHz 8088 coprocessor; GDOS/BASIC, North Star ASP, or MS-DOS; second 5.25-inch floppy disk drive; 5MB hard disk drive; serial or parallel interface; printer
Value: $35 to $95

The North Star Advantage ($35 to $95) featured a handsome all-in-one design.

Northwest Microcomputer Systems (Eugene, Oregon)

The 85/P featured an all-in-one design similar to the TRS-80 Model III, but in a natural finish wood enclosure. The "P" in its name referred to Pascal, and the 85/P was sold as a Pascal development svstem.

Northwest Microcomputer Systems 85/P (1978, early micro)
Original Retail Price: $7,495
Base Configuration: 8085 CPU, 54K RAM, two 5.25-inch floppy disk drives, integral monochrome CRT, integral keyboard/keypad, two serial ports, Pascal
Video: 24-line x 80-column text
Value: $50 to $125

Yes, that's a wood enclosure on this Northwest Microcomputer Systems 85/P ($50 to $125).

Noval Inc. (San Diego, California)

The Noval 760 was built into a wooden desk. The top of the desk was split length-wise and the computer, monitor, and cassette flipped up when needed. The keyboard was in a pull-out drawer. It looked sharp, but the combination probably made for a limited customer base. How many people would be looking for a desk and a computer at the same time? And what happened when you wanted to upgrade to a new computer?

Noval 760 (1977, early micro)
Base Configuration: 8080A CPU; 16K RAM (32K max); 3K ROM (16K max); integral PhiDeck cassette recorder, 12-inch monochrome CRT, keyboard, and printer; editor/assembler; debugger; operation manual **Video:** 28-line x 32-column text, 256 x 224 graphics **Important Options:** color monitor, paper tape reader, BASIC, EPROM programmer
Value: $300 to $550

What will they think of next?
A computer built into a desk, the Noval 760 ($300 to $550).

Ogivar Technologies Inc. (Montreal, Canada)

You might never have heard of Ogivar, but at one time it was Canada's leading PC manufacturer. What little success the company had in the U.S. came from its portable lines. All were well-designed and well-built.

Ogivar 286 Portable (June 1988, laptop PC)
Base Configuration: 12.5MHz 80286 CPU, OS/2 or MS-DOS, 640K RAM (2MB max), 3.5-inch floppy disk drive, EGA video port, 40MB hard disk drive, 10-inch monochrome gas plasma display, keyboard, RS-232 and parallel ports **Video:** EGA **Important Options:** keypad
Value: $5 to $22

Ohio Scientific Instruments (OSI) (Hudson, Ohio)

You could buy the Model 500 as a single-board system (the 500), as a bare-bones BASIC computer in an enclosure (the 500-1), or as an expandable BASIC computer in a larger OSI Challenger enclosure (the 500-8).

OSI had been selling the core components of the Challenger since 1975, but didn't integrate them into a single package until 1977. The OSI Challenger uses a non-standard Molex connector for its S-100 bus. The company believed that it provided a more reliable contact.

The Challenger II was housed in a large enclosure and required the addition of a terminal for keyboard input. It also did away with the BASIC in ROM, relying instead on the floppy drive. A Challenger II single-board computer, sans case, was also available. With the Challenger series you could have the biggest hard drive on the block—74MB—but it would set you back a cool $6,000.

Based on the Model 500 electronics, the Challenger IIP had a full-size, integrated keyboard housed in a case similar to the Processor Technology Sol-20. Subsequent IIP models came in different enclosures depending on configuration and expansion capability. The main floppy-disk-based C2-8P system, for example, was housed in a large enclosure with a separate keyboard.

With the Challenger III, OSI promised a system that could run all the popular software of the day. Challenger IIIs came in different enclosures depending on options and expansion capability.

Shown with the optional floppy drive, monitor, and keyboard, the Ohio Scientific Challenger ($85 to $175).

Much like the Sol-20, the Challenger 4P had an aluminum case with wooden sides. It was more of a home-user-friendly system than its predecessors with several options for home security. An 8P model used a larger enclosure and offered options for a hard drive, voice I/O, and telephone interface.

The Challenger I Series 2 was introduced after OSI had been sold to M/A-Com Office Systems.

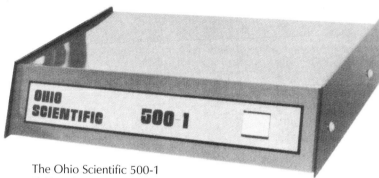

The Ohio Scientific 500-1
($40 to $100) was an inexpensive 6502-based micro.

OSI Model 500 Series
(1977, early micro)
Original Retail Price: $298 to $629
Base Configuration: 1MHz 6502 CPU, 4K RAM, 8K ROM, RS-232C port, BASIC **Size/Weight:** 12 x 15 x 4 inches (500-1) or 15 x 17 x 10 inches (500-8) **Important Options:** eight-slot chassis, power supply, two terminal connectors
Value: $40 to $100

OSI Challenger (1977, early micro)
Original Retail Price: $439 to $675
Base Configuration: 6502A CPU, OS-65, eight S-100 slots, 1K RAM (192K max), up to 16K ROM, external 5.25-inch floppy disk drive, serial interface, BASIC, editor/assembler **Video:** 16-line x 64-column text **Important Options:** 6502C or 6800 CPU; CPU expander board; external dual 5.25-inch floppy disk drives; keyboard terminal; Sanyo monitor; ADC, DAC, parallel, serial, and cassette interfaces
Value: $85 to $175

OSI Challenger IP (1978, early micro)
Original Retail Price: $349
Base Configuration: 6502 CPU, 4K RAM (8K max), 8K ROM, cassette interface, integral keyboard, BASIC in ROM **Video:** 24-line x 24-column text, 256 x 256 graphics **Important Options:** expander board, floppy disk drive interface, port adapter, editor/assembler
Value: $75 to $165

OSI Challenger II (1977, early micro)
Original Retail Price: $1,964
Base Configuration: 1MHz 6502 CPU, four S-100 slots, 16K RAM (192K max), 8-inch floppy disk drive, integral keyboard, serial or video interface, BASIC **Video:** 16-line x 64-column text **Important Options:** second 8-inch floppy disk drive, 74MB hard disk drive, video interface, line printer
Value: $125 to $350

The Ohio Scientific Challenger II ($125 to $350) had a form factor similar to the Sol-20.

OSI Challenger IIP (1977, early micro)
Original Retail Price: $598
Base Configuration: 2MHz 6502 CPU, four S-100 slots, 4K RAM (40K max), 8K ROM, cassette interface, integral keyboard, BASIC in ROM **Video:** 32-line x 64-column text **Important Options:** single or dual 8-inch floppy disk drives, 74MB hard disk drive, video interface, line printer
Value: $75 to $200

OSI Challenger III
(1977, early micro)
Original Retail Price: $3,481
Base Configuration: 6502A, 6800 and Z80 CPUs; OS-65D, 32K RAM; two 8-inch floppy disk drives; serial interface
Value: $100 to $275

Sitting amongst the many options available for it, the Ohio Scientific Challenger 4P ($75 to $200).

OSI Challenger 4P (1979, desktop)
Base Configuration: 6502 CPU; accessory bus; 8K RAM (48K max); integral keyboard; two RS-232, parallel, four game, and cassette ports; BASIC **Video:** 32-line x 64-column text, 512 x 256 graphics, 16 colors **Important Options:** 6502A CPU or 6502C "GT Option," external 5.25-inch floppy disk drive, Home Color TV set, joysticks, remote security console, modem
Value: $75 to $200

Ohio Scientific's Challenger III $100 to $275) shown with an output terminal.

OSI Challenger I Series 2 (desktop)
Original Retail Price: $479
Base Configuration: 6502 CPU, OS-65, 4K RAM (32K max), RS-232C port, BASIC **Video:** 24-line x 24-column text, 256 x 256 graphics
Value: $75 to $185

OSI Challenger II Series 2 (desktop)
Original Retail Price: $879
Base Configuration: 6502 CPU, OS-65, 8K RAM (48K max), integral keyboard, RS-232C and parallel ports, BASIC, music synthesizer
Video: 32-line x 64-column text, 15 colors
Value: $85 to $200

This Series 2 version ($85 to $200) of the Ohio Scientific Challenger II is markedly different from the original line.

Oki Electric Industry Co. (Tokyo, Japan)

BMC Systems sold the if800 in North America.

Oki Electric Oki if800 Model 30 (1982, desktop)
Base Configuration: 5MHz Z80B CPU; CP/M; ROM cartridge slot; three expansion slots; 128K RAM (256K max); two 8-inch floppy disk drives; integral 12-inch monochrome CRT, keyboard/keypad and printer; RS-232C and light-pen ports; Oki BASIC **Video:** 25-line x 80-column text, 640 x 400 graphics **Important Options:** parallel, IEEE-488, and ADC/DAC interfaces; light pen
Value: $22 to $65

At first glance, it appears that the monitor of this Oki Electric Ok if800 Model 30 ($22 to $65) is a separate unit, but it is in fact attached to the computer by two pedestals on either side of the built-in printer.

Oki IF COM7 (1982, laptop)
Base Configuration: 4.9MHz 80C86 CPU, 256K RAM, 3.5-inch floppy disk drive, monochrome LCD, integral keyboard, RS-232C port **Video:** 10-line x 40-column text, 600 x 200 graphics
Value: $35 to $70

Olivetti USA (Somerville, New Jersey)

Olivetti was a leading European manufacturer of office systems that often preferred to sell computers produced by other vendors under its own name. In particular, Olivetti PCs such as the M18 series and M19 were produced by Corona and Acorn, respectively. Kyocera produced the M10, which was the same system as the Tandy TRS-80 Model 100 and the NEC 8201.

Olivetti did design its earlier systems such as the P6060 and M20. The coprocessor model of the latter was called the Olivetti M20 BP, which offered the software suite as standard. PCOS (Professional Computer Operating System) was Olivetti's own and could run CP/M software through emulation.

In 1977, it was unusual to see both a keyboard and printer built into a computer like on this Olivetti P6060 Personal Minicomputer ($45 to $100).

Olivetti P6060 Personal Minicomputer
(1977, early micro)
Original Retail Price: $7,950
Base Configuration: 8K RAM (80K max), 5.25-inch floppy disk drive, integral keyboard/keypad, two serial and one RS-232C port, BASIC, integral thermal printer **Video:** 32-column text **Important Options:** second 5.25-inch floppy disk drive
Value: $45 to $100

Olivetti M20 (1983, desktop)
Original Retail Price: $2,295 to $5,295
Base Configuration: 4MHz Z8001 CPU, PCOS, five expansion slots, 128K RAM (512K max), 5.25-inch floppy disk drive, 10MB hard disk drive, 12-inch monochrome monitor, integral keyboard/keypad, RS-232C and parallel ports, M20 BASIC-8000 **Video:** 512 x 256 graphics **Important Options:** 8086 coprocessor, CP/M-86 or MS-DOS, IEEE-488 interface, application suite, printer
Value: $15 to $40

The Olivetti M20 ($15 to $40) was one of a few micros to use the Zilog Z8001 CPU.

Olivetti M19 (desktop PC)
Base Configuration: 8088 CPU, 256K RAM, monochrome monitor
Value: $5 to $35

Olivetti M24 (1985, desktop PC)
Original Retail Price: $2,745 to $3,395
Base Configuration: 8MHz 8086-2 CPU, MS-DOS 2.11, seven ISA slots, 128K RAM (640K max), two 5.25-inch floppy disk drives, 12-inch monochrome monitor, keyboard/keypad, serial and parallel ports **Video:** CGA, 640 x 400 graphics **Important Options:** 10MB hard disk drive
Value: $7 to $25

Olivetti's M10 notebook computer ($20 to $65) with the optional PL10 printer.

Olivetti M10 (May 1984, notebook)
Original Retail Price: $799 to $999
Base Configuration: 80C85 CPU; 8K RAM (32K max); monochrome LCD; integral keyboard; RS-232C, parallel, and cassette ports; application suite in ROM, internal modem **Video:** 8-line x 24-column text **Size/Weight:** 8.5 x 11.75 x 2.37 inches, 4.2 lbs. **Important Options:** PL10 printer
Value: $20 to $65

Olivetti M15 (Aug. 1987, laptop PC)
Original Retail Price: $1,995
Base Configuration: 80C88 CPU, MS-DOS 3.2, 512K RAM, two 3.5-inch floppy disk drives, 12-inch monochrome LCD, RS-232C and parallel ports, carrying case, battery pack, AC adapter **Size/Weight:** 11.5 lbs. **Important Options:** external 5.25-inch floppy disk drive
Value: $7 to $30

Olympia USA Inc. (Somerville, New Jersey)

The Olympia Boss was one of the sharper looking computers of 1981. It had a two-tone color scheme with a sloping front of the case and a separate but well-matched monitor.

The People computer was typical of the hybrid CP/M and MS-DOS systems introduced while the world was moving to PC compatibility.

The Olympia People ($15 to $35) ran both MS-DOS and CP/M.

Olympia Boss (1981, desktop)
Base Configuration: 4.9MHz 8085 CPU, Prologue, four expansion slots, 32K RAM (64K max), two 5.25-inch floppy disk drives, monochrome monitor, integral keyboard/keypad, parallel and cassette ports, printer **Video:** 25-line x 80-column text, 640 x 300 graphics **Value:** $17 to $50

Olympia People (1983, desktop)
Base Configuration: 8086 CPU, CP/M-86 and MS-DOS, 128K RAM (512K max), two 5.25-inch floppy disk drives, keyboard/keypad **Video:** 25-line x 80-column text, 640 x 475 graphics **Important Options:** Concurrent CP/M-86, 10MB hard disk drive, color monitor
Value: $15 to $35

Omnidata (Westlake Village, California)

The Omni Convertible could operate up to three processors at a time. That and its unusual but pleasing design make it an interesting collectible.

Omnidata Omni Convertible
(1984, desktop)
Original Retail Price: $6,000 **Base Configuration:** Z80H and TMS9995 CPUs, Omni-DOS, 128K RAM (1MB max), 5.25-inch floppy disk drive, integral monochrome CRT, keyboard/keypad, printer **Important Options:** 80186, 80286 or 68000 coprocessor; CP/M Plus, MS-DOS, Xenix, UCSD p-System, or Unix
Value: $15 to $50

Ontel Corp. (Woodbury, New York)

The computer and display of the Amigo were housed in the same unit. A 6502 processor drove the system's video.

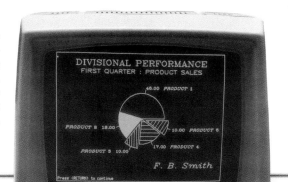

Ontel Amigo (1983, desktop)
Base Configuration: 4MHz Z80A CPU, CP/M with GSX-80, two external 5.25-inch floppy disk drives, integral 12-inch monochrome CRT, keyboard/keypad, RS-232C and parallel ports **Video:** 25-line x 80-column text, 640 x 300 graphics **Size/Weight:** 12 x 13 x 17 inches, 35 lbs. **Important Options:** 5MB hard disk drive, dot-matrix printer
Value: $17 to $45

The main electronics and monitor were combined in the same unit on the Ontel Amigo ($17 to $45).

Oric Products International Ltd. (Berkshire, U.K.)

The Oric was the first British color system to sell for less than £100. The system initially sold well, particularly in France. However, it was replaced by the Atmos within a year. The Atmos had similar specifications to the Oric-1, but came in a sexier looking black case with a real keyboard. It also fixed a few bugs in the ROM.

French firm Eureka Informatique bought Oric in 1985 and later introduced the Telestrat. This system was designed to be used with France's Minitel online information system (although it worked just fine as a standalone computer). The Telestrat was software and hardware compatible with both the Oric-1 and Atmos.

> Hard to find in North America, the Oric-I ($35 to $65) was a popular home computer in Europe where it has the most collector interest today.

Oric-I (1983, home computer)
Original Retail Price: £100 to £170
Base Configuration: 6502A CPU, expansion port, 16K RAM (48K max), 16K ROM, PAL and RGB video ports, integral Chiclet-style keyboard, parallel and cassette ports, three-voice sound **Video:** 28-line x 40-column text, 240 x 200 graphics, eight colors **Size/Weight:** 2 x 10.9 x 6.8 inches, 2.4 lbs. **Important Options:** external 3.5-inch floppy disk drive, modem, Speed Printer
Value: $35 to $65

Oric Atmos (Feb. 1984, home computer)
Base Configuration: 2MHz 6502A CPU, expansion port, 48K RAM, 16K ROM, PAL and RGB video ports, integral keyboard, parallel and cassette ports, Tangerine BASIC **Video:** 28-line x 40-column text, 240 x 200 graphics, eight colors **Important Options:** 3.5-inch floppy disk drive, modem, printer
Value: $37 to $75

Oric Telestrat (1986, home computer)
Base Configuration: 1MHz 6502 CPU; Stratsed operating system; expansion port; 64K RAM; 48K ROM; RGB video port; integral keyboard; RS-232C, parallel, MIDI, cassette, and two game ports; three-voice sound **Video:** 28-line x 40-column text, 240 x 200 graphics, eight colors **Size/Weight:** 13.6 x 10.1 x 2.8 inches **Important Options:** 3.5-inch floppy disk drive, printer, modem
Value: $75 to $125

ORIC-1™
Tomorrow's micro...today!

Osborne Computer Corp. (Hayward, California)

Computer book author and publisher Adam Osborne went into the hardware business in 1979 with a design for a transportable CP/M system. He put together an all-star team to launch the company and build the computer. CP/M creator Gary Kildall, CBASIC author Gordon Eubanks, and WordStar creator Seymore Rubenstein sat on his board of directors. Lee Felsenstein, who designed the Processor Technology Sol-20, developed the computer to Osborne's specifications.

Osborne was a victim of its own success. Launched in 1979, the company had sold 11,000 Osborne 1 systems by the end of 1981 with orders for 50,000 more. By the time the Executive came out in mid-1983, 100,000 Osborne 1 systems had been sold. A year later, Osborne was recording sales of $10 million a month. Osborne shipped nearly 150,000 Osborne 1 and Executive units worldwide by late 1984. Unfortunately, the company was unable to keep up with the backlog, which opened the door to competitors. In September 1983, Osborne filed for Chapter 11 bankruptcy, reorganized, and came out with several new models, none of which showed the innovation and customer loyalty that the Osborne 1 and Executive did. The company survived for several years post-bankruptcy, but produced mostly unremarkable PC-compatible desktop and transportable systems.

The earliest Osborne 1s had miniscule displays that were soon replaced by larger ones. The tan plastic case was replaced by a sturdier blue-grey case as well. Osborne improved the video display and boosted memory with the Executive. Unfortunately, it also added more than a pound of weight over the Osborne 1. The Executive II was Osborne's first attempt at a PC-compatible system.

The Vixen was introduced shortly after Osborne emerged from Chapter 11 bankruptcy protection. It was faster and had a bigger display than previous models, but was canceled shortly after its introduction.

The Osborne 3 (sold as Encore in the U.K.) is an unusual find today and features an odd design with a fold-down keyboard. It is the last true Osborne system. Vadem, a California company with management connections to Osborne, designed the Osborne 3. The Morrow Pivot and Zenith Z-171 used the same design.

Osborne 1 (1981, transportable)
Original Retail Price: $1,795
Base Configuration: Z80A CPU, CP/M, 5.25-inch floppy disk drive, integral monochrome CRT, keyboard/keypad, RS-232 and IEEE-488 ports, BASIC, application suite, carrying case **Video:** 24-line x 50-column text, 128 x 34 graphics **S ize/Weight:** 26 lbs. **Important Options:** 12-inch monochrome monitor, battery pack
Value: $25 to $125

The Osborne 1 ($25 to $125) wasn't the first transportable, but it defined a standard for many others to follow.

Osborne Executive/Executive II

(1983, transportable)
Original Retail Price: $2,495 (Executive)/$3,195 (Executive II)
Base Configuration: 4MHz Z80A CPU, 8088 coprocessor (Executive II), CP/M Plus (Executive)/CP/M-86 and MS-DOS (Executive II), 128K RAM (Executive)/256K RAM (Executive II), two 5.25-inch floppy disk drives, integral 7-inch monochrome CRT, keyboard/keypad, two RS-232C ports, MBASIC, CBASIC, application suite **Video:** 24-line x 80-column text **Size/Weight:** 20.5 x 13 x 9 inches, 28 lbs.
Value: $20 to $85

Not a big seller, the Osborne 4 Vixen ($45 to $175) is hard to find today.

Osborne 4 Vixen (1984, transportable)
Original Retail Price: $1,298
Base Configuration: 4MHz Z80A CPU, CP/M 2.2, 64K RAM, two 5.25-inch floppy disk drives, integral 7-inch monochrome CRT, keyboard, RS-232C and parallel ports, application suite, MBASIC **Video:** 25-line x 80-column text **Size/Weight:** 12.62 x 16.25 x 6.25 inches, 22 lbs.
Important Options: external 10MB hard disk drive
Value: $45 to $175

Osborne 3 (a.k.a. "Encore") (1985, transportable PC)
Original Retail Price: $1,895
Base Configuration: 3.5MHz 80C86 CPU, MS-DOS 2.11, 128K RAM (512K max), 5.25-inch floppy disk drive, monochrome LCD, integral keyboard, RS-232C and parallel ports, internal modem, AC adapter **Video:** 16-line x 80-column text, 480 x 128 graphics **Size/Weight:** 9.5 x 13 x 5.5 inches, 11.9 lbs. **Important Options:** NiCad battery pack
Value: $50 to $200

Otrona Advanced Systems (Boulder, Colorado)

Some considered the Otrona superior to the Osborne, as it was well made but smaller. The single-floppy drive model was called the Attache S. The Attache 8:16 used the same case as the Attache, but had updated electronics to accommodate a second 16-bit CPU. A Tempest version of the Attache 8:16 was introduced in 1984.

The Otrona 2001 could be configured as either a portable or a desktop PC. As a portable, its built-in CRT could tilt up for better viewing. As a desktop, a panel covered the slot for the built-in display and a standalone monitor was used.

The Osborne Executive ($20 to $85) made a number of incremental improvements over the Osborne 1, most notably a larger screen.

Otrona Attache (April 1982, transportable)

Original Retail Price: $3,995
Base Configuration: 4MHz Z80A CPU; CP/M; expansion slot; 64K RAM; 4K ROM; 5.25-inch floppy disk drive; integral 5.5-inch monochrome CRT; keyboard; two RS-232C ports; application suite; owner's, service, and software manuals **Video:** 24-line x 80-column text, 320 x 240 graphics **Size/Weight:** 12 x 5.75 x 13.6 inches, 19 lbs. **Important Options:** second 5.25-inch floppy disk drive, 10MB hard disk drive, parallel interface, carrying case, battery pack
Value: $20 to $75

At 19 pounds, the Otrona Attache ($20 to $75) was one of the smallest of the early transportables.

Otrona Attache 8:16 (July 1983, transportable)

Base Configuration: 8086 and Z80A CPUs; MS-DOS 2.0 and CP/M 2.2; expansion slot; 256K RAM; 5.25-inch floppy disk drive; integral 5.5-inch monochrome CRT; keyboard; two RS-232C ports; application suite; owner's, service, and software manuals **Video:** 24-line x 80-column text, 320 x 240 graphics **Size/Weight:** 5.75 x 12 x 13.6 inches, 19.5 lbs. **Important Options:** second 5.25-inch floppy disk drive, 10MB hard disk drive, parallel and IEEE-488 interfaces, carrying case, battery pack
Value: $20 to $60

Otrona 2001 (May 1984, transportable PC)

Original Retail Price: $2,495
Base Configuration: 4.77MHz 8088 CPU, MS-DOS, three ISA slots, 128K RAM (640K max), 5.25-inch floppy disk drive, integral 7-inch monochrome CRT, RGB port, keyboard/keypad, RS-232C and parallel ports **Video:** 25-line x 80-column text, 640 x 200 graphics **Size/Weight:** 7 x 15 x 14 inches, 19 lbs. **Important Options:** 4.77MHz Z80B coprocessor, CP/M 2.2, expansion chassis, second 5.25-inch floppy disk drive, 10MB hard disk drive, graphics upgrade card, 12-inch 2051 monochrome or 14-inch 2052 color monitor, GW-BASIC, 2031 printer, internal modem, carrying case, battery power
Value: $22 to $55

The built-in monitor of the Otrona 2001 ($22 to $55) had a unique tilt-up design.

Panasonic Co. (Secaucus, New Jersey)

Panasonic is a division of Japan's Matsushita Electric that specializes in consumer electronics. The company has made several unsuccessful attempts at establishing itself in the computer business with systems for professional and home use. Most Panasonic models were sold in Japan under the National brand with few differences.

The company was a big supporter of the MSX movement. The CF-2700 was one of the more popular MSX models. Panasonic was one of the last MSX holdouts, producing an FS-A1 series of MSX 2 systems and later an MSX 2+ system.

In the mid-1980s, Panasonic saw moderate success with several systems aimed at the professional market. Most notable were the transportable Sr. Partner and the Exec. Partner PC. Reviewers gave the Sr. Partner good grades on value and PC compatibility. Examples are relatively easy to find today. The company also offered a PC AT-compatible Business Partner 286.

The Panasonic JD-850M ($15 to $40) with the optional JK-7600 hard drive.

Panasonic JD-850M (1982, desktop)
Original Retail Price: $8,000
Base Configuration: CP/M, two 8-inch floppy disk drives, integral 12-inch monochrome CRT, keyboard/keypad **Important Options:** external JK-7600 8.4MB hard disk drive
Value: $15 to $40

Panasonic JR-200U Personal Computer
(1982, home computer)
Base Configuration: MN1800A CPU; external expansion bus; 32K RAM; 16K ROM; RGB and TV video ports; integral Chiclet-style keyboard; parallel, game speaker, and cassette ports; JR-BASIC 5.0; music synthesizer **Size/Weight:** 13.65 x 8.15 x 2.2 inches, 5.5 lbs. **Important Options:** RQ-8300 cassette recorder, CT-1300D color monitor, RS-232C interface, JR-U08U joysticks, JR-PO2U printer
Value: $20 to $45

Not well known in the U.S., the Panasonic JR-200U ($20 to $45) was a well-designed home computer.

Panasonic CF-2700 (1984, MSX home computer)
Base Configuration: 3.58MHz Z80A CPU; two ROM cartridge slots; 64K RAM; 48K ROM; TV video port; integral keyboard; parallel, cassette, and two game ports; MSX BASIC **Video:** 26-line x 40-column text, 256 x 192 graphics, 16 colors
Value: $17 to $42

Panasonic Business Partner (1986, desktop PC)
Base Configuration: 7.16MHz 8086-2 CPU, MS-DOS, two 5.25-inch floppy disk drives, keyboard/keypad
Important Options: CGA card
Value: $7 to $25

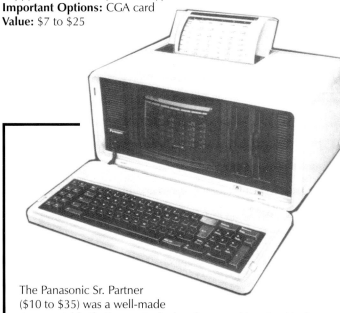

The Panasonic Sr. Partner ($10 to $35) was a well-made transportable that's easy to find and reasonably priced today.

Panasonic Sr. Partner
(late 1983, transportable PC)
Original Retail Price: $2,495
Base Configuration: 8088 CPU, MS-DOS 2.0, one ISA slot, 128K RAM (512K max), 5.25-inch floppy disk drive, integral 9-inch monochrome CRT, RGB video port, keyboard/keypad, RS-232 and parallel ports, GW-BASIC, application suite, integral thermal printer
Video: 25-line x 132-column text, 640 x 200 graphics **Size/Weight:** 18.25 x 13.2 x 8.25 inches, 28.7 lbs. **Important Options:** second 5.25-inch floppy disk drive
Value: $10 to $35

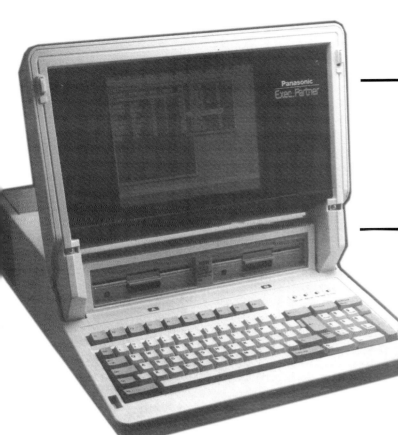

Panasonic Exec. Partner
(1985, transportable PC)
Base Configuration: 7.16MHz 8086-2 CPU, MS-DOS, expansion slot, 256K RAM (640K max), two 5.25-inch floppy disk drives, monochrome gas plasma display, integral keyboard/keypad and printer **Important Options:** carrying case
Value: $12 to $35

The Panasonic Exec. Partner ($12 to $35).

Paradyne Corp. (Lago, Florida)

The PortaBrain was a small unit housing a motherboard and storage devices. It had a handle for easy carrying but required a connection to a terminal for video and a keyboard. Paradyne was primarily a manufacturer of Unix-based multi-user systems.

Paradyne PortaBrain
(1983, desktop)
Base Configuration: 4MHz Z80A CPU, CP/M, ROM cartridge slot, 256K RAM, 16K ROM, 5.25-inch floppy disk drive, two RS-232C and one parallel port **Size/Weight:** 6 lbs.
Value: $15 to $37

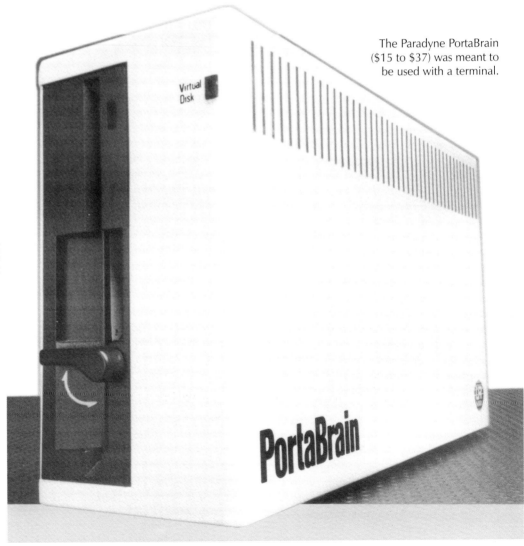

The Paradyne PortaBrain ($15 to $37) was meant to be used with a terminal.

Parasitic Engineering (Albany, California)

COPE was Parasitic's Cassette Operating Executive software.

Parasitic Engineering Equinox 100 (1977, early micro)
Original Retail Price: $699
Base Configuration: 8080A CPU, COPE, 20 S-100 slots, 4K RAM, cassette interface, LED readout , integral hex keyboard, RS-232 and parallel ports, EQU/ATE, BASIC-EQ, power supply
Value: $100 to $235

PCM (San Ramon, California)

PCM apparently expected owners of the PCM-12 to get their own software to run this PDP-8/E-compatible system from DEC. This might have been the first microcomputer to use the Intersil IM6100 CPU.

PCM-12 (1976, early micro)
Original Retail Price: $400 to $600 kit
Base Configuration: IM6100 CPU, 4K RAM (32K max), front panel switches, serial and cassette ports, enclosure, power supply
Value: $100 to $450

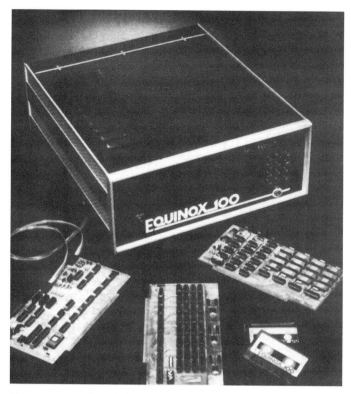

Up to 20 S-100 boards like those shown could be placed in the Parasitic Engineering Equinox 100 ($100 to $235).

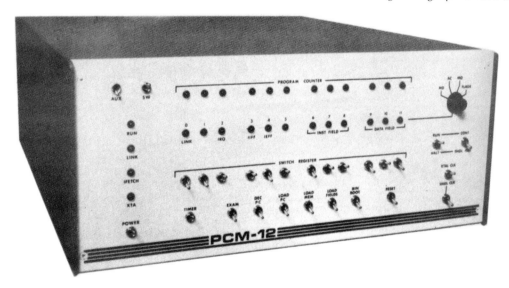

The PCM-12 ($100 to $450) was compatible with the DEC PDP-8/E.

PC's Limited (Austin, Texas)

PC's Limited became Dell Computer Corp. in 1987, and at this writing is the world's leading seller of PC systems. Michael Dell started the company in 1984 selling PC clones from his dorm room at the University of Texas. The company grew because it offered a solidly built PC compatible at a reasonable price. Nothing fancy—just the basic options that most people would want.

PC's Limited Turbo (1985, desktop PC)
Original Retail Price: $799 to $1,899
Base Configuration: 8MHz 8088 CPU, MS-DOS, eight ISA slots, 640K RAM, 5.25-inch floppy disk drive, keyboard/keypad, parallel port
Important Options: 20- or 40MB hard disk drive, monochrome monitor, EGA card
Value: $20 to $45

Personal Microcomputers Inc. (PMC) (Mountain View, California)

PMC is best known for selling the PMC-80 and PMC-81 TRS-80 clones (see "Eaca International Video Genie EG-3003"). The MicroMate, however, was different. It was similar in concept to the Paradyne PortaBrain in that it was designed to turn any dumb terminal into a CP/M computer.

PMC MicroMate (March 1983, desktop)
Original Retail Price: $1,495
Base Configuration: 4MHz Z80A CPU, CP/M Plus or CP/M-80, 128K RAM, 4K ROM, 5.25-inch floppy disk drive, two serial and four parallel ports, T/Maker III **Video:** 24-line x 80-column text **Size/Weight:** 3.5 x 6 x 13 inches, 8 lbs . **Important Options:** 10MB hard disk drive, MMT-102 terminal
Value: $15 to $35

It looks like an external floppy drive, but inside the PMC MicroMate ($15 to $35) is a complete CP/M-based microcomputer.

Philips Electronics (Eindhoven, The Netherlands)

The first micro that Philips sold appears to be the P2000. It came in two versions: The P2000T had a TV interface, and the P2000M used a standard computer monitor. The P2000 probably was not sold in North America.

Designed by the French company RTC, the VG5000 was Philips's first home computer. The VG5000 was also sold as the Radiola VG5000 and the Schneider VG5000.

Philips moved directly to the VG-8000 MSX systems from the VG5000. The VG-8000 did not implement all of the MSX standard—it had no audio, for example. It was replaced by the Kyocera-built VG-8020 (also sold under the Yashica name), which was later followed by the MSX 2-compatible VG 8220.

Philips P2000 (1982, desktop)
Base Configuration: Z80 CPU, 16K RAM (48K max), 4K ROM, integral cassette recorder and keyboard/keypad, serial port **Video:** 24-line x 80-column text **Important Options:** 12-inch monochrome monitor
Value: $17 to $45

Philips VG5000 (1984, home computer)
Base Configuration: 4MHz Z80 CPU, expansion port, 24K RAM (56K max), 18K ROM, integral Chiclet-style keyboard/keypad, cassette port, Microsoft BASIC, AC adapter **Video:** 25-line x 40-column text **Size/Weight:** 10.9 x 12.4 x 1.6 inches **Important Options:** expansion unit, joysticks and interface, printer
Value: $20 to $65

Philips VG-8000 (1985, MSX home computer)
Base Configuration: 3.58MHz Z80 CPU, ROM cartridge slot, 16K RAM (32K max), 32K ROM, RGB video port, integral Chiclet-style keyboard, cassette and two game ports **Video:** 256 x 192 graphics, 16 colors
Value: $15 to $35

Pioneer Electronics (Long Beach, California)

Pioneer designed the MSX-based Palcom PX-7 to be used with a videodisc player and provided a number of games in videodisc format.

Pioneer Palcom PX-7 (1984, MSX home computer)
Original Retail Price: $370
Base Configuration: Z80 CPU, two ROM cartridge slots, composite and RGB video ports, integral keyboard, videodisc controller, MSX-BASIC **Video:** 24-line x 40-column text, 256 x 192 graphics
Value: $20 to $45

Polymorphic Systems (Goleta, California)

Polymorphic introduced the Micro-Altair, an early S-100 bus system that attempted to capitalize on the popularity of the Altair and IMSAI computers, in 1976. Unfortunately, none apparently were ever sold. The Poly 88 and System 8813, however, were produced.

Several configurations of the Poly 88 were available. The System 2 was the main processor unit in kit form, and the System 8 and System 16 were assembled systems with 8K and 16K RAM, respectively. They also came with a monitor, cassette recorder, and keyboard.

Polymorphic Systems Poly 88 (1977, early micro)
Original Retail Price: $2,250
Base Configuration: 1MHz 8080 CPU, 16K RAM (48K max), 1K ROM (3K max), cassette recorder, monochrome TV monitor, keyboard, BASIC, assembler **Video:** 16-line x 64-column text, 128 x 48 graphics
Value: $125 to $325

Everything shown here came standard with the Polymorphic Systems Poly 88 ($125 to $325).

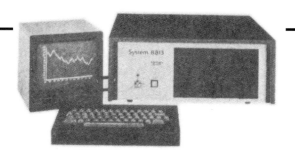

Polymorphic Systems System 8813
(mid-1977, early micro)
Original Retail Price: $3,250
Base Configuration: Z80 and 8080 CPUs, CP/M, 16K RAM (104K max), 5.25-inch floppy disk drive, 9-inch monochrome monitor, keyboard/keypad, RS-232C port, BASIC **Video:** 16-line x 64-column text, 128 x 48 graphics **Important Options:** second and third 5.25-inch floppy disk drives, 12-inch monochrome monitor **Value:** $135 to $375

The Polymorphic Systems System 8813 ($135 to $375) used both Z80 and 8080 CPUs.

Processor Technology Corp. (Emeryville, California)

Processor Technology was launched in 1975 by Bob Marsh as a manufacturer of 4K memory boards for the MITS Altair. Lee Felsenstein, who would later design the Osborne 1, created the Sol-20 the following year for Marsh. It was one of the more attractive computers of the era, with a bright blue metal case and finished wood sides. An estimated 20,000 Sol-20s were made before Processor Technology went out of business in 1980. The optional Helios drives had a reputation as being unreliable, and many Sol-20 owners opted for 5.25-inch drives made by North Star. A Sol-10, which lacked the S-100 bus, was also sold as a terminal.

Processor Technology Sol-20 (1976, early micro)
Original Retail Price: $995 kit, $2,129 assembled
Base Configuration: 8080A CPU, SOLOS, five S-100 slots, 2K RAM (64K max), 1K ROM (2K max), cassette recorder, 12-inch monochrome TV/monitor, integral keyboard, RS-232 and cassette ports **Video:** 16-line x 64-column text **Important Options:** 8080A or 9080A CPU, external Helios II dual 8-inch floppy disk drives **Value:** $150 to $1,200

Pronto Computers Inc. (Torrance, California)

The Series 16 won an award from Industrial Design magazine for superior design in the business and scientific category. Although it was software compatible with the PC, the Series 16 had a proprietary expansion bus.

Pronto claimed that the Transportable Solution was the first portable to offer an 80186 CPU, but others had it at about the same time.

Pronto Series 16 (Aug. 1983, desktop PC)
Original Retail Price: $3,200 to $6,190
Base Configuration: 8MHz 80186 CPU, MS-DOS 2.11, 256K RAM (1MB max), 16K ROM, 5.25-inch floppy disk drive, keyboard/keypad, two RS-232C and one parallel port, Executec application suite **Video:** 25-line x 80-column text **Important Options:** second 5.25-inch floppy disk drive, 5.6MB removeable hard disk drive, monochrome monitor, 640 x 480 graphics card **Value:** $15 to $40

Pronto Transportable Solution (Nov. 1983, transportable PC)
Original Retail Price: $3,950 to $8,690
Base Configuration: 8MHz 80186 CPU, MS-DOS 2.11, proprietary expansion slot, 256K RAM, 16K ROM (64K max), 5.25-inch floppy disk drive, integral 9-inch monochrome CRT, keyboard/keypad, two RS-232 and one parallel port, application suite **Video:** 25-line x 80-column text **Size/Weight:** 7.5 x 17.25 x 18 inches, 30 lbs. **Important Options:** 5.6- to 35MB hard disk drive, enhanced graphics upgrade **Value:** $15 to $35

Quadram Corp. (Norcross, Georgia)

The lunchbox-style Datavue 25 was typical of the genre.

Quadram Datavue 25 (March 1985, transportable PC)
Original Retail Price: $2,195
Base Configuration: 4.77MHz 80C88 CPU, MS-DOS 2.11, external expansion port, 256K RAM (1.23MB max), 64K ROM, 3.5-inch floppy disk drive, 20MB hard disk drive, monochrome LCD, RGB and composite video ports, keyboard/keypad, RS-232C and parallel ports, AC adapter, external lead-acid battery pack **Video:** 640 x 200 graphics, four colors **Size/Weight:** 12.75 x 6.25 x 10.5 inches, 16 lbs. **Important Options:** external 5.25-inch floppy disk drive, WriteStyle printer **Value:** $5 to $25

This photo not only shows all the options available for the Processor Technology Sol-20 ($120 to $1,200), but its internal components as well.

Quasar Data Products
(N. Olmstead, Ohio)

Quasar Data Products QDP-100 (1980, desktop)
Original Retail Price: $4,795
Base Configuration: 4MHz Z80A CPU, CP/M 2.2, S-100 bus, 64K RAM, two 8-inch floppy disk drives, monochrome CRT terminal, two serial and two parallel ports, PROM programmer
Value: $20 to $65

Quasar Data Products QDP-8100 (1980, desktop)
Original Retail Price: $6,395
Base Configuration: 4MHz Z8000 CPU, CP/M 2.2, S-100 bus, 64K RAM, two 8-inch floppy disk drives, intelligent monochrome terminal, two serial and one parallel port, BASIC, Z80 software emulator
Important Options: Z8000 Pascal
Value: $20 to $65

R2E of America
(Minneapolis, Minnesota)

The Micral N, designed by Francois Gernelle and Andre Thi Truong, has a solid claim to being the first commercial microcomputer. Unlike the Kenbak-1, it used a real processor. However, Intel's Intellec series was produced at about the same time. Philippe Kahn, who would later found Borland Software in the U.S., wrote the software for the Micral. Made and sold almost exclusively in France, the Micral is difficult to find in the U.S. About 500 units were made. R2E upgraded the original Micro to the Intel 8080 CPU in 1975, calling it the Micral S. France's Group Bull bought R2E in 1979, discontinued the original Micral line, and renamed the company Bull Micral.

The standard monitor of the Series 80 had a retro-looking, tall pedestal mount.

R2E Micral N (1973, early micro)
Original Retail Price: $1,750
Base Configuration: 8008 CPU, 2K RAM (64K max), LED readout, front panel switches, assembler
Value: $2,500 to $5,000

R2E Series 80 (1979, desktop)
Base Configuration: Z80 CPU, 32K RAM (64K max), two 5.25-inch floppy disk drives, monochrome monitor, integral keyboard/keypad, BASIC **Important Options:** CP/M, external 10MB removeable hard disk drive, graphics upgrade, tabletop monochrome monitor
Value: $20 to $55

RCA (Lancaster, Pennsylvania)

Sold as an inexpensive hobbyist system, the Cosmac VIP was a single-board computer in a simple enclosure with graphics capability. You might call it the first home computer, since the Cosmac VIP was designed to be used by the whole family. A collection of 20 games was included with every unit. The user had to supply a monitor, cassette recorder, speaker, and enclosure.

The Elf II was a popular entry-level, single-board computer. It was followed by the Super Elf.

RCA Cosmac VIP (1977, computer trainer)
Original Retail Price: $275
Base Configuration: CDP 1802 CPU, 2K RAM (32K max), 512 bytes ROM, cassette interface, hex keypad, CHIP-8 programming language, microprocessor and operation manuals **Video:** 128 x 64 graphics **Size/Weight:** 8.5 x 11 inches **Important Options:** VP-590 color video board, keyboard, parallel interface, Tiny BASIC, VP-595 sound and VP-550 music boards, EPROM programmer
Value: $75 to $200

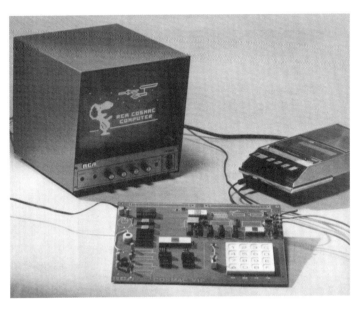

The user had to supply the monitor and cassette recorder for this RCA Cosmac VIP ($75 to $200). *Reused with permission CMP Media LLC, Byte.com (Byte Magazine), Manhasset NY. All rights reserved.*

RCA Cosmac Elf II (computer trainer)
Original Retail Price: $100
Base Configuration: CDP-1802 CPU, five expansion slots, 256 bytes RAM (64K max), video interface, integral hex keyboard **Video:** 128 x 64 graphics
Value: $65 to $175

The RCA Cosmac Elf II ($65 to $175) shown with an optional full keyboard and various add-on boards installed.

Realistic Controls Corp. (Cleveland, Ohio)

Realistic Controls Z//100 (1977, early micro)
Original Retail Price: $7,995 to $9,795
Base Configuration: 8080 CPU, 33K RAM (64K max), 3K ROM, two 5.25-inch floppy disk drives, two RS-232C ports **Important Options:** external dual 5.25-inch floppy disk drives, monochrome monitor, FORT//80 FORTRAN compiler, printer
Value: $100 to $225

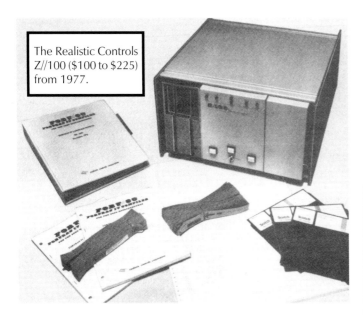

The Realistic Controls Z//100 ($100 to $225) from 1977.

Realistic Controls REX (early micro)
Base Configuration: Z80 CPU, five S-100 slots, 24K RAM, 5.25-inch floppy disk drive, keyboard, walnut cabinet **Important Options:** second 5.25-inch floppy disk drive
Value: $50 to $125

RGS Electronics (Santa Clara, California)

At $375, the RGS 008A was a good deal for hobbyists. You got everything you needed to build a working computer—almost. A cabinet, the fuses, and a power cord were not included. The 008A is a rare find today, but not as sought-after as the MITS Altair, Sphere, or Scelbi systems.

RGS Electronics RGS 008A (1975, early micro)
Original Retail Price: $375 kit
Base Configuration: 8008 CPU, front panel switches, manual, schematic **Important Options:** cassette and parallel interfaces, keyboard
Value: $100 to $500

Rockwell International (Milwaukee, Wisconsin)

Rockwell AIM-65 (1976, computer trainer)
Base Configuration: R6500 CPU, expansion bus, 1K RAM (5K max), 4K ROM (20K max), 20-character display, keyboard, two I/O ports, integral thermal printer **Important Options:** editor/assembler, BASIC, power supply
Value: $75 to $150

Royal Business Machines Inc. (Windsor, Connecticut)

Royal was a subsidiary of Germany's Triumph-Adler, which in turn was owned by Volkswagen. Triumph-Adler had the distinction of being the last company to own MITS, which produced the famous Altair 8800.

Parent company Triumph Adler sold the Alphatronic PC in Europe under its own brand.

Royal Alphatronic Personal Computer
(PC) (early 1984, home computer)
Original Retail Price: $695
Base Configuration: Z80A CPU; ROM cartridge slot; 64K RAM, 32K ROM; RGB and TV video ports; integral keyboard/keypad; RS-232C, parallel, and cassette ports; Microsoft BASIC and word processor in ROM **Video:** 24-line x 80-column text **Size/Weight:** 16.25 x 10.25 x 3 inches, 7.75 lbs. **Important Options:** CP/M, external 5.25-inch floppy disk drive, Alpha 2002 or 2015 typewriter/printer
Value: $5 to $30

Also sold under the Triumph Adler brand, the Royal Alphatronic Personal Computer ($5 to $30) with its optional floppy drive and monitor.

Sage Computer Technology
(Reno, Nevada)

The Sage II was the single-user offering from multi-user system vendor Sage. The company provided an upgrade path to convert the Sage II for multi-user capability. Purchasers of the Sage II system supplied their own terminals for video and keyboard or purchased the optional Sage Terminal. Later versions of the Sage II shared the same smaller enclosure as the Sage IV, which was configured similarly to the Sage II. The Sage Terminal was actually a relabeled Qume 102.

By 1984, the company changed its name to Stride Micro and concentrated on multi-user systems based on the VMEbus.

Sage Computer Technology's Sage II ($45 to $100) sitting beneath a Sage IV multi-user system.

Sage Computer Technology Sage II
(1982, desktop)
Original Retail Price: $3,600 to $4,800
Base Configuration: 8MHz 68000 CPU; UCSD p-System; two Sage Bus slots; 128K RAM (512K max); 8K ROM (32K max); 5.25-inch floppy disk drive; two RS-232C, parallel, and IEEE-488 slots; FORTRAN-77; BASIC; four-volume manual set **Size/Weight:** 6.5 x 12.5 x 16.75 inches, 16 lbs. **Important Options:** CP/M-68K, second 5.25-inch floppy disk drive, RAM disk, Sage terminal
Value: $45 to $100

Sanyo Business Systems Corp.
(Moonachie, New Jersey)

Consumer electronics company Sanyo made several interesting CP/M and PC-based systems. The CP/M systems combined the main electronics, video, and storage in one unit, while the MS-DOS systems used a typical PC design. Although the MBC-55 ran MS-DOS, it did not use the standard PC disk format. Sanyo began selling the MBC-55 in North America in mid-1983.

Sanyo cut a few corners to get the base price of the MBC-550 under $1,000. Speed was the main trade-off, and lack of a standard serial port was another. Nonetheless, the MBC-550 developed a loyal following. The dual-floppy-drive model was called the MBC-555.

Sanyo's home computer line begins with the PHC-10. Sanyo also sold the PHC-20, a cheaper, less capable version of the PHC-25. The PHC-27 is Sanyo's first MSX-compatible system, and the PHC-35J is its first MSX 2 computer.

Sanyo MBC-2000/MBC-3000/FDS-1000
(1982, desktop)
Original Retail Price: $1,995 (FDS-1000)/$3,495 (MBC-2000)/$6,495 (MBC-3000)
Base Configuration: Z80A (FDS-1000)/8085A (MBC-2000 and MBC-3000) CPU, CP/M, one (FDS-1000)/two (MBC-2000) 5.25-inch floppy disk drives, two 8-inch floppy disk drives (MBC-3000), integral monochrome CRT, keyboard/keypad, Sanyo BASIC
Value: $15 to $40

A family of Sanyos, from left to right: the MBC-2000, the MBC-3000, and the FDS-1000 ($15 to $40 for each system).

Sanyo MBC-1000 (1982, desktop)
Base Configuration: CP/M 2.2, three expansion slots, 5.25-inch floppy disk drive, integral 12-inch monochrome CRT, keyboard/keypad, serial and parallel ports **Video:** 25-line x 80-column text **Important Options:** second 5.25-inch floppy disk drive
Value: $15 to $45

Sanyo MBC-1150 Creative Computer (1983, desktop)
Base Configuration: Z80A CPU, CP/M 2.2, 64K RAM, two 5.25-inch floppy disk drives, integral 12-inch monochrome CRT, keyboard/keypad, RS-232C and parallel ports, Sanyo Enhanced BASIC **Video:** 25-line x 80-column text **Important Options:** PR5000 printer
Value: $15 to $40

Sanyo MBC-55 (1983, desktop)
Base Configuration: 8088 CPU; MS-DOS, CP/M-86, or Concurrent CP/M-86; 64K RAM (256K max); 4K ROM; two 5.25-inch floppy disk drives, keyboard/keypad
Value: $17 to $45

Inside the somewhat unusual configuration of the Sanyo MBC1150 Creative Computer ($15 to $40) is a typical CP/M system.

Sanyo MBC-550 (1983, desktop PC)
Original Retail Price: $995
Base Configuration: 3.6MHz 8088 CPU, MS-DOS 1.25, 128K RAM (256K max), 5.25-inch floppy disk drive, RGB and monochrome video ports, keyboard/keypad, parallel port, BASIC, application suite, owner and software manuals **Video:** 25-line x 80-column text, 640 x 200 graphics **Size/Weight:** 15 x 4.4 x 14.2 inches **Important Options:** second 5.25-inch floppy disk drive, monochrome or color monitor, RS-232C interface, Apple joystick
Value: $15 to $50

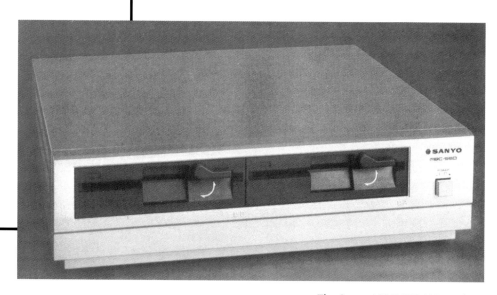

The Sanyo MBC-550 ($15 to $50) was a low-end PC-compatible system.

Sanyo MBC-885

(1985, desktop PC)
Base Configuration: 256K RAM (640K max), two 5.25-inch floppy disk drives, RGB and composite video ports, keyboard/keypad, RS-232C and parallel ports
Value: $10 to $30

Sanyo MBC-675

(1985, transportable PC)
Base Configuration: 256K RAM (640K max), two 5.25-inch floppy disk drives, integral monochrome CRT, RGB and composite video ports, keyboard/keypad, RS-232C and parallel ports **Important Options:** hard disk drive, printer, monitor
Value: $15 to $40

Sanyo MBC-775

(Jan. 1985, transportable PC)
Original Retail Price: $2,599 **Base Configuration:** two ISA slots, 256K RAM (640K max), two 5.25-inch floppy disk drives, integral 9-inch color CRT, RGB and composite video ports, keyboard/keypad, RS232C and parallel ports **Video:** 16 colors
Value: $17 to $45

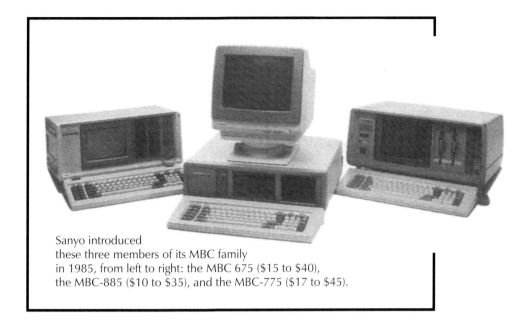

Sanyo introduced these three members of its MBC family in 1985, from left to right: the MBC 675 ($15 to $40), the MBC-885 ($10 to $35), and the MBC-775 ($17 to $45).

Sanyo PHC-25 (1983, home computer)
Original Retail Price: $264 **Base Configuration:** 4MHz Z80A CPU, 16K RAM, 28K ROM, RGB and TV video ports, integral Chiclet-style keyboard, parallel and cassette ports **Video:** 16-line x 32-column text, 256 x 192 graphics, eight colors
Value: $17 to $40

Sanyo Wavy MPC-5/MPC-10/MPC-11 (1984, MSX home computer)
Original Retail Price: $225 (MPC-5)/$310 (MPC-10)/$415 (MPC-11) **Base Configuration:** Z80 CPU, 16K RAM (MPC-5)/32K RAM (MPC-10 and MPC-11), composite video port, RGB video port (MPC-11), integral keyboard, parallel port, light pen (MPC-10 and MPC-11), superimpose capability (MPC-11), eight-octave sound **Video:** 24-line x 40-column text, 256 x 192 graphics
Value: $10 to $45

Scelbi-8H (1974, early micro)
Original Retail Price: $695 to $1,249 kit, $750 to $1,295 assembled
Base Configuration: 8008 CPU, 1K RAM (4K max), LED readout, front panel switches **Important Options:** cassette, magnetic tape, and oscilloscope interfaces; manual
Value: $850 to $2,500

Scelbi-8B (June 1975, early micro)
Original Retail Price: $499 kit, $849 assembled
Base Configuration: 8008 CPU, 1K RAM (16K max), LED readout, front panel switches, programming manuals **Important Options:** cassette, oscilloscope, keyboard, and TTY interfaces; assembler; text editor; monitor software
Value: $750 to $2,200

Scelbi Computer Consulting Inc. (Milford, Connecticut)

Like the Altair 8800, the Scelbi-8H and 8B were innovative in the way they were packaged. They came as a complete, upgradeable units and had enough software tools for hobbyists to program useful applications. Scelbi supported the systems well with interfaces that allowed owners to add a variety of third-party peripherals.

Many of the early computer hobbyists were ham radio operators. They would program the systems to control repeater stations and other ham equipment. Scelbi made a point of targeting hams in its advertising, touting its ability to send Morse code and send/receive data.

Scelbi-8H and 8B systems are rare today and treasured by enthusiasts. The company eventually switched to a software vendor, selling programming tools for 8008 and 8080 systems.

An important but rare early microcomputer, the Scelbi 8B ($750 to $2,200).

Seals Electronics (Concord, Tennessee)

The main chassis of the PUP-1 (Peripheral Universal Processor) slid out of the back of the enclosure for easy access.

Seals Electronics PUP-1 (1977, early micro)
Base Configuration: 2MHz Z80 CPU, DOS, 11 S-100 slots, 32K (512K max), two 5.25-inch floppy disk drives, two serial and two parallel ports, Extended BASIC **Important Options:** 4MHZ Z80 CPU
Value: $75 to $200

Seequa Computer Corp. (Odenton, Maryland)

A Chameleon Plus model offered dual floppy drives, 256K RAM, better compatibility with PC software, and the Condor I and Perfect Speller applications. Seequa also offered several PC-compatible desktop models.

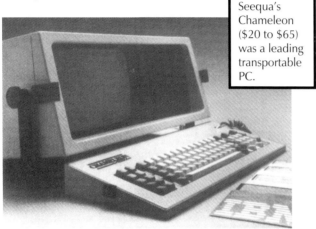

Seequa's Chameleon ($20 to $65) was a leading transportable PC.

Seequa Chameleon (1983, transportable PC)
Original Retail Price: $1,995 to $2,895
Base Configuration: 5MHz 8088 and 2.5MHz Z80A CPUs; MS-DOS; 128K RAM (256K max); 16K ROM integral 9-inch monochrome CRT display; keyboard/keypad; RS-232C, parallel, and RGB video ports; M-BASIC-86; PerfectCalc and PerfectWriter; user's manual **Video:** 640 x 200 graphics **Size/Weight:** 8 x 18 x 15.5 inches, 28 lbs. **Important Options:** CP/M-80 or CP/M-86, second 5.25-inch floppy disk drive, 10MB hard disk drive, IEEE-488 and ADC/DAC ports

Value: $20 to $65

Sega Corp. (Japan)

The SC 3000H was also sold under the Yeno brand.

Sega SC-3000/SC-3000H (1983, home computer)
Base Configuration: 3.58MHz D780C-1 CPU; ROM cartridge slot; expansion port; 48K RAM; 32K ROM; TV and composite video ports; integral Chiclet-style keyboard (SC-3000)/integral keyboard (SC-3000H); serial, cassette, and two game ports; Sega BASIC **Video:** 25-line x 40-column text, 256 x 220 graphics, 16 colors
Value: $20 to $75

SEI Inc. (Northbrook, Illinois)

SEI CAT-100 (1983, Apple II-class desktop)
Original Retail Price: $850
Base Configuration: Z80 and 6502 CPUs, four Apple-compatible slots, 64K RAM, 5.25-inch floppy disk drive, composite video port, keyboard/keypad, game port **Video:** 280 x 92 graphics, six colors
Value: $10 to $40

Seiko Instruments Inc. (Japan)

The 5900B was designed for BASIC programmers, as each key had a BASIC command as an alternative value. The unit looked similar to an Hewlett-Packard HP-85.

One of the 9500's 8088 processors handled I/O chores while the other was dedicated to communications tasks.

Seiko 5900B (desktop)
Base Configuration: 8085A CPU; Seiko bus; 128K RAM; 2K ROM; 5.25-inch floppy disk drive; integral monochrome CRT, keyboard/keypad, and printer; RS-232C, GP-IB, and BCD ports; Seiko BASIC **Size/Weight:** 18.7 x 7.3 x 23 inches, 42.5 lbs.
Value: $17 to $45

The Seiko 5900B ($17 to $45) had an all-in-one design similar to that found on the Hewlett-Packard 80 series.

Seiko 7500 (desktop)
Base Configuration: 8085A CPU, Seiko bus, 64K RAM, 72K ROM, 5.25-inch floppy disk drive, integral monochrome CRT and keyboard/keypad, GP-IB and BCD ports, Seiko BASIC **Size/Weight:** 20.3 x 14.6 x 21.45 inches, 55.9 lbs.
Value: $17 to $45

Seiko 9500 (1983, desktop)
Base Configuration: 8086 and two 8088 CPUs, RMX/86, 256K RAM (512K max) **Video:** 512 x 480 graphics
Value: $17 to $50

The Seiko 9500 ($17 to $50) used three CPUs, one 8086 and two 8088s.

Sekon Systems Inc. (Santa Monica, California)

A dual-processor version of the Sekon 64, the Sekon 64Z, was Apple II compatible. The Sekon 64Z came in two configurations: a single unit with the keyboard integrated and a unit with dual floppy drive bays and a separate IBM-style keyboard.

Sekon 64 (desktop)
Original Retail Price: $695
Base Configuration: Z80 CPU, CP/M, seven Apple-compatible slots, 64K RAM, integral or separate keyboard/keypad **Video:** 40-column text **Important Options:** 6502 coprocessor, 5.25-inch floppy disk drive, 80-column card
Value: $15 to $40

Sharp Corp. (Osaka, Japan), Sharp Electronics Corp. (Paramus, New Jersey)

The MZ-80 series was Sharp's first microcomputer, introduced as early as 1979 (although some sources place it as late as 1981). It had several incarnations during its production run. The MZ-80K was first and featured an odd keyboard similar to the original Commodore PET. It was followed by the MZ-80C, which had a more standard keyboard. The MZ-80A (sold as the MZ-1200 in Japan) had an even better keyboard and a more streamlined design. Finally, the MZ-80B had a redesigned case that could more easily accommodate a floppy drive, and it had hi-res graphics capability.

Sharp replaced the MZ-80 series with the MZ-700 in 1983. It had a separate monitor but retained the built-in cassette recorder. The MZ-800 series supplanted the MZ-700 in 1985. It was partially compatible with the early MZ systems and could optionally run CP/M.

The Sharp X1 series aimed to bridge home computing and television technologies. It could function as both, and users could superimpose computer-generated images over TV images. Consumers could chose among three colors for the Model CZ-800C: snow white, rose red, and metallic silver. Only the latter two colors were available for the other models. The X1 line seems to have been developed for the Japanese market, but a few might have been sold in the U.S. through a California distributor. Sharp literature also refers to a C1 Microcomputer Television, but this was probably an early designation for the X1.

The MZ-700 series had three models: the MZ-711, MZ-721, and MZ-731. The MZ-711 used a TV for video and required a separate cassette recorder for storage. Both the MZ-721 and MZ-731 had cassette recorders built in, and the MZ-731 also had a built-in printer/plotter. The two MZ-3500 models were the MZ-3531 and MZ-3541.

Sharp MZ-80 Series (1979, desktop)
Base Configuration: Z80 CPU, integral monochrome CRT and keyboard, BASIC **Important Options:** external dual floppy disk drives
Value: $25 to $140

Sharp MZ-700 Series (1983, desktop)
Base Configuration: Z80A CPU, 64K RAM, 4K ROM, integral keyboard **Size/Weight:** 17.2 x 11.9 x 3.4 inches, 7.9 lbs. **Important Options:** integral cassette recorder, integral printer
Value: $15 to $40

The Sharp MZ-700 ($15 to $40) was an important system, particularly in Asia and Europe.

Sharp MZ-800 Series (1985, desktop)
Base Configuration: 3.5MHz Z80A CPU, 64K RAM, 16K ROM, RGB video port, integral cassette recorder and keyboard, parallel and two game ports, three-voice sound **Video:** 25-line x 80-column text, 640 x 200 graphics, four colors **Important Options:** CP/M, external 5.25-inch floppy disk drive, 2.8-inch Quick disk drive
Value: $15 to $40

Sharp MZ-3500 Series (desktop)
Base Configuration: Z80A CPU, 128K RAM (256K max), 8K ROM, keyboard/keypad, RS-232C and GP-IB ports **Video:** 640 x 400 graphics **Size/Weight:** 18.3 x 14.6 x 5.7 inches, 26.4 lbs.
Value: $15 to $40

The CP/M-based Sharp MZ-3500 ($15 to $40).

Sharp MZ-5500 Personal Computer (1983, desktop)
Original Retail Price: $1,285 to $1,730
Base Configuration: 5MHz 8086 CPU, CP/M-86, 256K RAM (512K max), 5.25-inch floppy disk drive, 12-inch monochrome monitor, keyboard/keypad, two RS-232C and one parallel port, BASIC, sound generator **Important Options:** MS-DOS, expansion unit, second 5.25-inch floppy disk drive, 10MB hard disk drive, 12-inch color monitor, mouse
Value: $15 to $45

Sharp YX-3200 Business Computer
(Oct. 1980, desktop)
Original Retail Price: $6,000
Base Configuration: Z80 CPU, 64K RAM (128K max), 32K ROM (72K max), two 5.25-inch floppy disk drives, 12-inch monochrome monitor, program generator, BASIC, printer **Video:** 24-line x 80-column text
Value: $17 to $45

The Sharp YX-3200 Business Computer ($17 to $45).

Who says a computer has to be beige?
"Rose red" suits this Sharp X1 ($17 to $45) just fine.

Sharp X1 Series (1982, desktop)
Base Configuration: 4MHz Z80A CPU, 64K RAM, 6K ROM, integral cassette drive, CZ-800D or CZ-801D 14-inch color TV, RGB video port, keyboard/keypad, parallel and two game ports, Sharp-Hu BASIC, sound synthesizer **Video:** 25-line x 80-column text, 640 x 200 graphics **Size/Weight:** 15.4 x 13.1 x 4.25 or 16.5 x 13.5 x 4.5 inches **Important Options:** expansion chassis, integral printer **Value:** $17 to $45

Sharp OA-8100 (late 1983, desktop)
Base Configuration: 68000 CPU, Unix System III, 512K RAM (4MB max), 5.25-inch floppy disk drive, keyboard/keypad, RS-232C and Ethernet ports **Video:** 1152 x 750 graphics, 16 colors **Important Options:** 10- to 135MB hard disk drive, second 5.25-inch floppy disk drive, color monitor **Value:** $12 to $35

Sharp MZ-6500 (1984, desktop PC)
Original Retail Price: $2,800
Base Configuration: 8MHz 8086-2 CPU, MS-DOS and CP/M-86, 512K RAM, two 5.25-inch floppy disk drives, keyboard/keypad, two RS-232C ports, BASIC, application suite **Important Options:** 10MB hard disk drive
Value: $15 to $45

Sharp's MZ-6500 ($15 to $45) desktop PC had an interesting tower enclosure. This is the Model 50 HD with a hard drive.
Photo courtesy of Sellam Ismail, Vintage Computer Festival.

Sharp PC-7500 (desktop PC)
Base Configuration: 8MHz 80286, MS-DOS 3.1, 512K RAM (1MB max), 5.25-inch floppy disk drive, keyboard/keypad, serial and parallel ports, GW-BASIC 3.1 **Important Options:** second 5.25-inch floppy disk drive, 20MB hard disk drive, monochrome or color monitor **Value:** $10 to $35

Sharp's PC-7500 ($10 to $35) was one of the company's first PC-compatible offerings.

Sharp PC-7000 Series Compact Personal Computer (1985, transportable PC)
Original Retail Price: $1,995 to $2,995
Base Configuration: 7.27MHz 80C86-2 CPU, MS-DOS 2.11, 320K RAM (740K max), 5.25-inch floppy disk drive, 20MB hard disk drive, monochrome ELD, keyboard/keypad, RS-232C and parallel ports
Video: 25-line x 80-column text, 640 x 200 graphics **Size/Weight:** 16.1 x 6.3 x 8.5 inches, 20.6 lbs.
Important Options: expansion unit, CGA card, GW-BASIC, internal modem, printer, carrying case
Value: $7 to $25

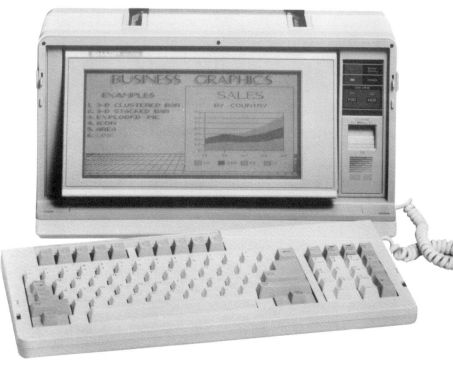

Sharp opted for a lunchbox-style for its PC-compatible portable PC-7100 HD ($7 to $25).

Sharp PC-7200 Compact Personal Computer
(1987, transportable PC)
Original Retail Price: $2,995 to $3,995
Base Configuration: 10MHz 80286, MS-DOS 3.2, ISA slot, 640K RAM (1.6MB max), 5.25-inch floppy disk drive, monochrome ELD, RGB video port, keyboard/keypad, RS-232C and parallel ports, GW-BASIC 3.2 **Video:** 25-line x 80-column text, 640 x 200 CGA graphics **Size/Weight:** 16.1 x 9.5 x 6.25 inches, 21 lbs. **Important Options:** expansion unit, second 5.25-inch floppy disk drive, 20MB or 40MB hard disk drive, internal modem, carrying case, CE-700P printer
Value: $5 to $25

Sharp PC-5000 Portable Computer
(Nov. 1983, laptop)
Original Retail Price: $1,995
Base Configuration: 80C88 CPU; MS-DOS 2.0; two expansion slots; 128K RAM (256K max), 192K ROM; monochrome LCD; integral keyboard; RS-232C, parallel, and cassette ports; BASIC; battery pack; AC adapter **Video:** 8-line x 80-column text, 640 x 80 graphics **Size/Weight:** 12.75 x 12 x 3.5 inches, 11 lbs. **Important Options:** dual external 5.25-inch floppy disk drives, 128K to 256K bubble memory, internal modem, integral CE-150 printer
Value: $50 to $175

When introduced in 1983, the Sharp PC-5000 ($50 to $175) was ahead of its time.

Sharp PC-4500 Series (1987, laptop PC)
Original Retail Price: $995 to $3,195
Base Configuration: 7.16MHz 80188-compatible CPU, MS-DOS 2.11, two expansion slots, 256K RAM (640K max) and 32K ROM, 3.5-inch floppy disk drive, monochrome LCD, parallel port, lead-acid battery pack, AC adapter **Video:** 25-line x 80-character text **Size/Weight:** 12.12 x 3 x 13.75 inches, 10 lbs. **Important Options:** MS-DOS 3.2, second 3.5-inch floppy disk drive, external 5.25-inch floppy disk drive, 20MB hard disk drive, GW-BASIC 3.2
Value: $8 to $30

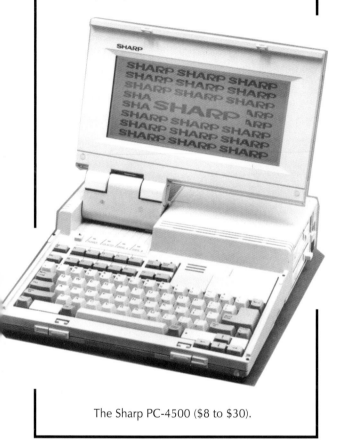

The Sharp PC-4500 ($8 to $30).

Silicon Valley Micro Inc.

Silicon Valley Micro introduced both models listed below at the 1983 Fall Comdex show, and they were two of a very few microcomputers to use the National Semiconductor 32032 CPU.

Silicon Valley Micro $5000 Model/$10,000 Model
(late 1983, transportable)
Original Retail Price: $5000/$10,000
Base Configuration: NS32032 and 8080 CPUs, Unix and MS-DOS, 512K RAM (2MB max), two 5.25-inch floppy disk drives, 140MB hard disk drive ($10,000 Model), tape backup drive ($10,000 Model) integral 9-inch monochrome CRT display, serial and parallel ports, thermal printer **Video:** 25-line x 80-column text
Value: $17 to $75

Sinclair Research Ltd. (Cambridge, U.K.)

Clive Sinclair's company made microcomputers affordable for the masses. At just under $200, the ZX80 allowed many students and other people of limited means to learn about computing. By 1984, Sinclair had sold 2 million computers, including all models, worldwide. Sinclair's success earned him a knighthood.

At one point, Sinclair was selling more computers per month than Apple, Commodore, or Tandy/Radio Shack. The company sold 250,000 ZX81s worldwide in the first 10 months of production, with 50,000 of those sales in the U.S. The company hit hard times by 1985, however, and was forced to consider buyout offers as unsold inventory began to fill warehouses. Amstrad purchased the rights to the Sinclair line.

Sinclair sold more than100,000 ZX80s. The ZX80 inspired several clones, including the $150 (in kit form) MicroAce. ZX80s had the habit of blanking the screen while performing background tasks, so don't be concerned if this happens with yours.

It wasn't a lot of computer—it had a lousy membrane keyboard and only 1K RAM—but at $150 the ZX81 was the only one that many people could afford. The ZX81 was a great teaching computer, especially in kit form. It wasn't unusual for Sinclair owners, after building and learning to program their ZX81s, to start a new career in the computer field. Timex, which manufactured the ZX81 for Sinclair at its plant in Scotland, sold the system in the U.S. under its own brand as the Timex Sinclair 1000. Mitsui sold the ZX81 in Japan. A number of ZX81 clones were made, including the Lambda IQ 8300, Prologica CP 200S, and the Your Computer. Unbuilt ZX81 kits appear from time to time, although reviewers of the system recommended against novices assembling them. ZX80s and ZX81s without the memory expansion modules are capable of very little, so look for units with the option.

Sinclair sold 100,000 ZX Spectrums in the first nine months of its production in the U.K. alone. The Spectrum was sold in the U.S. by Timex as the Timex Sinclair 2000. Many Spectrum clones were made around the world, including the, Microdigital TK85 (Brazil), Inves Spectrum+ (Spain), and from Russia the Hobbit, Robik, Peters MC 64, and Spektr 48.

In 1984, Sinclair introduced the ZX Spectrum+, which replaced the Chiclet keyboard with the full-travel keyboard used on the QL. It also came with 48K RAM standard. A year later, Sinclair replaced the Spectrum+ with the ZX Spectrum 128. This was the first significant revision of the Spectrum line since its introduction. Aside from a boost in memory capacity, the Spectrum 128 had vastly improved sound capability, including MIDI output. Sinclair sold the Spectrum 128 for about a year before replacing it with the ZX Spectrum +2.

The Spectrum +2 was the first computer produced under Amstrad, and it had a form factor similar to the Amstrad CPC-464. The motherboard, however, was a slightly modified version of the one used in the Spectrum 128. Spectrum +2A and +2B were later available. They were essentially cassette-based Spectrum +3s. The original Spectrum +2 had a grey case, while the +2A and +2B had black cases.

The most obvious change that the +3 made to the Spectrum line was a built-in three-inch floppy drive. The +3 used an operating system similar to the one used on Amstrad's CPC line. The company also redesigned the motherboard and revised the system ROMs, but maintained software compatibility with all previous Spectrum models.

Priced like a home computer, the QL (for Quantum Leap) was aimed at a small-business market. It used the 32-bit 68008 processor, which is the same processor used in the original Macintosh but with only an 8-bit data bus. The Microdrive was a Sinclair-designed tape storage device with a capacity of about 100K per cartridge. QDOS was Sinclair's multitasking operating system based on its own SuperBASIC programming language. British Telecom produced an enhanced version of the QL called the Merlin Tonto.

Sinclair's lone PC-compatible model was the PC-200, a relabeled Amstrad PC-20.

Sinclair ZX80

(1980, home computer)
Original Retail Price: $200
Base Configuration: Z80A CPU, 1K RAM (16K max),
TV video interface, integral membrane keyboard,
BASIC, AC adapter, manual **Video:** 24-line x 32-
column text **Size/Weight:** 6.5 x 8.5 x 1.5 inches, 12
oz. **Important Options:** enhanced BASIC
Value: $75 to $275

Although it had limited capabilities, the Sinclair ZX80 ($75 to $275)
made computing affordable for thousands of people.

Sinclair ZX81

(1981, home computer)
Original Retail Price: $100 kit, $150 assembled
Base Configuration: 3.5MHz Z80A CPU, 1K RAM
(16K max), 8K ROM, integral, TV video port, mem-
brane keyboard, BASIC, programming course, AC
adapter **Video:** 24-line x 32-column text
Size/Weight: 6 x 6.5 x 1.5 inches, 12 oz.
Important Options: ZX Printer
Value: $5 to $40

The Sinclair ZX81
($5 to $40) was cheaper
and better than the ZX80,
and sold in the millions worldwide.

Sinclair ZX Spectrum

(April 1982, home computer)
Original Retail Price: £125 to £175
Base Configuration: 3.5MHz Z80A CPU, expansion
port, 16K RAM (48K max), integral Chiclet-style keyboard, cassette port, ZX Spectrum BASIC, BASIC and
owner's manuals **Video:** 24-line x 32-column text,
256 x 192 graphics, eight colors **Size/Weight:** 9.2 x
5.7 x 1.2 inches **Important Options:** Microdrive,
RS-232 interface, ZX printer
Value: $10 to $45

The Sinclair ZX Spectrum ($10 to $45) had limited color capabilities.

Sinclair ZX Spectrum + (1984, home computer)
Base Configuration: 3.5MHz Z80A CPU, expansion slot, 48K RAM, 16K ROM, RF video port, integral keyboard, cassette port, Sinclair BASIC, AC adapter **Video:** 24-line x 32-column text, 256 x 192 graphics, eight colors
Value: $10 to $45

Sinclair ZX Spectrum 128 (1985, home computer)
Base Configuration: 3.5MHz Z80A CPU; expansion slot; 128K RAM; 32K ROM; RGB video port; integral keyboard; RS-232, keypad, cassette, and MIDI ports; Sinclair BASIC; AC adapter; three-voice sound **Video:** 24-line x 32-column text, 256 x 192 graphics, eight colors
Size/Weight: 12.5 x 5.9 x 1.8 inches
Value: $12 to $50

Sinclair ZX Spectrum +2 (1986, home computer)
Base Configuration: 3.5MHz Z80A CPU; expansion slot; 128K RAM; integral cassette recorder; PAL and RGB video ports; integral keyboard; RS-232, parallel, two game, and MIDI ports; Sinclair BASIC; three-voice sound; AC adapter **Video:** 24-line x 32-column text, 256 x 192 graphics, eight colors **Size/Weight:** 17.2 x 6.8 x 2.1 inches
Value: $5 to $25

Sinclair ZX Spectrum +3 (1987, home computer)
Original Retail Price: £249
Base Configuration: 3.5MHz Z80A CPU; +3DOS; expansion slot; 128K RAM; 64K ROM; 3-inch floppy disk drive; RGB and PAL video ports; integral keyboard; RS-232, parallel, two game, cassette, and MIDI ports; Sinclair and ZX+3 BASIC; AC adapter; three-voice sound **Video:** 24-line x 32-column text, 256 x 192 graphics, eight colors **Size/Weight:** 17.2 x 6.8 x 2 inches **Important Options:** second floppy disk drive
Value: $5 to $25

Sinclair QL (April 1984, desktop)
Original Retail Price: $499
Base Configuration: 7.5MHz 68008 CPU; QDOS; expansion and one ROM cartridge slot; 128K RAM (640K max), 32K ROM (64K max); two Microdrives; TV and RGB video ports; integral keyboard; two RS-232C, two game, and two network ports; SuperBASIC; application suite **Video:** 25-line x 85-column text, 512 x 256 graphics **Size/Weight:** 5.37 x 1.75 x 18.75 inches, 3 lbs. **Important Options:** hard disk drive, parallel and IEEE-488 interfaces, modem, ADC converter
Value: $20 to $85

Sirius Systems Technology (see "Victor Technologies")

Smoke Signal Broadcasting (Hollywood, California)
Smoke Signal Broadcasting would become an important early manufacturer of multi-user systems.

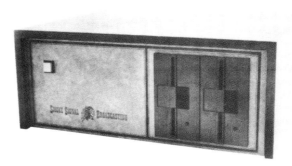

Smoke Signal Broadcasting's Chieftain ($100 to $325) was one of the best SS-50 systems made.

Smoke Signal Broadcasting Chieftain (1978, early micro)
Original Retail Price: $2,595
Base Configuration: 6800 CPU, DOS-68, SS-50 bus, 32K RAM (60K max), two 5.25-inch floppy disk drives, two serial ports **Important Options:** 8-inch floppy disk drive
Value: $100 to $325

Sinclair hoped that the QL ($20 to $85would catch on with business. It didn't, and examples are uncommon finds today.

Sony Corp. of America (Park Ridge, New Jersey)

Sony invented the 3.5-inch floppy disk drive, and its first computer, the SMC-70, was the first to use them. In fact, the SMC-70 might have been the only CP/M system to use the smaller storage devices as standard equipment. Other small form-factor drives were produced at the time, but Sony's design was eventually accepted as standard. Sony also offered the SMC-70G, which had enhanced graphics/imaging capability and was designed to work with video editing systems.

Sony Filer was an operating system compatible with CP/M 1.4. The SMC-777 was the last non-MSX home computer Sony produced. Units with enhanced color graphics capability were designated the SMC-777C.

The company produced many MSX models, all with the nickname "HiTBiT," which comes from the Japanese word for "people," *hitobito*. Sony offered the HiTBiT in several color choices. The HB-55P and HB-75P seem to be the most common examples today. The "P" designation refers to a model sold internationally.

Sony SMC-70 (July 1983, desktop)
Original Retail Price: $1,475
Base Configuration: 4MHz Z80A CPU; CP/M 2.2; two proprietary expansion slots; 64K RAM (256K max); 32K ROM; TV, RGB, and composite video ports; keyboard; RS-232C, parallel, light-pen, and cassette ports; Sony BASIC **Video:** 25-line x 80-column text, 640 x 400 graphics, 16 colors **Size/Weight:** 14.5 x 17.5 x 3.5 inches, 10.5 lbs. **Important Options:** 8086 coprocessor, expansion box, one or two 3.5- or 8-inch floppy disk drives, hard disk drive, 12-inch monochrome or color monitor, keypad, SMI-7020 printer, 256K memory cache
Value: $55 to $100

Sony SMC-777 (late 1983, home computer)
Original Retail Price: $650
Base Configuration: Z80A CPU, Sony Filer, 64K RAM, 3.5-inch floppy disk drive, RF modulator, TV video port, integral keyboard and touchpad pointing device, BASIC, sound generator **Video:** 25-line x 80-column text, 640 x 200 graphics, 16 colors **Important Options:** external 3.5-inch floppy disk drive, graphics upgrade
Value: $15 to $45

Sony's SMC-777 ($15 to $45) home computer.

Sony SMC-2000 (desktop PC)
Base Configuration: 6MHz 80186 CPU; MS-DOS; 256K RAM (512K max); 64K ROM; 3.5-inch floppy disk drive; RGB video port; keyboard/keypad; RS-232C, parallel, and light-pen ports **Video:** 640 x 400 graphics, 16 colors **Important Options:** mouse, IEEE-488 interface
Value: $10 to $30

The SMC-70 ($55 to $100) was a popular CP/M system. The example shown here has the optional expansion box.

Sony M35 (1986, laptop PC)
Original Retail Price: $2,695
Base Configuration: 80C88 CPU, MS-DOS, 640K RAM, two 3.5-inch floppy disk drives, monochrome LCD, RGB and composite video ports, integral keyboard, serial and parallel ports, internal modem **Size/Weight:** 13 lbs. **Important Options:** external 5.25-inch floppy disk drive, 25-line LCD
Value: $5 to $25

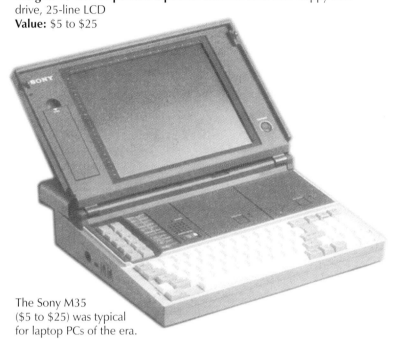

The Sony M35 ($5 to $25) was typical for laptop PCs of the era.

Sony HB-55P/HB75P HiTBiT (late 1983, MSX home computer)
Original Retail Price: $230
Base Configuration: Z80 CPU, ROM cartridge slot, 16K RAM (HB-55P)/64K RAM (HB-75P), composite video port, integral keyboard, parallel port, MSX BASIC **Video:** 24-line x 40-column text, 256 x 192 graphics
Value: $15 to $50

Sord Computer Corp. (Tokyo, Japan)

As early as 1974, Sord was selling a microcomputer—the SM80X—in Japan. By the time Sord began exporting its products to the U.S. in the early 1980s, it had captured about 7 percent of the Japanese computer market. The name Sord was a quasi-acronym for "SOftware/haRDware."

Sord sold the M5 in two configurations with different software offerings. The M5 Fun Computer was designed for games and came with the BASIC-I cartridge, while the M5 Multi-Computer was for users interested in both games and productivity applications. It came with the M5 FALC spreadsheet program, BASIC-G, and a carrying case.

Although sold as a portable, the M23P wasn't much different from most other 8-bit micros—an all-in-one unit with a small flip-up LCD.

The Z80A coprocessor in the M68 allowed it to run 8-bit software, or it could be configured as an I/O processor. Fuji-Xerox sold an OEM version of the M68.

The key feature of the M343 was its outstanding graphics capability. The M343SX used a modular rather than the integrated design found with other M343 systems. It could serve as either a single- or multi-user system. Sord also sold the M343SX jr. on an OEM basis either as a complete computer or just the system boards.

Sord later sold a version of the IS-11 Consultant with an 80-column display.

Sord M23 (1979, desktop)
Base Configuration: 4MHz Z80A CPU, Sord Operating System, two expansion slots, 128K RAM, 5.25-inch floppy disk drive, integral keyboard/keypad, two RS-232C and one parallel port, PIPS spreadsheet, BASIC **Video:** 25-line x 80-column text, 640 x 256 graphics, eight colors **Size/Weight:** 16.6 x 4.15 x 11.15 inches, 8.4 lbs. **Important Options:** SB-80, second 5.25-inch floppy disk drive, external dual 8-inch floppy disk drives, external 7.5MB hard disk drive, 12-inch monochrome or 14-inch color monitor
Value: $35 to $75

Sord M23P (1983, transportable)
Original Retail Price: $2,200
Base Configuration: 4MHz Z80A CPU, Sord Operating System, three expansion slots, two 3.5-inch floppy disk drives, monochrome LCD, integral keyboard/keypad, two RS-232C and one parallel port, PIPS spreadsheet, BASIC **Video:** 8-line x 80-column text, 640 x 256 graphics, eight colors **Size/Weight:** 17.25 x 5.15 x 15.5 inches, 16.5 lbs. **Important Options:** 8088 coprocessor; SB-80, UCSD p-System, or MS-DOS; 12-inch monochrome or 14-inch color monitor
Value: $20 to $55

Sony produced many different MSX-based HiTBiT systems ($15 to $50). This is one of the last, the MSX2+ HB-F1XDJ. *Photo courtesy of Sellam Ismail, Vintage Computer Festival.*

Sord M5 (1982, home computer)
Original Retail Price: $200
Base Configuration: Z80A CPU; ROM cartridge slot; 4K RAM (36K max), 8K ROM; TV video port; RF modulator; integral keyboard; parallel and cassette ports; M5 BASIC-I, BASIC-G, or BASIC-F, AC adapter **Video:** 25-line x 40-column text, 256 x 192 graphics, 16 colors **Size/Weight:** 10.3 x 7.3 x 1.4 inches, 1.75 lbs. **Important Options:** expansion box, RS-232C interface, game controllers, carrying case, battery pack
Value: $12 to $40

Hard to find in North America, the Sord M5 ($12 to $40) home computer had strong followings in Asia and Europe.

Sord M68/M68MX (1982 [M68]/1984 [M68MX], desktop)
Original Retail Price: $4,490 to $13,000 (M68)
Base Configuration: 10MHz 68000 and 4MHz Z80A (68000 only for M68MX); CP/M-68K; three expansion slots; 256K RAM (4MB max) plus 64K RAM and 4K ROM for the Z80A (M68)/512K RAM (3.5MB max) and 16K ROM (M68MX); one (M68MX) or two (M68) 5.25-inch floppy disk drives; RAM disk (M68MX); 20MB hard disk drive (68MX); 12-inch monochrome monitor; keyboard/keypad; two serial, parallel, and IEEE-488 ports (M68)/parallel port (M68MX); system manuals **Video:** 25-line x 80-column text, 640 x 400 graphics (M68)/640 x 500 graphics (M68MX), 16 colors **Size/Weight:** 18.9 x 15.7 x 4.7 inches, 33 lbs. **Important Options:** 7.5MB or 20MB hard disk drive (M68), 8-inch floppy disk drive (M68), color monitor (M68), mouse (M68MX)
Value: $18 to $55

Sord M243 Series (1983, desktop)
Base Configuration: 4MHz Z80A CPU; RDOS/RMDOS, MS-DOS, CP/M-86, or UCSD p-System; four S-100 slots; 192K RAM (1MB max); 5.25- or 8-inch floppy disk drive; integral 12-inch monochrome CRT; keyboard/keypad; four RS-232C and one parallel port; PIPS spreadsheet **Video:** 25-line x 80-column text, 640 x 400 graphics **Important Options:** second 5.25- or 8-inch floppy disk drive, 7.9MB hard disk drive, integral 12-inch color CRT
Value: $17 to $50

Sord M343 Series (1983, desktop)
Base Configuration: 5MHz 8086 CPU; RDOS/RMDOS, MS-DOS, CP/M-86, or UCSD p-System; four S-100 slots; 256K RAM (768K max); 5.25- or 8-inch floppy disk drive; integral 12-inch monochrome CRT; keyboard/keypad; four RS-232C and one parallel port; PIPS spreadsheet **Video:** 25-line x 80-column text, 640 x 400 graphics **Size/Weight:** 22.2 x 17.9 x 18.6 inches, 70 lbs. **Important Options:** second 5.25- or 8-inch floppy disk drive, 7.9MB hard disk drive, integral 12-inch color CRT
Value: $17 to $50

The Sord M68 ($18 to $55) was a well-made CP/M system.

Sord M343SX

(Nov. 1984, desktop PC)
Original Retail Price: $4,000
Base Configuration: 8086 CPU; MS-DOS, CP/M, UCSD p-System, or RMDOS; 256K RAM (6MB max); 5.25- or 8-inch floppy disk drive, 12-inch monochrome monitor, keyboard/keypad
Video: 720 x 500 graphics **Important Options:** 20MB hard disk drive, 14-inch color monitor
Value: $10 to $32

Sord's M343SX ($10 to fered four options for a ating system, includir DOS and CP/M.

Sord M343SX jr. (1984, desktop PC)
Base Configuration: 8088 CPU, MS-DOS, 256K RAM
Value: $7 to $27

Sord IS-11 Consultant

(April 1984, notebook)
Original Retail Price: $995
Base Configuration: Z80A CPU, TOS, 32K RAM (64K max), 128K ROM, integral microcassette drive, monochrome LCD, integral keyboard, RS-232C port, application suite in ROM, NiCad battery pack, AC adapter **Video:** 8-line x 40-column text **Size/Weight:** 11.75 x 8.45 x 1.45 inches, 4.4 lbs. **Important Options:** external floppy disk drive, monochrome monitor, keypad, data transfer utility, thermal printer, bar-code reader, internal modem
Value: $20 to $65

The Sord IS-11 Consultant ($20 to $65) had a built-in microcassette drive.

Sord IS-11C (1985, notebook)
Original Retail Price: $1,495
Base Configuration: 3.4MHz Z80A CPU; ROM cartridge slot; 80K RAM (144K max); 72K ROM; integral microcassette drive; monochrome LCD; integral keyboard; RS-232C, parallel, and bar-code reader ports; application suite; NiCad battery pack; AC adapter **Video:** 25-line x 80-column text, 640 x 200 graphics **Size/Weight:** 11.75 x 8.45 x 3.37 inches, 6.4 lbs. **Important Options:** 3.5-inch floppy disk drive, keypad, mouse, I-BASIC, printer
Value: $15 to $45

The Sord IS-IIC ($15 to $45) had similar electronics to the IS-11 Consultant, but offered a larger fold-up LCD.

Southwest Technical Products Corp. (SWTPC) (San Antonio, Texas)

The SWTPC 6800 was one of the first micros based on the 6800 processor, which eventually evolved to the 6809 used in the Tandy/Radio Shack Color Computer, and then the 68000 series that powered the Apple Macintosh. The SWTPC 6800 was heavily documented with large applications and programming manuals. MIKBUG was a rudimentary operating system in ROM from Motorola that allowed data entry immediately after turning on the computer. Other systems required you to first load the software that enabled data entry. Owners could use any ASCII terminal with the SWTPC 6800. The motherboard (marked MP-B) contains the slots that the other components plug into.

SWTPC created the SS-50 bus, which was cheaper and easier for hobbyists to build. Several other important computer makers adopted the SS-50 bus including Smoke Signal Broadcasting.

Spectravideo Inc. (Great Neck, New York)

Spectravideo produced several lines of well-regarded home computers in the early 1980s. It also produced a popular line of games for Atari systems under the Spectravision name. The company, like many others of the time, ran into difficulty in 1984 and was forced to sell a controlling interest to Bondwell Holding Ltd. of Hong Kong. The Spectravideo brand and products were discontinued, and a restructured company began selling Bondwell-branded PC-compatible laptop and desktop computers.

The SVI-728 was the first U.S.-made MSX computer.

SWTPC 6800 Computer System (Nov. 1975, early micro)
Original Retail Price: $450 kit
Base Configuration: 6800 CPU; 15 SS-50 slots; 2K RAM; serial interface; Mikbug; assembly, operation, and programming manuals; power supply **Size/Weight:** 15.13 x 7 x 15.25 inches **Important Options:** CT-1024 Video Terminal, MP-S serial and MP-L parallel interfaces
Value: $250 to $1,250

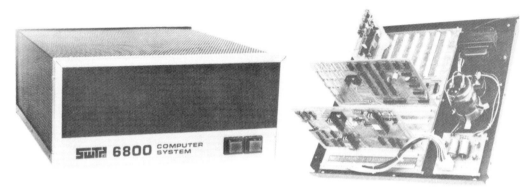

Perhaps the most popular 6800-based system of its time, the SWTPC 6800 ($250 to $1,250) is popular among enthusiasts today, too. On the right is a photo of the 6800's electronics.

Spectravideo SV-318 (1983, home computer)
Original Retail Price: $300
Base Configuration: Z80A CPU, CP/M, ROM cartridge slot, 32K RAM (256K max), 32K ROM (96K max), integral Chiclet-style keyboard, integral joystick, Extended BASIC, three-voice sound **Video:** 24-line x 40-column text, 256 x 192 graphics **Important Options:** MSX compatibility, SV-601 Super Expander, SV-902 5.25-inch floppy disk drive, SV-105 cassette recorder, mouse, SV-901 printer
Value: $20 to $85

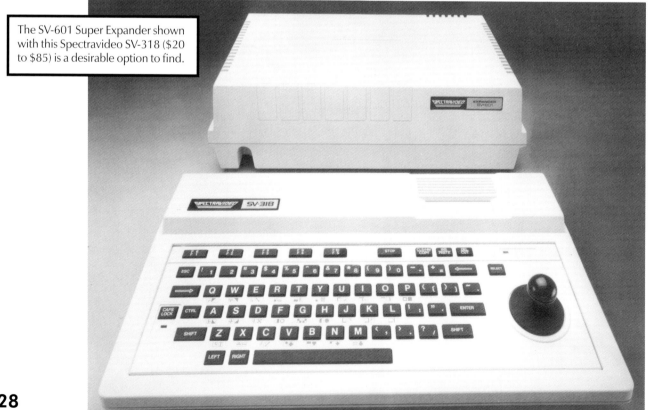

The SV-601 Super Expander shown with this Spectravideo SV-318 ($20 to $85) is a desirable option to find.

Spectravideo SV-328 (1983, home computer)
Original Retail Price: $595
Base Configuration: Z80A CPU, ROM cartridge port, 64K RAM (256K max), 48K ROM (96K max), TV video interface, integral keyboard/keypad, Super Extended Microsoft BASIC, word processing and terminal software, three-voice sound **Video:** 24-line x 80-column text, 256 x 192 graphics **Important Options:** SV-601 Super Expander, SV-902 5.25-inch floppy disk drive, SV-903 cassette recorder, mouse, SV-901 printer, SV-700 modem
Value: $30 to $85

The Spectravideo SV-328 ($30 to $85) was a great game system.

Spectravideo SVI-328 Mark II (1983, home computer)
Base Configuration: Z80A CPU, CP/M, ROM cartridge port, 80K RAM (144K max), 32K ROM (96K max), integral keyboard/keypad, word processor, Super Extended Microsoft BASIC, three-voice sound **Video:** 80-column text, 256 x 192 graphics **Important Options:** SV-601 Super Expander, SV-902 floppy disk drive, SVI-904 cassette recorder, mouse, SV-901 printer, SV-700 modem
Value: $17 to $40

Spectravideo SVI-728 (1983, MSX home computer)
Base Configuration: 3.6MHz Z80A CPU, ROM cartridge port, 80K RAM, 32K ROM (96K max), integral keyboard/keypad, parallel and cassette ports, three-voice sound **Video:** 24-line x 40-column text, 256 x 192 graphics, 16 colors **Important Options:** SVI-707 floppy disk drive, SVI-727 80-column cartridge, RS-232 interface, SVI-737 modem, SVI-101 joystick
Value: $25 to $65

Spectravideo MSX Xpress Model SVI-738
(Sept. 1985, MSX home computer)
Original Retail Price: $595
Base Configuration: 64K RAM, 3.5-inch floppy disk drive, integral keyboard **Video:** 80-column text
Value: $35 to $100

Sperry Corp. (Blue Bell, Pennsylvania)
The Sperry PC was manufactured by Mitsubishi in Japan and is the same system as the Leading Edge PC. One difference, however, is that Sperry provided better graphics and display options. Sperry sold its PC in a transportable configuration as well. Sperry merged with Burroughs in 1986 to form Unisys Corp.

Sperry Personal Computer (PC) (Jan. 1984, desktop PC)
Original Retail Price: $2,643 to $5,753
Base Configuration: 7.16MHz 8088 CPU, MS-DOS 1.25, seven ISA slots, 128K RAM (640K max), 5.25-inch floppy disk drive, 12-inch monochrome monitor, keyboard/keypad, serial and parallel ports, GW-BASIC, owner's and DOS manuals **Video:** 25-line x 80-column text, 640 x 200 graphics **Important Options:** MS-DOS 2.0, Xenix 3.0, second 5.25-inch floppy disk drive, 10MB hard disk drive, CGA card, 12- or 15-inch color monitor, Model 5 printer
Value: $12 to $45

Sphere Corp. (Bountiful, Utah)
Perhaps the most interesting aspect about this company's first computer, the Sphere 1, is how it marketed the system. Although the earliest ads targeted hobbyists, later advertising reached out to a more general consumer audience. It promoted using the Sphere 1 for the home and business to perform tasks such as balancing a checkbook or writing a resume. This effort pre-dated by nearly two years the first mass-marketing of microcomputers by Commodore, Tandy, and Apple. Apparently, the company believed that home and business users had deeper pockets, as it raised prices by more than $200 for each model.

A bit more expensive than the Altairs, Scelbis, and other competitors, the Sphere 1 did not sell in great numbers. They are rare and prized finds today.

The Sphere 1 was one of the first "modern" looking microcomputers. Hook it up to a TV and you have a system similar in its physical configuration to, say, a Commodore 64. Gone are the switches and LEDs that other systems of the era used for input and readout. Sphere offered a full line of peripherals including a floppy disk drive with a disk operating system—a luxury in 1975. In late 1975, the Sphere 2, 3, and 4 were introduced. All were based on the Sphere 1 and were packaged with different features. The Sphere 2 had a serial communications and a cassette or modem interface. The Sphere 3 added 20K of memory to the Sphere 2 configuration. The Sphere 4 replaced the cassette interface of the Sphere 3 with a dual IBM-compatible floppy disk drives. It also provided a disk operating system, BASIC, and a line printer. A One Card Computer was simply the bare Sphere 1 CPU board packaged for the hobbyist.

Sphere 1/Sphere 2/Sphere 3/Sphere 4 (1975, early micro)
Original Retail Price: $650 kit or $1,345 assembled (Sphere 1)/$1,499 (Sphere 2)/$2,250 (Sphere 3)/$7,995 (Sphere 4)
Base Configuration: 6800 CPU, 4K RAM (64K max), 1K PROM, TV video port, integral keyboard, cassette and modem ports, BASIC, Program Development System, monitor in ROM, operations and programming manuals **Video:** 512-character display **Important Options:** disk operating system, floppy disk drive, paper tape reader, serial port, line printer
Value: $100 to $750

Sphere was ahead of its time (1975) in how it marketed and packaged its Sphere I ($100 to $750) computer, but it's likely that very few were sold. *Reused with permission CMP Media LLC, Byte.com (Byte Magazine), Manhasset NY. All rights reserved.*

Sphere Micro-Sphere 200

(1976, early micro)
Original Retail Price: $860 to $1,645 assembled
Base Configuration: 6800 CPU, Sphere Cassette Operating System (SCOS), 4K RAM (8K max), cassette interface, integral keyboard, Advanced Program Development System, Monte Carlo game, operation manual **Video:** 16-line x 21-column text **Important Options:** 9-inch monochrome TV display, mouse
Value: $125 to $550

Stearns Computer Systems Corp. (Minneapolis, Minnesota)

The Desktop Computer was not fully IBM compatible. Although it had an ISA expansion slot, it could use only Stearns-supplied cards in it. Stearns shipped 110 systems in the first month of production, and anticipated sales of 10,000 for the first year.

Stearns Desktop Computer

(May 1983, desktop PC)
Original Retail Price: $2,945 to $5,650
Base Configuration: 8MHz 8086 CPU, MS-DOS 1.25, ISA slot, four proprietary expansion slots, 128K RAM (896K max), 16K ROM, 5.25-inch floppy disk drive, 12-inch monochrome monitor, keyboard/keypad, RS-232C port, owner's and MS-DOS manuals **Video:** 25-line x 80-column text **Size/Weight:** 5.5 x 21.7 x 15.7 inches, 33 lbs. **Important Options:** Concurrent CP/M, second 5.25-inch floppy disk drive, 5- to 20MB hard disk drive, 15-inch monochrome monitor, CGA card, parallel port
Value: $10 to $30

STM Electronics Corp. (Menlo Park, California)

The Pied Piper I was sold as a lightweight portable computer, but it's not a true portable without its own video display. A two-line LCD was available as an option.

The portable and desktop versions of the STM Personal Computer used similar enclosures. On the portable, the detachable keyboard attached to the case upside-down covering the LCD. A cover replaces the area where the LCD and keyboard attach on the desktop case.

STM's Pied Piper I ($20 to $55) was a video display-less portable.

STM Electronics Pied Piper I (March 1983, desktop)

Original Retail Price: $1,299
Base Configuration: 4MHz Z80A CPU, CP/M 2.2, two expansion slots, 64K RAM, 4K ROM, 5.25-inch floppy disk drive, TV video port, integral keyboard, parallel port, application suite **Video:** 24-line x 80-column text **Size/Weight:** 4 x 20.2 x 10.8 inches, 12.5 lbs. **Important Options:** second 5.25-inch floppy disk drive, 5- or 10MB hard disk drive, monochrome LCD, RS-232C interface, internal modem, integral printer
Value: $20 to $55

The Stearns Desktop Computer ($10 to $30) was designed so the keyboard could slide under the case when not in use.

STM Electronics Personal Computer

(April 1984, desktop PC)
Original Retail Price: $3,000 (transportable)/$2,500 (desktop)
Base Configuration: 8MHz 80186 CPU, MS-DOS 2.0, external expansion slot, 256K RAM (512K max), 8K ROM, two 5.25-inch floppy disk drives, monochrome LCD (portable), composite video port, keyboard/keypad, two serial and one parallel port, application suite, internal modem **Video:** 16-line x 84-column text (portable), 540 x 200 graphics **Size/Weight:** 20.3 x 10.8 x 4 inches, 17 lbs. (portable) **Important Options:** integral printer
Value: $15 to $45 (transportable)/$12 to $37 (desktop)

STM Electronics LapTop (1986, laptop PC)

Original Retail Price: $2,999
Base Configuration: 4.77MHz 80C88 CPU, ROM cartridge slot, 256K RAM (640K max), 3.5-inch floppy disk drive, monochrome ELD, integral keyboard/keypad, serial and parallel ports **Video:** 25-line x 80-column text, CGA **Important Options:** LapMate expansion unit, 384K bubble memory, backlit LCD, dual NiCad battery packs, AC adapter
Value: $8 to $30

STM Systems Inc.
(Mont Vernon, New Hampshire)

Byte magazine called the Baby! 1 the world's first portable computer, but it had more in common with the Commodore 64 than, say, the GRiD Compass. The main unit was unusually small and light, but required a separate monitor for display. Still, the Baby! 1 did push the size envelope and is a significant system.

STM Systems Baby! 1 (Aug. 1976, transportable)

Original Retail Price: $850 assembled
Base Configuration: 6502 CPU, 4K RAM (64K max), 1K ROM, cassette interface, video interface, integral keyboard, RS-232, serial, and four parallel ports, monitor in ROM, Tiny BASIC, TECO **Video:** 16-line x 32-column text **Size/Weight:** 14.75 x 10.63 x 3.63 inches, 10 lbs.
Value: $175 to $550

The portable version of the STM Electronics Personal Computer ($15 to $45). The desktop version replaced the LCD with a cover.

Strategic Technologies Inc.
(Norcross, Georgia)

The PC Traveler was built into a briefcase and had several advanced features. The company claimed to be the first to use a gas plasma display in a commercial microcomputer. The removeable disk cartridges were made by Amlyn, but were never widely used. Finding a cartridge today would be difficult. One of the PC Traveler's CPUs was devoted to I/O operations.

Strategic Technologies PC Traveler

(Nov. 1983, transportable PC)
Original Retail Price: $4,495
Base Configuration: two 80186 CPUs, MS-DOS 2.0, 128K RAM (1MB max), 6.2MB removeable disk cartridge, 9.25-inch monochrome gas plasma display, keyboard/keypad, GW-BASIC 2.0, integral printer
Video: 25-line x 80-column text, 256 x 128 graphics **Size/Weight:** 14 x 19 x 6 inches, 27 lbs. **Important Options:** CP/M-86, 5.25-inch floppy disk drive, internal modem
Value: $20 to $55

Built into a briefcase, the Strategic Technologies PC Traveler ($20 to $55) apparently was aimed at the executive with a hankering for the latest tech toys.

In an exceptionally small package for 1976, the STM Systems Baby! 1 ($175 to $550) was sold as a portable computer. The monitor and cassette recorder were not standard equipment.

Sumicom Inc. (Tustin, California)

Sumicom was a division of Japan's Sumitomo Corp., one of the largest companies in the world. It introduced the System 330 to the U.S. market in late 1983

.

Sumicom System 330 (1982, desktop)

Original Retail Price: $1,795 to $6,475
Base Configuration: 8088 CPU, CP/M-86 or MS-DOS, three expansion slots, 96K RAM (224K max), 16K ROM, 5.25- or 8-inch floppy disk drive, 12-inch monochrome monitor, keyboard/keypad, parallel port **Video:** 25-line x 80-column text, 640 x 400 graphics **Important Options:** expansion unit, second 5.25- or 8-inch floppy disk drive, 5MB or 16MB hard disk drive, RS-232C interface
Value: $12 to $35

Sumicom System 830 (1982, desktop)

Original Retail Price: $4,295 to $7,117
Base Configuration: 5MHz Z80B CPU, CP/M 2.2, three expansion slots, 128K RAM (256K max), two 8-inch floppy disk drives, integral 12-inch monochrome CRT, integral keyboard/keypad, RS-232C port, Enhanced BASIC, integral printer **Video:** 25-line x 80-column text, 640 x 400 graphics **Size/Weight:** 22 x 27.5 x 20 inches **Important Options:** 5MB or 16MB hard disk drive; integral 12-inch color CRT; parallel, IEEE-488, and DA/AD interfaces
Value: $12 to $40

Symbiotic Systems Inc. (Santa Cruz, California)

The main Stratos system and its separate keyboard were built into Teak enclosures. A nice touch, but wood makes a lousy RFI shield.

Symbiotic Systems Stratos (1981, desktop)

Base Configuration: Z80 CPU, CP/M 2.2, 80K RAM, two 5.25-inch floppy disk drives, keyboard/keypad, application suite
Value: $15 to $40

Synertek Systems Corp. (Sunnyvale, California)

The SYM-1 rhymed with KIM-1 and was hardware compatible with the popular system from MOS Technology.

Synertek SYM-1 (1977, computer trainer)

Base Configuration: expansion bus; 1K RAM (4K max); 4K ROM (24K max); integral membrane hex keypad; TV video, RS-232, TTY, and cassette interfaces; Supermon monitor in ROM
Value: $75 to $200

Tandy Corp. (Fort Worth, Texas)

When the Tandy brass gave the go-ahead to market the Model I, company president Lewis Kornfeld rationalized that if they didn't sell, the company would use them in its retail outlets. The initial run of 5,000 systems sold out quickly, and Tandy suddenly found itself in the computer business. Apple, Commodore, and Tandy fans will often argue about which company was first to mass market a personal computer, but the three were within a couple of months of each other with the edge going to Apple.

Although Tandy never formally designated its original TRS-80 system as such, "Model I" was the name by which everyone, including Tandy, called the computer. Tandy was notorious among electronics suppliers for negotiating the lowest possible prices, and that skill was no doubt a factor in the low price of the Model I. Legend has it that Tandy bought thousands of obsolete black-and-white TV components on the cheap and converted them for the Model I displays.

In the mid-1970s, Tandy was debating whether to manufacture and sell a microcomputer. One problem: The company lacked knowledge of the market. By chance, two Tandy executives walked into a computer store on the West Coast and met a young man named Steve Leininger. Leininger had a degree in electronics and a handle on the hobbyist market. Tandy eventually hired Leininger and moved him to Texas, where he designed the TRS-80 Microcomputer System. By 1979, Tandy had sold 100,000 of them. Tandy discontinued the Model I at the end of 1980.

The original TRS-80 is the most sought-after, and desirable options such as the Expansion Interface (which, among other things, allowed for up to 48K RAM), monitor, and floppy drive can push values to $300 or more. The earliest models had only a keyboard, but by 1978 Tandy was selling the Model I with a keyboard/keypad. The edge connectors on the main unit and Expansion Interface were prone to corrosion. If you find a system or peripheral that doesn't work, clean the connectors and try again. Rubbing the connector with a pencil eraser often does the trick.

The Model III is an all-in-one system that is software compatible with the Model I. Improvements over the Model I include a built-in power supply, 1,500-baud cassette I/O mode, and a more robust BASIC in ROM. It's more common to find Model IIIs with floppy drives than without. Check the monitor of examples you find to make sure it is secure. Sharp jolts to the system often broke the internal plastic mounts.

The most noticeable difference between the Model III and Model 4 is the switch from a silver-grey color to "fawn grey" (more off-white than grey) for the case. The new finish doesn't wear off as easily as the silver-grey paint, but it collects dirt. Cleaning the off-white models is complicated by the textured surface. Tip: Use a mild spray-on cleaner and let it soak; then gently wipe it clean in a circular motion. Harsh chemicals and brute force will damage the surface.

The TRS-80 Model 4P was a Model 4 reconfigured as a portable. It was a durable system with a proven, stable design. The detachable cover that holds the keyboard during transport is sometimes lost on examples found today. All versions of the Model 4 could run the software of its predecessor in Model III mode.

The Model 4D was the last of the TRSDOS-based line. It was a regular Model 4 with dual floppy drives, 64K RAM, the DeskMate application suite, and an RS-232C interface as standard. By the time the 4D was introduced, the TRS-80 line was a small part of Tandy's computer business. Tandy sold only 3,750 TRSDOS systems in the first quarter of 1986, for example.

Tandy introduced the Model II as a more serious business system, and did a good job of providing software support for it. Taranto & Associates sold Model IIs under its own brand with its suite of business software pre-installed. The Model 12 was compatible with the Model II and could be upgraded to the Model 16B multi-user system. Tandy released a Model 16B in 1983 that was primarily a multi-user system. The Tandy 6000, a multi-user system running Xenix, eventually replaced the Model 16.

In terms of fanatical devotion, Color Computer (or CoCo, as it was commonly referred to) owners were second to none. The computer, designed by a young engineer by the name of Dale Chatham, didn't appear that special, but it had what was arguably the most powerful 8-bit processor available at the time, a good implementation of BASIC, and much potential for expansion. With the optional Extended Color BASIC, the CoCo could display 256 x 192 graphics.

Tandy rarely released sales figures, but it is believed that the company sold several million CoCos of all types, and they are common and inexpensive today. Peripherals and software are plentiful, too, which makes the CoCo a great hobby computer today. A Multi-Pak Interface, which allows for system expansion, and the floppy drives might cost more today than the main system, but they make the CoCo much more usable. In late 1980, Tandy introduced a 16K model with Extended Color BASIC as standard.

The 64K CoCo was a short-run transition model between the original system and the Color Computer 2. It came in two forms: the old-style silver/grey color with a badge labeled "64K" on the right of the keyboard area, and with an off-white old-style case with the label above the keyboard. Few were made, and it is the rarest CoCo.

The CoCo 2 and 3 were arguably the best deal of the day in a low-cost computer. With the optional OS-9 operating system and memory expansion, their capabilities and performance rivaled that of some 16-bit systems. They even had multitasking and multi-user capabilities, but were also backward-compatible with the original CoCo. Even today, these systems are fun to use and make a great starter collectible. Availability for both the Color Computer 2 and 3 are high and prices are low. Tandy sold 36,000 CoCo 2s in the first quarter of 1986.

The CoCo 3 had a faster processor and better graphics than the CoCo 2. It also broke the 64K barrier for the CoCo with a maximum memory capacity of 512K, giving the powerful OS-9 operating system some breathing room. Tandy apparently produced more Color Computer 3s than it could easily sell, and by the late 1980s was discounting them heavily. It's not uncommon to find little used or unused examples still in their original boxes.

The MC-10 was a belated and short-lived attempt to offer an even less-expensive Color Computer to compete with the Timex Sinclair systems. Matra Hachette sold the same system in Europe as the Alice.

Although the 2000 ran MS-DOS, it was not fully PC-compatible. Programs that were written to accommodate the PC hardware specifications would not run on the 2000 without modification. Those applications that did work on the 2000 ran faster and sometimes looked better than on the IBM PC. In October 1986, Tandy sold off its remaining 2000 inventory in a blow-out sale.

The Tandy 1200, however, was your classic PC XT-compatible. Systems sold with hard drives were labeled Tandy 1200HD, which was actually introduced before the floppy-drive-only 1200. The latter first appeared in November 1985. When Tandy announced the 3000 HL in July 1986, the 1200 models were designated SOWG (sold out when gone), Tandy's euphemism for "discontinued."

Much to the alarm of the TRSDOS faithful, the Tandy 1000 was a rousing success. In 1985, research firm Future Computing ranked it as the top-selling low-cost PC compatible, and Tandy put 1000 unit sales at 125,000 for that year alone. Production ended in July 1986.

Although the TRS-80 Model 2000 appeared earlier, the Tandy 1000 represented the company's shift from its proprietary TRSDOS systems to true PC compatibility. For the first time, the TRS-80 label disappeared from a Tandy computer's brand name. Systems sold with hard drives were labeled Tandy 1000HD. Today, the Tandy 1000 is an inexpensive collectible, although many have become separated from their monitors or keyboards. Also, the 1000 was not 100 percent hardware compatible with the PC; many PC-standard add-on boards won't work with it. If you get a Tandy 1000 from a school, look under the cover for a possible bonus: a Diamond Trackstar Apple II emulator board.

The 1000 EX was a reconfigured 1000 SX aimed at the home and school markets. Tandy decided to go with its proprietary PLUS expansion slots in the 1000 EX, which forced users to buy add-on boards from Tandy or a limited number of third-party vendors. Both the 1000 EX and 1000 SX were supposed to ship within a week of their July 30, 1986, announcement, but Tandy ran into trouble with FCC RFI (radio frequency interference) certification. The systems didn't ship until September.

The 1000 SX replaced the Tandy 1000 and provided greater compatibility with PC add-on cards and better overall performance. It was a good seller for Tandy. By January 1987, backorders for the system topped 30,000. Subsequent models included the 8086-based 1000 SL, the 8088-based 1000 HX, and the 80286-based 1000 TX. The latter two were launched in 1987. An 80286-based 1000 TL appeared in 1988 and was the last of the Tandy 1000 line.

The Tandy 3000 was the company's first IBM PC AT compatible and one of the top sellers in its class. Like many other manufacturers, it competed with IBM on price and performance, using a faster 80286 processor. Units sold with hard drives were designated Tandy 3000HD. The 3000 HL replaced the Tandy 1200.

Many people consider the Model 100 the first truly useable portable. The size of a hardcover book, it had a screen just large enough to do word processing or spreadsheet calculations. Reporters in particular grew fond and dependent on the Model 100, and many of the systems remained in use for years. In fact, part of the demand for the Model 100 today is from people looking to replace their worn-out units. Japan's Kyocera manufactured the Model 100 for Tandy.

An uncommon but desirable Model 100 option is the Disk/Video Interface, which provides one or two floppy drives and the option to use either a TV or a monitor for the display. Third-party ROMs containing more sophisticated software can enhance the value and usability of a Model 100. The system runs on four AA batteries. Tandy discontinued the Model 100 in June 1986. The smaller Tandy 102 replaced the Model 100, and it was functionally the same.

Tandy added a little thickness to the Model 100/102 design to accommodate a flip-up LCD in the 200. The result was a notebook computer better suited for common applications such as word processing and spreadsheets. Like the 100/102, the 200 runs off either an AC adapter or four AA batteries.

Tandy Radio Shack TRS-80 Microcomputer System (Model I) (Aug. 1977, desktop)
Original Retail Price: $400 to $600
Base Configuration: Z80 CPU, 4K RAM (16K max), 4K ROM (12K max), integral keyboard, Level I BASIC, user manual, AC adapter **Video:** 16-line x 64-column uppercase text, 128 x 48 graphics **Size/Weight:** 16.5 x 8 x 3.5 inches **Important Options:** TRS-80 Expansion Interface, CTR-41 cassette recorder, external 5.25-inch floppy disk drive with TRSDOS, 12-inch monochrome monitor, Level II BASIC, RS-232 interface, Modem I
Value: $20 to $125

A decked-out Tandy/Radio Shack TRS-80 Microcomputer System ($20 to $125), commonly called the Model I. The Expansion Interface, the monitor that sits atop it, the floppy drives, and the Line Printer were options.

Tandy Radio Shack TRS-80 Model III

(1980, desktop)
Original Retail Price: $699 to $2,495
Base Configuration: 2MHz Z80 CPU, 4K RAM (48K max), 4K ROM (14K max), integral 12-inch monochrome CRT and keyboard/keypad, Model III BASIC, parallel port
Video: 16-line x 64-column text **Important Options:** TRSDOS, 5.25-inch floppy disk drive, RS-232C interface, CTR-41 cassette recorder, modem
Value: $20 to $75

A dependable workhorse, the Tandy/Radio Shack TRS-80 Model III ($25 to $75).

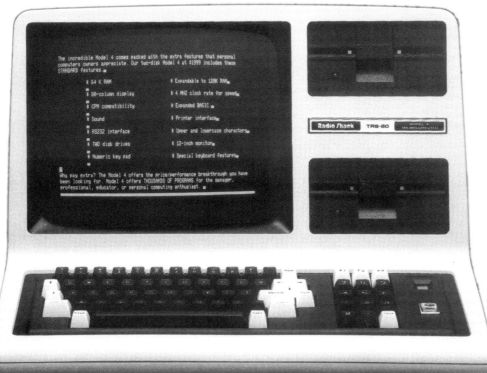

Tandy Radio Shack TRS-80 Model 4/Model 4D

(1983 [Model 4], desktop)
Original Retail Price: $999 to $1,999
Base Configuration: 4MHz Z80A CPU, 16K RAM (128K max), 14K ROM, integral 12-inch monochrome CRT and keyboard/keypad, Microsoft BASIC 5.0, parallel port, owner's and programming manuals, system introduction, reference card **Video:** 24-line x 80-column text
Size/Weight: 12.5 x 18.87 x 21.5 inches
Important Options: one or two 5.25-inch floppy disk drives, TRSDOS 6.0, cassette recorder, external 5- or 15MB hard disk drive, RS-232C interface, internal modem, DeskMate software
Value: $20 to $75

The Tandy/Radio Shack TRS80 Model 4 ($20 to $75) offered better performance and greater memory capacity than the Model III, not to mention a better-looking off-white case.

Tandy Radio Shack TRS-80 Model 4P

(Sept. 1983, transportable)
Original Retail Price: $1,799
Base Configuration: 4MHz Z80A, TRSDOS 6.0, 64K RAM (128K max), two 5.25-inch floppy disk drives, integral 9-inch monochrome CRT, keyboard/keypad, parallel port, Microsoft BASIC 5.0 **Video:** 24-line x 80-column text **Size/Weight:** 16.5 x 13.5 x 9.75 inches, 26 lbs. **Important Options:** CP/M Plus, high-resolution graphics, RS-232C port, internal modem
Value: $20 to $50

Tandy made only one transportable TRSDOS-based system, the TRS-80 Model 4P ($20 to $50).

134

Tandy Radio Shack TRS-80 Model II
(May 1979, desktop)
Original Retail Price: $3,450 to $3,899
Base Configuration: TRSDOS, 32K RAM (64K max), 8-inch floppy disk drive, integral 12-inch monochrome CRT, keyboard/keypad, two RS-232C and one parallel port, Level III BASIC
Video: 24-line x 80-column text **Important Options:** external 8-inch floppy disk drive, Line Printer II or III
Value: $25 to $85

Shown with the optional external Disk System, Line Printer III, and custom desk, the Tandy/Radio Shack TRS-80 Model II ($25 to $85).

Tandy Radio Shack TRS-80 Model 12
(Jan. 1983, desktop)
Original Retail Price: $2,799 to $3,499 **Base Configuration:** 4MHz Z80A CPU, TRSDOS 4.2, 80K RAM (144K max), 8-inch floppy disk drive, integral 12-inch monochrome CRT, keyboard/keypad, two RS-232C and one parallel port, Microsoft BASIC **Video:** 24-line x 80-column text, 640 x 240 graphics **Important Options:** CP/M Plus, six-slot card cage, second internal or external dual 8-inch floppy disk drives, 15MB hard disk drive
Value: $20 to $55

Tandy Radio Shack TRS-80 Model 16
(Jan. 1982, desktop)
Original Retail Price: $4,999 to $5,798
Base Configuration: 6MHz 68000 and 4MHz Z80A CPUs; TRSDOS-16; 128K RAM (512K max); 8-inch floppy disk drive; keyboard/keypad; two RS-232C and one parallel port **Important Options:** TRS-Xenix, TRSDOS 4.2, or CP/M Plus; 8.4- or 15MB hard disk drive; second 8-inch floppy disk drive; external dual 8-inch floppy disk drives
Value: $15 to $55

Tandy Radio Shack TRS-80 Color Computer

(July 1980, home computer)
Original Retail Price: $399
Base Configuration: 0.894MHz 6809E CPU; ROM cartridge slot; 4K RAM (16K max); 8K ROM; TV switch box, integral Chiclet-style keyboard; RS-232C, cassette, and two game ports; TRS-80 Color BASIC; operation and Color BASIC manuals; reference card **Video:** 16-line x 32-column text, 64 x 32 graphics **Important Options:** Multi-Pak Interface, external floppy disk drive, CTR-80A cassette recorder, enhanced graphics, joysticks, Quick Printer II, modem, Extended Color BASIC ROM
Value: $15 to $45

The Tandy/Radio Shack TRS-80 Color Computer ($15 to $45) could be used with any color TV.

Tandy Radio Shack TRS-80 64K Color Computer

(1983, home computer)
Original Retail Price: $400
Base Configuration: 6809E CPU; ROM cartridge slot; 64K RAM; integral Chiclet-style keyboard; RS-232C, cassette, and two game ports; TRS-80 Extended Color BASIC **Video:** 16-line x 32-column text, eight colors max, 196 x 256 maximum graphics **Important Options:** Multi-Pak Interface, external floppy disk drive, cassette recorder, joysticks, Quick Printer II, modem, Extended Color BASIC ROM
Value: $20 to $40

Tandy TRS-80 Color Computer 2

(Sept. 1983, home computer)
Original Retail Price: $160 to $260
Base Configuration: 0.894MHz 6809E CPU; ROM cartridge slot; 16K RAM (64K max); 8K ROM (16K max); RF modulator; integral keyboard; RS-232C, cassette, and TV video ports; Color BASIC **Video:** 16-line x 32-character text, 256 x 192 graphics, eight colors **Size/Weight:** 3 x 10.37 x 14.75 inches **Important Options:** OS-9, Multi-Pak Interface, CCR-82 or CCR-81 cassette recorder, FD-501 Color Thinline 5.25-inch floppy disk drive, mouse, Extended Color BASIC, joysticks
Value: $5 to $25

Tandy TRS-80 Color Computer 3

(July 1986, home computer)
Original Retail Price: $219
Base Configuration: 1.7MHz 6809 CPU; ROM cartridge slot; 128K RAM (512K max); 32K ROM; RF modulator; integral keyboard; RS-232C, cassette, TV and RGB video ports; BASIC; DeskMate 3 **Video:** 24-line x 80-column text, 640 x 192 graphics, 16 colors **Size/Weight:** 3 x 10.37 x 14.75 inches **Important Options:** OS-9 2.0, Multi-Pak Interface, FD-502 Color Thinline 5.25-inch floppy disk drive, cassette recorder, 13-inch CM-8 color monitor, mouse, joysticks
Value: $10 to $50

Tandy offered more options for the TRS-80 Color Computer 3 ($10 to $50), including the CM-8 monitor, monitor stand, and floppy drive shown here.

Tandy Radio Shack TRS-80 Model MC-10 (1983, home computer)
Original Retail Price: $120
Base Configuration: 4K RAM (20K max), integral Chiclet-style keyboard
Value: $5 to $15

Tandy's TRS-80 Model MC-10 ($5 to $15) was sold as a low-end Color Computer, but it was never popular.

The Tandy 1200 ($5 to $25) was the closest the company got to producing a true IBM PC "clone." This is the 1200 HD model with a hard drive and the optional VM-3 monitor.

Tandy 1200 (Sept. 1984, desktop PC)
Original Retail Price: $1,499 to $2,999
Base Configuration: 4.77MHz 8088 CPU, MS-DOS 2.11, seven ISA slots, 256K RAM (640K max), 5.25-inch floppy disk drive, keyboard/keypad, parallel port, Microsoft BASIC, owner's manual **Important Options:** second 5.25-inch floppy disk drive, 10MB hard disk drive, 12-inch VM-3 monochrome or 13-inch CM-2 color monitor
Value: $5 to $25

Tandy TRS-80 Model 2000
(Nov. 1983, desktop PC)
Original Retail Price: $2,750 to $4,250
Base Configuration: 8MHz 80186 CPU; MS-DOS 2.0; four proprietary expansion slots; 128K RAM (768K max); 5.25-inch floppy disk drive; keyboard/keypad; RS-232C, parallel, and composite video ports; Microsoft BASIC **Video:** 640 x 400 graphics **Size/Weight:** 18.75 x 21.25 inches, 41 lbs. **Important Options:** second 5.25-inch floppy disk drive, 10MB hard disk drive, Disk Cartridge System, 12-inch monochrome VM-1 or 14-inch color CM-1 monitor, graphics upgrade, mouse, floor stand
Value: $10 to $45

The TRS-80 Model 2000 ($10 to $45) was Tandy's first MS-DOS system, but it wasn't entirely PC-compatible. The CM-1 monitor was optional.

Tandy 1000 (Nov. 1984, desktop PC)
Original Retail Price: $1,199
Base Configuration: 4.77MHz 8088 CPU; MS-DOS 2.11; three ISA slots; 128K RAM (640K max); 5.25-inch floppy disk drive; keyboard/keypad; parallel, game, and light-pen ports; DeskMate software; BASIC; three-voice sound **Video:** 640 x 200 graphics, CGA
Important Options: internal or external 10MB hard disk drive, 10MB Bernoulli drive, monochrome VM-2 or color CM-2 CRT display, RS-232C interface, modem
Value: $7 to $35

The Tandy 1000 ($7 to $35)
was one of the top-selling PCs of its day.

Tandy 1000 EX (Sept. 1986, desktop PC)
Original Retail Price: $799
Base Configuration: 7.16MHz 8088-2; MS-DOS 2.11; PLUS slot; 256K RAM (640K max); 5.25-inch floppy disk drive; integral keyboard/keypad; parallel, RGB, composite video, and two game ports; headphone jack; Personal DeskMate software; GW-BASIC **Video:** 25-line x 80-column text, CGA, eight colors **Important Options:** PLUS Expansion Adapter; 12-inch monochrome VM-4, 13-inch color CM-5, or color CM-10 CRT display; mouse; RS-232C interface; modem
Value: $5 to $25

Tandy 1000 SX (Sept. 1986, desktop PC)
Original Retail Price: $1,199
Base Configuration: 7.16MHz 8088; MS-DOS 3.2; five ISA slots; 384K RAM (640K max); two 5.25-inch floppy disk drives; keyboard/keypad; parallel, two game, light-pen, and RGB and composite video ports; DeskMate II; GW-BASIC **Video:** 25-line x 80-column text, 640 x 200 graphics, eight colors **Important Options:** 80286 processor upgrade, 10- or 20MB hard disk drive, monochrome VM-4 or color CM-5 or CM-10 monitor, mouse, RS-232C interface, modem
Value: $5 to $30

Tandy 3000 (Nov. 1985, desktop PC)
Original Retail Price: $2,599 to $3,599
Base Configuration: 8MHz or 12MHz 80286 CPU, MS-DOS 3.1, 10 ISA slots (eight open), 512K RAM (1MB max), 5.25-inch floppy disk drive, keyboard/keypad, RS-232C and parallel ports, Professional DeskMate software, utilities disk, installation and operation manual **Video:** CGA **Size/Weight:** 6.5 x 19 x 18 inches, 42 lbs. **Important Options:** OS/2 or Xenix 5.0, 3.5-inch floppy disk drive, 20- or 40MB hard disk drive, tape backup unit, 12-inch monochrome VM-1 or 14-inch color CM-1 monitor, EGA card, modem
Value: $5 to $25

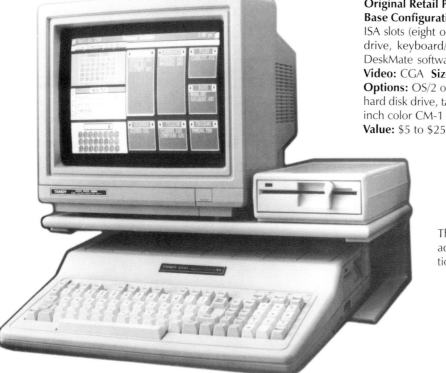

The Tandy 1000 EX ($5 to $25) required special PLUS add-on boards. This example is shown with the optional CM-4 monitor, monitor stand, and floppy drive.

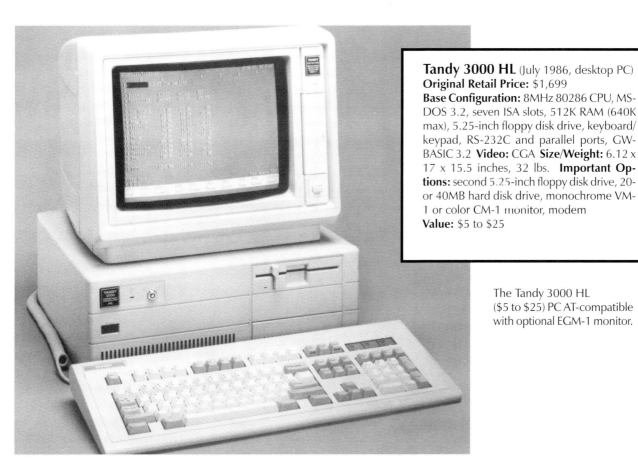

Tandy 3000 HL (July 1986, desktop PC)
Original Retail Price: $1,699
Base Configuration: 8MHz 80286 CPU, MS-DOS 3.2, seven ISA slots, 512K RAM (640K max), 5.25-inch floppy disk drive, keyboard/keypad, RS-232C and parallel ports, GW-BASIC 3.2 **Video:** CGA **Size/Weight:** 6.12 x 17 x 15.5 inches, 32 lbs. **Important Options:** second 5.25-inch floppy disk drive, 20- or 40MB hard disk drive, monochrome VM-1 or color CM-1 monitor, modem
Value: $5 to $25

The Tandy 3000 HL ($5 to $25) PC AT-compatible with optional EGM-1 monitor.

Tandy Radio Shack TRS-80 Model 100
(March 1983, notebook)
Original Retail Price: $799 to $999
Base Configuration: 2.4MHz 80C85 CPU; proprietary operating system in ROM; ROM socket; 8K RAM (32K max); 32K ROM; monochrome LCD; integral keyboard; RS-232C, parallel, cassette, and bar-code ports; BASIC; application suite in ROM; internal modem; AC adapter; slipcover **Video:** 8-line x 40-column text **Size/Weight:** 2 x 11.87 x 8.5 inches, 3.9 lbs. **Important Options:** Disk/Video Interface, external 3.5- or 5.25-inch floppy disk drive, carrying case
Value: $25 to $100

Many people still use their Tandy/Radio Shack TRS-80 Model 100 ($25 to $100), which was introduced in 1983.

Tandy 102 (June 1986, notebook)
Original Retail Price: $499
Base Configuration: 2.4MHz 80C85 CPU; expansion bus; ROM socket; 24K RAM (32K max); monochrome LCD; integral keyboard; RS-232C, parallel, cassette, and bar-code reader ports; BASIC and application suite in ROM; internal modem; AC adapter; slipcover
Video: 8-line x 40-column text **Size/Weight:** 1.5 x 11.8 x 8.5 inches, 3 lbs. **Important Options:** Disk/Video Interface, external 3.5-inch floppy disk drive, carrying case
Value: $25 to $100

Tandy 200 (1984, notebook)
Original Retail Price: $799
Base Configuration: 2.4MHz 80C85 CPU; 24K RAM (72K max); 72K ROM (104K max); monochrome LCD; integral keyboard; RS-232C, parallel, bar-code, and cassette ports; application suite, internal modem **Video:** 16-line x 40-column text, 240 x 128 graphics **Size/Weight:** 2.15 x 11.75 x 8.5 inches, 4.5 lbs. **Important Options:** Disk/Video Interface, external 3.5-inch floppy disk drive
Value: $20 to $85

The Tandy 200 ($20 to $85) had similar electronics to the Model 100, but offered a larger fold-up LCD.

Tandy 600 (Oct. 1985, notebook)
Original Retail Price: $1,599
Base Configuration: 3.07MHz 80C88 CPU, expansion slot, 32K RAM (224K max), 3.5-inch floppy disk drive, monochrome LCD, RS-232C and parallel ports, application suite, internal modem, NiCad battery pack, AC adapter **Video:** 16-line x 80-column text, 480 x 128 graphics **Size/Weight:** 2.75 x 12 x 13 inches, 9.5 lbs. **Important Options:** Disk/Video Interface, BASIC
Value: $15 to $55

The Tandy 600 ($15 to $55) had great proportions for a laptop, but did not run MS-DOS.

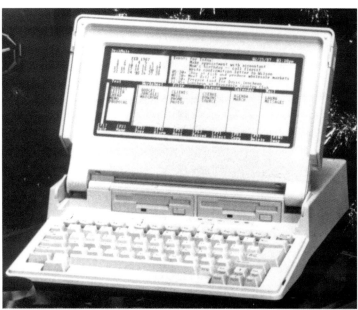

Tandy 1400 LT (Aug. 1987, laptop PC)
Original Retail Price: $1,599
Base Configuration: 7.16MHz V-20 CPU, MS-DOS 3.2, 768K RAM, 16K ROM, two 3.5-inch floppy disk drives, RGB and composite video ports, keyboard, RS-232C and parallel ports, GW-BASIC, battery pack, AC adapter **Video:** 25-line x 80-column text, 640 x 200 graphics **Size/Weight:** 14.5 x 12.37 x 3.5 inches, 13.5 lbs. **Important Options:** internal modem, carrying case
Value: $8 to $30

As a collectible, the Tandy 1400 LT ($8 to $20) is under-appreciated. It was a solid laptop PC.

Tangerine (U.K.)

Tangerine would eventually change its name to Oric Products International and become better known for its Oric line of computers. The Microtan 65 could be considered a predecessor to the Oric 1. It was sold in kit form, and users had to supply their own video display.

Tangerine Microtan 65 (1979, desktop)
Base Configuration: 0.75MHz 6502 CPU, expansion slot, 1K RAM (48K max), 1K ROM (14K max), hex keypad, cassette port, TANBUG monitor in ROM **Video:** 16-line x 32-column text, 64 x 64 graphics **Important Options:** keyboard/keypad
Value: $100 to $225

Tano Corp. (Matairie, Louisiana)

The Tano Outpost II ($35 to $100) was an early all-in-one unit.

Tano Outpost II (1978, desktop)
Original Retail Price: $1,995
Base Configuration: 6800 CPU, Flex 2.0, 32K RAM (64K max), 5.25-inch floppy disk drive, integral 12-inch monochrome CRT, RS-232C port, BASIC, manuals **Video:** 24-line x 80-column text **Size/Weight:** 13 x 24 x 25 inches, 60 lbs. **Important Options:** second 5.25-inch floppy disk drive, printer interface
Value: $35 to $100

Tatung Co. (Taiwan)

Tatung Einstein TC-01 (1984, home computer)
Base Configuration: 4MHz Z80A CPU; Xtal/DOS; 64K RAM; 8K ROM (32K max); 3.5-inch floppy disk drive; integral keyboard; RS-232C, parallel, and two game ports; three-voice sound **Video:** 24-line x 40-column text, 256 x 192 graphics, 16 colors **Important Options:** 80-column card
Value: $20 to $50

Tava Corp. (Irvine, California)

Tava ran ads for the Tava PC pricing it at $995, but that didn't include disk drives or a monitor.

Tava PC (1983, desktop PC)
Original Retail Price: $2,395
Base Configuration: 4.77MHz 8088 CPU; MS-DOS, CP/M-86, or UCSD p-System; 64K RAM (512K max); two 5.25-inch floppy disk drives; monochrome monitor; keyboard/keypad; two RS-232C and one parallel port **Important Options:** 5- to 15MB hard disk drive; color monitor; CGA card
Value: $10 to $30

Tava Triumph LT (March 1985, laptop PC)
Original Retail Price: $2,495
Base Configuration: 80186 CPU, 256K RAM (640K max), two 5.25-inch floppy disk drives, integral keyboard, serial and parallel ports, AC adapter **Video:** 25-line x 80-column text, 640 x 200 graphics **Size/Weight:** 15.4 x 12.2 x 3.5 inches, 14.5 lbs. **Important Options:** internal modem, battery pack
Value: $5 to $25

Technical Design Labs (TDL) (Princeton, New Jersey)

The Xitan came in two configurations: the base Alpha 1 model and the Alpha 2, which added a 16K RAM board and a software package including the Zapple Text Editor and the Relocating Macro-Assembler.

The General was aimed at the business market and featured a more user-friendly design than the Xitan. It also abandoned the S-100 bus architecture. Although several prototypes are known to have been made, it is not clear if the General ever made it into production.

Technical Design Labs Xitan (1977, early micro)
Original Retail Price: $769 to $1,369 kit, $1,039 to $1,749 assembled
Base Configuration: 2K RAM, 2K ROM, S-100 bus, cassette interface, two serial and one parallel port, BASIC
Value: $85 to $225

Technical Design Laboratories The General (1978, desktop)
Original Retail Price: $3,500
Base Configuration: 4MHz Z80A CPU, 32K RAM, 5.25-inch floppy disk drive, integral 12-inch monochrome CRT, keyboard/keypad, serial and two parallel ports, BASIC, word processor **Video:** 25-line x 80-column text **Important Options:** printer, plotter
Value: $75 to $185

The General ($75 to $185) from Technical Design Laboratories was a big beast with a built-in monitor.

Telcon Industries (see "Modular Micros")

Teleram Communications Corp. (White Plains, New York)

All three Teleram models used the same design and configuration, but with varying screen sizes. The T-3000 was one of the earliest notebook computers. The T-3500 Office Station converted all Teleram models to full-fledged desktop computers with hard and floppy disk drives.

Teleram T-3000 (1982, notebook)
Original Retail Price: $2,795 to $3,495
Base Configuration: Z80 CPU, CP/M 2.2, 64K RAM, 4K ROM, 128K bubble memory, monochrome LCD, integral keyboard/keypad, RS-232C port **Video:** 4-line x 80-column text **Size/Weight:** 13 x 9.75 x 3.5 inches, 9.75 lbs. **Important Options:** T-3500 Office Station, additional 128K bubble memory
Value: $35 to $100

Its LCD was minimal, but the Teleram T-3000 ($35 to $100) was a remarkably small laptop for 1982.

Teleram T-4000/T-5000 (early 1984, notebook)
Original Retail Price: $1,995 (T-4000)/$2,495 (T-5000)
Base Configuration: Z80L CPU, CP/M-80 or UCSD p-System, 64K RAM, 4K ROM, 128K bubble memory storage (256K max), monochrome LCD, integral keyboard/keypad, RS-232C port, teleText software **Video:** 8-line (T-4000)/16-line (T-5000) x 80-column text **Size/Weight:** 10 lbs. **Important Options:** T-3500 desktop expansion unit
Value: $15 to $50

Televideo TS 802 (1982, desktop)
Original Retail Price: $3,495
Base Configuration: 4MHz Z80A, CP/M-80 with GSX-80, 64K RAM (128K max), 5.25-inch floppy disk drive, integral monochrome CRT, keyboard/keypad, two RS-232C ports, application suite **Video:** 24-line x 80-column text, 640 x 240 graphics **Important Options:** second 5.25-inch floppy disk drive, 10MB hard disk drive, mouse, RS-422 interface, printer
Value: $15 to $35

Televideo Systems Inc. (Sunnyvale, California)

Known mainly for its terminals, Televideo also offered a line of CP/M systems in the early 1980s. The TS 802 was its entry-level model. The TS 803 had a sleek keyboard with a wrist rest, and its CPU and storage housing attached to the side of the monitor in a sidecar fashion. Televideo used the same general configuration for its first PC compatible, the TeleColor-XT.

Although nearly identical functionally, the TS 1602G and TS 1603 had markedly different external designs. The former had a low-profile design that integrated the CRT with the floppy drives and main circuitry. The TS 1603 also integrated those components, but had a larger CRT and mounted the drives vertically in sidecar fashion.

Televideo also sold similarly configured XT versions of the 1605 series—the Tele-XT and TeleColor-XT—with the same value range.

A pleasing design makes the Televideo TS-802 ($15 to $35) stand out among CP/M systems.

142

Two CP/M systems from Televideo: the TPC I transportable (left, $15 to $45) and the TS 803 ($15 to $35). Behind them is a TS-800 diskless workstation.

Televideo TS 803 (Oct. 1983, desktop)
Original Retail Price: $3,995
Base Configuration: 4MHz Z80A CPU, CP/M-80 with GSX-80, 64K RAM (128K max), 5.25-inch floppy disk drive, integral 14-inch monochrome CRT, keyboard/keypad, two RS-232C ports, application suite **Video:** 24-line x 80-column text, 640 x 240 graphics **Important Options:** second 5.25-inch floppy disk drive, 10MB hard disk drive, mouse, RS-422 port, printer
Value: $15 to $35

Televideo TS 1602G/TS 1603 (1983, desktop)
Original Retail Price: $2,495
Base Configuration: 5MHz 8088, CP/M-86 with GSX-86, 128K RAM (256K max), 4K ROM, two 5.25-inch floppy disk drives, integral 12-inch (TS 1602G) or 14-inch (TS 1603) monochrome CRT, keyboard/keypad, two RS-232C and one RS-422 port **Video:** 24-line x 80 column text, 576 x 424 graphics (TS 1602G)/640 x 240 graphics (TS 1603)
Size/Weight: 13.5 x 22 x 14.4 inches (TS 1602G)/14.5 x 18.5 x 14.5 inches (TS 1603) **Important Options:** MS-DOS, 7.5MB hard disk drive (TS 1602G), enhanced graphics (TS 1603), mouse
Value: $15 to $40

Televideo Tele-PC Plus Model TS/1605/TeleColor-PC Model TS 1605C (late 1983 [TelePC Plus]/1984 [TeleColor-PC], desktop PC)
Original Retail Price: $2,995 (TelePC Plus)
Base Configuration: 4.77MHz 8088, TeleDOS (PC-DOS 2.11 compatible), one ISA slot, 256K RAM (640K max), 8K ROM, one (Tele-PC Plus) or two (TeleColor-PC) 5.25-inch floppy disk drives, 10MB hard disk drive (Tele-PC Plus), integral 14-inch monochrome (Tele-PC Plus) or 14-inch color (TeleColor PC) CRT, RGB and composite video ports (Tele-PC Plus), keyboard/keypad, RS-232C and parallel ports, GW-BASIC, application suite **Video:** 640 x 200 graphics **Size/Weight:** 14.5 x 18.5 x 14.5 inches, 52 lbs. **Important Options:** Concurrent CP/M-86, second 5.25-inch floppy disk drive (Tele-PC)
Value: $12 to $35

Televideo TPC I (1984, transportable)
Base Configuration: Z80A CPU, CP/M, 5.25-inch floppy disk drive, integral 9-inch monochrome CRT, keyboard/keypad, RS-232C and parallel ports **Video:** 24-line x 80-column text **Important Options:** second 5.25-inch floppy disk drive, mouse, RS-422 interface
Value: $15 to $45

Televideo TPC II (early 1984, transportable PC)
Base Configuration: 4.77MHz 8088 CPU, TeleDOS (PC-DOS 2.11 compatible), one ISA slot, 256K RAM (640K max), 8K ROM, 5.25-inch floppy disk drive, integral 9-inch monochrome CRT, RGB and composite video ports, keyboard/keypad, RS-232C and parallel ports, GW-BASIC, application suite **Video:** 640 x 200 graphics **Size/Weight:** 8 x 18 x 15 inches, 30 lbs.
Important Options: second 5.25-inch floppy disk drive
Value: $12 to $40

Terak Corp. (Scottsdale, Arizona)

Terak 8510 (1977, desktop)
Original Retail Price: $5,000
Base Configuration: LSI-11 CPU, RT-11, 64K RAM, 8-inch floppy disk drive, 12-inch monochrome CRT, RS-232C and parallel ports, BASIC **Video:** 24-line x 80-column text, 320 x 240 graphics **Important Options:** 12-inch color CRT, 640 x 480 graphics upgrade
Value: $150 to $550

Texas Electronic Instruments Inc. (TEI) (Houston, Texas)

The Processor Terminal was sold through CMC Marketing. A Model PT112/32 offered 32K of RAM.

An early CP/M machine, the TEI Processor Terminal Model MCS-PT ($110 to $375).

TEI Processor Terminal Model MCS-PT
(1977, early micro)
Original Retail Price: $2,995 kit, $3,495 assembled
Base Configuration: 8080 CPU, CP/M, 12 expansion slots, 16K RAM, 5.25-inch floppy disk drive, integral 15-inch monochrome CRT, integral keyboard/keypad, three serial and three parallel ports, BASIC **Video:** 24-line x 80-column text
Value: $110 to $375

Texas Instruments Inc. (Austin, Texas)

Before releasing the TI-99/4 and TI-99/4A in 1979, TI was best known as a manufacturer of semiconductors and small engineering/industrial systems. In fact, these early home computers used a TI-made CPU, the TMS 9900.

TI improved on the TI-99/4 design shortly after its introduction by adding a full-travel keyboard and slightly more memory capacity with the TI-99/4A. More important, the company expanded its software catalog for the system. The TI-99/4A came in either a silver or a less common cream color. The Peripheral Expansion System is an important option that allows the addition of disk drives, an RS-232 interface, and additional memory. It can easily double the value of a TI-99/4A system.

In 1983, TI developed a lower-cost version of the TI-99/4A, the TI-99/2. Like the Timex Sinclair 1000, the TI-99/2 was a bare-bones system designed as an inexpensive introduction to computing. It was loosely based on the TI-99/4A design and could use the same peripherals. However, it required its own cartridges. The TI-99/2 apparently was produced but never officially sold by TI. Examples are rare, which is why their value is so much higher than the TI-99/4 or TI-99/4A.

TI boasted that its Professional Computer had better graphics than the IBM PC. The company also used its experience to develop a speech synthesis/recognition card for the system. The Business Pro used a tower enclosure and offered performance far superior to the IBM PC AT.

One interesting feature of the Pro-Lite was that its keyboard pops up at a better typing angle when you flip up the LCD. TI promised that the CC-40 would run 200 hours on four AA alkaline batteries. The CC-40 is small enough that some might consider it a handheld computer.

Texas Instruments TI-99/4
(June 1979, home computer)
Base Configuration: TMS 9900 CPU, ROM cartridge slot, 16K RAM (48K max), 26K ROM, integral Chiclet-style keyboard, cassette port, TI BASIC, three-voice sound, AC adapter **Video:** 24-line x 32-column text, 256 x 192 graphics, 16 colors **Size/Weight:** 10.2 x 15 x 2.5, 5 lbs. **Important Options:** external 5.25-inch floppy disk drive, 13-inch color monitor, RF modulator, RS-232 interface, joysticks, Speech Synthesizer, thermal printer
Value: $50 to $125

Texas Instruments sold millions of TI-99/4A ($5 to $20) systems, making them inexpensive to acquire today.

Texas Instruments TI-99/4A
(1979, home computer)
Original Retail Price: $525
Base Configuration: TMS 9900 CPU, ROM cartridge slot, 16K RAM (52K max), 26K ROM, integral keyboard, cassette port, TI BASIC, three-voice sound, AC adapter **Video:** 24-line x 32-column text, 256 x 192 graphics, 16 colors **Important Options:** Peripheral Expansion System, external 5.25-inch floppy disk drive, 10-inch color monitor, RF modulator, 80-column card, Speech Synthesizer, acoustic coupler, joysticks, thermal printer
Value: $5 to $20

Texas Instruments TI-99/2
(1983, home computer)
Original Retail Price: $99
Base Configuration: TMS-9995 CPU, external TI Hex-Bus expansion port, ROM cartridge slot, 4.2K RAM (36.2K max), 24K ROM, TV video ports, integral keyboard, TI BASIC **Video:** 24-line x 28-column text **Important Options:** Program Recorder cassette drive, HX-2000 Wafertape drive, RS-232C interface, HX-1000 printer/plotter
Value: $50 to $150

The rare Texas Instruments TI-99/2 ($50 to $150).

Texas Instrument Professional Computer
(1983, desktop PC)
Original Retail Price: $2,595
Base Configuration: 8088 CPU; MS-DOS 1.25, CP/M-86, Concurrent CP/M-86, or UCSD p-System; five slots; 64K RAM (256K max), 8K ROM (16K max); two 5.25-inch floppy disk drives; 12-inch monochrome monitor; keyboard/keypad; parallel port **Video:** 25-line x 80-column text, 720 x 300 graphics **Important Options:** Z80 coprocessor, 5- or 10MB hard disk drive, 13-inch color monitor, graphics upgrade, RS-232C interface, Omni 800 Model 850 or 855 printer, internal modem, speech synthesizer
Value: $15 to $40

Some reviewers at the time thought that the Texas Instruments Professional Computer ($15 to $40) was an improvement over the IBM PC.

Texas Instruments Business Pro (1985, desktop PC)
Base Configuration: 80286 CPU, MS-DOS 3.1, 14 ISA slots, 512K RAM (640K max), 5.25-inch floppy disk drive, keyboard/keypad, serial and parallel ports **Video:** 720 x 300 graphics, eight colors **Important Options:** Microsoft Xenix System V, 21MB hard disk drive, monochrome or color monitor, CGA or hi-res monochrome graphics card, mouse
Value: $7 to $25

Texas Instruments Portable Professional Computer
(1984, transportable PC)
Original Retail Price: $2,395
Base Configuration: NEC 8088 CPU, MS-DOS, five ISA slots, 64K RAM (768K max), 5.25-inch floppy disk drive, integral 9-inch monochrome monitor, keyboard/keypad **Video:** 25-line x 80-column text, 720 x 300 graphics **Size/Weight:** 34 lbs. **Important Options:** second 5.25-inch floppy disk drive, 10MB hard disk drive, integral 9-inch color CRT
Value: $15 to $40

The Texas Instruments Pro-Lite ($10 to $35) laptop PC.

Texas Instruments Pro-Lite
(Jan. 1985, laptop PC)
Original Retail Price: $2,995
Base Configuration: 5MHz 80C88 CPU, MS-DOS 2.13, two expansion slots, 256K RAM (768K max), 3.5-inch floppy disk drive, 12-inch monochrome LCD, RGB and composite video ports, integral keyboard, RS-232C and parallel ports, battery pack, AC adapter **Video:** 25-line x 80-column text, 640 x 200 graphics **Size/Weight:** 2.75 x 11.5 x 13 inches, 10.5 lbs. **Important Options:** expansion box, external floppy disk drive, internal modem, thermal printer, carrying case
Value: $10 to $35

Texas Instruments Compact Computer 40 (CC-40)
(1983, notebook)
Base Configuration: ROM cartridge port, 6K RAM (22K max), 34K ROM, monochrome LCD, integral keyboard/keypad, TI Enhanced BASIC, AC adapter **Video:** 31-column text **Size/Weight:** 9.25 x 5.75 x 1 inches, 1.4 lbs. **Important Options:** Wafertape drive, RS-232C interface, printer/plotter
Value: $20 to $60

The tiny Texas Instruments CC-40 ($20 to $60) with its optional printer, floppy drive, and modem modules.

Timex Computer Corp. (Waterbury, Connecticut)

Timex manufactured Sinclair computers for the company and sold them in North America under its own brand. The TS1000 was the Sinclair ZX81 in North American garb. Production of the TS1000 and the TS1500 ceased in February 1984. The Spectrum-based TS2000 was discontinued at the same time.

The TS2068 offered a larger keyboard than the TS2000, more memory capacity, and an enhanced graphics mode.

Timex Sinclair 1000 (TS1000)
(1982, home computer)
Original Retail Price: $50
Base Configuration: 3.25MHz Z80A CPU, 2K RAM (16K max), 8K ROM, integral membrane keyboard, cassette port, BASIC, BASIC tutorial, AC adapter **Size/Weight:** 6 x 6.5 x 1.5 inches, 12 oz. **Important Options:** TS2050 modem, TS2040 printer
Value: $5 to $40

Timex Sinclair 1500 (TS1500) (May 1982, home computer)
Original Retail Price: $80
Base Configuration: 3.5MHz Z80A CPU, 16K RAM (32K max), 8K ROM, TV video port, integral keyboard, cassette port, Extended BASIC, BASIC tutorial, AC adapter **Video:** 24-line x 32-column text **Size/Weight:** 9 x 5.5 x 1.5 inches, 1.25 lbs. **Important Options:** TS2050 modem, TS2040 printer
Value: $7 to $50

The Timex Sinclair 2000 ($3 to $30) weighs just a little more than a pound.

Timex Sinclair 2000 (TS2000) (1983, home computer)
Original Retail Price: $150 to $200
Base Configuration: 3.5MHz Z80A CPU, 16K RAM (48K max), TV video port, RF modulator, integral Chiclet-style keyboard, cassette port, Timex Extended BASIC, programming and system manuals, AC adapter **Video:** 24-line x 32-column text, 256 x 192 graphics, eight colors **Size/Weight:** 9.12 x 5.62 x 1.25 inches, 1.25 lbs. **Important Options:** TS2040 printer
Value: $3 to $30

Timex Sinclair 2068 (TS2068) (1983, home computer)
Original Retail Price: $200
Base Configuration: 3.5MHz Z80A CPU, ROM cartridge slot, 48K RAM (256K max), 23K ROM, TV and RGB video ports, integral keyboard, cassette and two game ports, Sinclair Extended BASIC, AC adapter **Video:** 24-line x 64-column text, 512 x 192 graphics, eight colors **Size/Weight:** 14.75 x 7.5 x 1.37, 3.3 lbs. **Important Options:** Bus Expansion unit, Microdrive, RS-232C and parallel interfaces, TS2040 printer, TS2050 modem
Value: $4 to $35

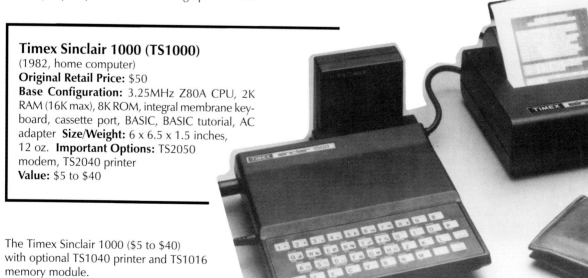

The Timex Sinclair 1000 ($5 to $40) with optional TS1040 printer and TS1016 memory module.

TLF (Littleton, Colorado)

Both the Mini 12 and the Data 12 were compatible with the DEC PDP-8E minicomputer, and the Data 12's operating system was based on DEC's OS-8.

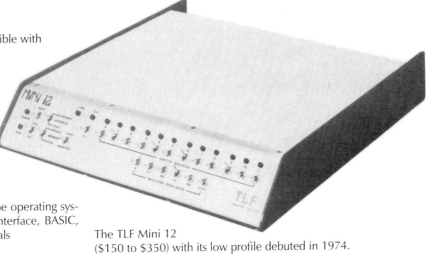

TLF Mini 12 (1974, early micro)
Base Configuration: 8K RAM (32K max), Extended BASIC **Important Options:** FORTRAN, Algol
Value: $150 to $350

TLF Data 12 (1977, early micro)
Original Retail Price: $1,695
Base Configuration: 4MHz IM6100, proprietary tape operating system, 4K RAM (32K max), digital tape drive, serial interface, BASIC, Algol **Important Options:** display and ASCII terminals
Value: $125 to $300

The TLF Mini 12
($150 to $350) with its low profile debuted in 1974.

Tomcat Computer Inc. (Los Angeles, California)

It's not clear if the Tomcat PCX-1600 was sold in North America. However, the company's U.S. division distributed literature for the 3000, which was designed in part to act as a server to multiple PCX-1600s.

Tomcat 3000 (desktop)
Base Configuration: 5MHz 8086 CPU, CP/M-86, four Multibus slots, 128K RAM (1MB max), 16K ROM, two 5.25-inch floppy disk drives, color monitor, keyboard/keypad, two RS-232C ports **Video:** 640 x 400 graphics, eight colors
Value: $12 to $35

Tomcat PCX-1600
(desktop)
Base Configuration: 5MHz 8086 and 4MHz Z80A CPUs; CP/M-86, MS-DOS, RDOS, or UCSD p-System; 128K RAM (384K max); 16K ROM, two 5.25-inch floppy disk drives; integral 12-inch monochrome CRT; keyboard/keypad; RS-232C port **Size/Weight:** 17.2 x 12.8 x 12.9 inches
Value: $12 to $35

With both 8086 and Z80A CPUs, the Tomcat PCX-1600 ($12 to $35) could accommodate several operating systems.

Tomy (Japan)

The Tomy Tutor was partially compatible with the Texas Instruments TI-99/4A. Although sold worldwide, the Tutor found little success outside of Japan, where it was known as the Pyuuta.

Tomy Tutor (1983, home computer)
Original Retail Price: $385
Base Configuration: 2.7MHz TMS9995NL CPU, ROM cartridge slot, 16K RAM (64K max), 32K ROM, TV and composite video ports, integral Chiclet-style keyboard, cassette and game ports, Tomy BASIC and GBASIC, three-voice sound **Video:** 24-line x 32-column text, 256 x 192 graphics, 16 colors
Value: $50 to $85

Partially compatible with the TI-99/4A, the Tomy Tutor ($50 to $85) was a popular home computer in Europe and Asia. *Photo courtesy of Sellam Ismail, Vintage Computer Festival.*

Torch Computers Ltd. (Cambridge, U.K.)

The Torch Computer was optimized for network and dial-in communications. Its 6502 coprocessor was dedicated to handling communications tasks. Torch also offered the SuperTorch upgrade, which replaced the Z80A board with a combination Motorola 68000/Z80 board.

Torch Computer (1983, desktop)
Base Configuration: 6MHz Z80A and 2MHz 6502 CPUs; CP/M; 64K RAM and 4K ROM (Z80A); 32K RAM and 48K ROM (6502); two 5.25-inch floppy disk drives; integral 12-inch color CRT; keyboard/keypad; RS-232C, parallel, and A-D ports; BBC BASIC; internal modem; three-voice sound, speech synthesizer
Value: $20 to $85

The Torch Computer ($20 to $85) was made in the U.K. and designed for communications tasks.

Toshiba America Inc. (Tustin, California)

Toshiba was and still is a leading manufacturer of laptop and notebook computers, but it has also produced desktop systems since the early 1980s. The T100 was an inexpensive BASIC-based system that, with the LCD option, became a small but powerful portable computer. The main form of storage for the T100 was a removeable 32K RAM pack that used static RAM. Toshiba literature indicates that the T100 was made in two colors: white and silver/grey. The T200 and PC-compatible T300 followed the T100. Toshiba sold a system similar to the T300 in Japan as the Pasopia 16.

The company also sold the popular HX-10 MSX system. Toshiba referred to the 16K model as the HX-10S and the 64K model as the HX-10D. An HX-10DN model offered a parallel interface. The HX-10 came in one of three colors: red, black, or white.

The T1100 Plus represented a breakthrough in laptop design in terms of the power-to-size ratio and established Toshiba's reputation for quality small computers. It was a small 10-pound unit that could nearly match the performance of a PC XT. To top it off, its screen could display 25 lines of text—the same as a desktop PC. The lower cost T1000 and faster, more expandable T1200 followed the T1100. Toshiba also offered a dual-floppy-drive T1200F. Toshiba later offered a T3100/20, which had a 20MB hard drive as standard.

Toshiba T100 (1982, desktop)
Original Retail Price: $795
Base Configuration: 4MHz Z80A CPU; ROM/RAM cartridge slot; 64K RAM, 32K ROM; RAM pack storage; integral keyboard/keypad; RS-232C, parallel, and cassette ports; TBASIC **Video:** 25-line x 80-column text **Size/Weight:** 16.5 x 4 x 11 inches **Important Options:** CP/M, external dual 5.25-inch floppy disk drives, 12-inch monochrome or 14-inch color monitor, LCD, T-Disk BASIC, P1010 or P1350 printer, modem, carrying case
Value: $35 to $75

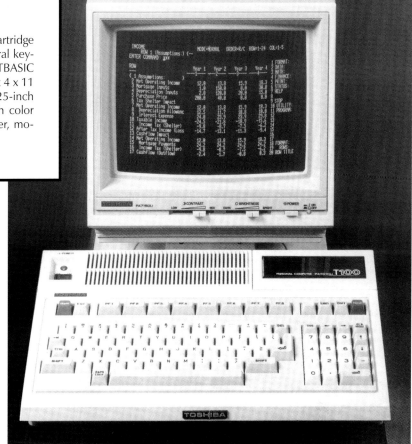

Shown with the optional PA7150U
monitor, the Toshiba T100 ($35 to $75).

Toshiba T200/T250 (1982, desktop)
Original Retail Price: $5000 (T200)/$6,000 (T250)
Base Configuration: TMP 8085A CPU, CP/M, 64K RAM, 5.25-inch (T200)/8-inch (T250) floppy disk drive, integral 12-inch monochrome CRT, keyboard/keypad, RS-232C and parallel ports, BASIC-80, dot-matrix printer **Video:** 24-line x 80-column text **Size/Weight:** 21.75 x 13 x 17 inches, 66 lbs. (T200)/ 24 x 15 x 19 inches, 88 lbs. (T250) **Important Options:** second 5.25-inch (T200)/8-inch (T250) floppy disk drive
Value: $15 to $40

Toshiba T300 (1983, desktop PC)
Original Retail Price: $3,090
Base Configuration: 6MHz 8088 CPU, MS-DOS 2.0, seven expansion slots, 192K RAM (512K max), 4K ROM, 5.25-inch floppy disk drive, RGB and composite video ports, keyboard/keypad, RS-232C and parallel ports, T-BASIC16 **Size/Weight:** 16.5 x 5.5 x 16.5 inches **Important Options:** CP/M-86, second 5.25-inch floppy disk drive, 10MB hard disk drive, 12-inch monochrome or 14-inch Color Display monitor, graphics card, IEEE-488 interface, P1350 or P1010 printer
Value: $15 to $40

With the T300 ($15 to $40), Toshiba's
desktop line became PC-compatible.

Toshiba HX-10 (1984, MSX home computer)
Original Retail Price: $230 to $275
Base Configuration: Z80 CPU, ROM cartridge slot, 16K RAM (64K max), composite video port, integral keyboard **Video:** 24-line x 40-column text, 256 x 192 graphics **Important Options:** parallel interface
Value: $7 to $40

Toshiba T1100/T1100 Plus (1986, laptop PC)
Original Retail Price: $1,999 to $2,399
Base Configuration: 7.16MHz 80C86 CPU; MS-DOS 2.11; 256K RAM (640K max); two 3.5-inch floppy disk drives; monochrome LCD; CGA, RGB, and composite video ports; integral keyboard; RS-232C and parallel ports; SideKick; carrying case; AC adapter; battery charger; NiCad battery pack **Video:** 25-line x 80-column text, 640 x 200 graphics **Size/Weight:** 12.1 x 2.6 x 12 inches, 10 lbs. **Important Options:** expansion chassis, external 5.25-inch floppy disk drive, keypad, internal modem
Value: $5 to $50

Toshiba T1000 (July 1987, laptop PC)
Original Retail Price: $1,199
Base Configuration: 4.77MHz 80C88 CPU, MS-DOS 2.11, 512K RAM (1.25MB max), 3.5-inch floppy disk drive, RGB and composite video ports, monochrome LCD, integral keyboard, RS-232C and parallel ports, SideKick, NiCad battery pack, AC adapter, charger **Video:** CGA **Size/Weight:** 12.2 x 2 x 11 inches, 6.4 lbs. **Important Options:** external 5.25-inch floppy disk drive, keypad, internal modem, carrying case
Value: $10 to $35

Toshiba T1000SE (laptop PC)
Base Configuration: 9.54MHz 80C86 CPU, MS-DOS 3.3, expansion slot, 1MB RAM (3MB max), 3.5-inch floppy disk drive, RGB and composite video ports, monochrome LCD, integral keyboard, RS-232C and parallel ports, hypertext manual, NiCad battery pack, AC adapter, charger **Video:** CGA **Size/Weight:** 12.4 x 10.16 x 1.78 inches, 5.9 lbs. **Important Options:** external 5.25-inch floppy disk drive, internal modem, carrying case
Value: $10 to $35

Toshiba T1200 (1987, laptop PC)
Original Retail Price: $3,499
Base Configuration: 9.54MHz 80C86 CPU; MS-DOS 3.2; external expansion bus; 1MB RAM; 3.5-inch floppy disk drive; 10MB hard disk drive; monochrome LCD; CGA, RGB, and composite video ports; integral keyboard; RS-232C and parallel ports; SideKick; NiCad battery pack; AC adapter **Video:** 25-line x 80-column text **Size/Weight:** 12.2 x 2.6 x 12 inches, 10.8 lbs. **Important Options:** expansion chassis, external 5.25-inch floppy disk drive, keypad, internal modem
Value: $5 to $35

Toshiba T3100 (July 1986, laptop PC)
Original Retail Price: $4,499
Base Configuration: 8MHz 80286 CPU, MS-DOS 2.11, expansion slot, 640K (2.6MB max), 3.5-inch floppy disk drive, 10MB hard disk drive, monochrome gas plasma display, RGB port, integral keyboard, RS-232C and parallel ports, carrying case **Video:** 25-line x 80-column text, CGA **Size/Weight:** 12.2 x 3.1 x 14.2 inches, 15 lbs. **Important Options:** expansion chassis, external 5.25-inch floppy disk drive, keypad, internal modem
Value: $7 to $32

U-Microcomputers Ltd. (Cheshire, U.K.)

The U-Man Series 1000 used a 6809 processor to manage I/O functions.

U-Microcomputers U-Man Series 1000 (1985, desktop)
Original Retail Price: £2,499
Base Configuration: 68000 CPU; CP/M-68K or UCSD p-System; 128K RAM (1MB max); two 5.25-inch floppy disk drives; monochrome and RGB video ports; keyboard/keypad; two serial, parallel port, and game ports; speech synthesizer; sound generator **Video:** 680 x 270 graphics **Important Options:** hard disk drive
Value: $15 to $40

> A group of laptop classics, from left to right: the Toshiba T1000 ($10 to $35), T1200 ($5 to $35), T3100/20 ($7 to $32), and T1100 Plus ($5 to $50).

Umtech Inc. (Sunnyvale, California)

The VideoBrain was one of the earliest home computers and one of the first systems to use ROM cartridges as a software medium. Sold through retail outlets, the VideoBrain suffered from poor graphics capability and inadequate software support. Finding compatible ROM cartridges today is difficult.

Umtech VideoBrain (1978, home computer)
Original Retail Price: $500
Base Configuration: F8 CPU, ROM cartridge slot, 1K RAM, 4K ROM, TV video interface and switchbox, integral keyboard, two joysticks, three ROM cartridge programs, AC adapter **Video:** 7-line x 16-column text
Value: $45 to $175

Universal Data Inc. (Clarkston, Michigan)

An aluminum case helped keep the weight down on the UDI-500.

Universal Data UDI-500 (1983, laptop)
Base Configuration: CMOS 2.5MHz Z80 and CMOS 1805 CPUs, CP/M 2.2 and MicroDOS, two RCA microboard slots (one open), 64K RAM (256K max), two 3.5-inch floppy disk drives, monochrome LCD, keyboard, RS-232C and parallel ports, Perfect Software suite, NiCad battery, AC adapter **Video:** 8-line x 40-column text **Size/Weight:** 11 x 13 x 3.12 inches, 12.8 lbs. **Important Options:** internal modem
Value: $17 to $45

Vector Graphic Inc. (Thousand Oaks, California)

Like many other early microcomputer vendors, Vector Graphic started out selling S-100 boards of its own design. The Vector 1 was a well-regarded S-100-based system. A later Vector 1+ model came with an internal 5.25-inch floppy drive.

The Memorite was sold as a text processing system for the office. The System 3005 was one of the better 8-bit business class micros made in the early 1980s. Although not a PC-compatible system, the Vector 4-S could read PC-format floppy disks.

Vector Graphic Vector 1 (1977, early micro)
Base Configuration: 8080A CPU, S-100 bus
Value: $150 to $400

Vector Graphic Memorite (1977, early micro)
Original Retail Price: $7,950
Base Configuration: 8080A CPU, S-100 bus, 5.25-inch floppy disk drive
Value: $125 to $350

Vector Graphic System B (1979, desktop)
Base Configuration: Z80A CPU, CP/M, S-100 bus, 56K RAM, integral 12-inch monochrome CRT, integral keyboard/keypad, RS-232C and parallel ports, BASIC **Video:** 24-line x 80-column text, 160 x 72 graphics
Value: $75 to $200

Vector Graphic System 3005 (1981, desktop)
Original Retail Price: $7,950
Base Configuration: 4MHz Z80A CPU, CP/M 2.2, six S-100 slots (four open), 56K RAM, 5.25-inch floppy disk drive, 5MB hard disk drive, integral monochrome CRT, integral keyboard/keypad, RS-232C and parallel ports, BASIC-80 **Video:** 24-line x 80-column text **Important Options:** external dual 5.25-inch floppy disk drives
Value: $65 to $150

Vector Graphic Vector 3 (desktop)
Original Retail Price: $3,695
Base Configuration: Z80 CPU, CP/M, S-100 bus, 56K RAM, 12-inch monochrome CRT, RS-232C and parallel ports, BASIC **Video:** 24-line x 80-column text, 160 x 72 graphics
Value: $50 to $75

Vector Graphic Vector 4/Vector 4-S (1982 [4]/1984 [4-S], desktop)
Original Retail Price: $3,295 to $9,995 (4-S)
Base Configuration: Z-80 and 8088 CPUs, CP/M (4)/CP/M-86 with GSX-86 (4-S); two S-100 slots (4-S); 128K RAM (256K max); floppy disk drive, integral monochrome CRT; keyboard; RS-232C, serial, and two parallel ports **Important Options:** MS-DOS or Oasis, second floppy disk drive, 5- to 36MB hard disk drive, color monitor, communications card
Value: $45 to $75

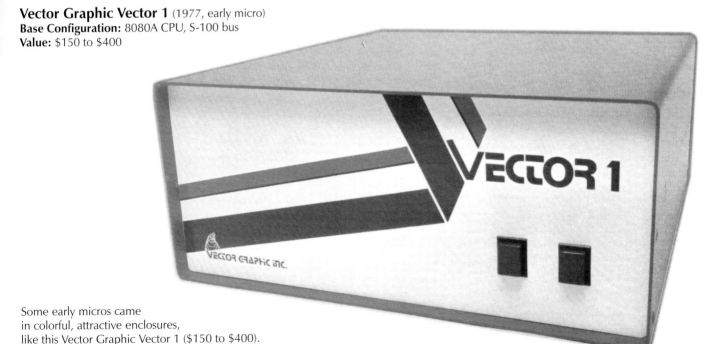

Some early micros came
in colorful, attractive enclosures,
like this Vector Graphic Vector 1 ($150 to $400).

Victor Technologies Inc. (Scotts Valley, California)

The Victor 9000 was developed by Sirius Systems Technology and sold in the U.S. by Victor Business Systems, a company known for its calculators and cash register systems. Sirius sold the computer as the S1 in France and as the Sirius 1 elsewhere. Sirius bought Victor Business Systems in 1982 and changed its name to Victor Technologies. Chuck Peddle, who created the MOS Technologies 6502 and designed the Commodore PET series, became Victor's president. Sirius produced 1,150 Victor 9000/Sirius 1 systems in March 1982, and 3,000 the following month.

Victor Technologies Victor 9000
(Jan. 1982, desktop PC)
Original Retail Price: $5,000
Base Configuration: 5MHz 8088 CPU, MS-DOS and CP/M-86, four expansion slots, 128K RAM (896K max), two 5.25-inch floppy disk drives, 12-inch monochrome monitor, keyboard/keypad, two RS-232C and one parallel port, voice synthesizer **Video:** 40-line x 132-column text, 800 x 400 graphics **Size/Weight:** 7 x 15 x 13 inches, 28 lbs. **Important Options:** Z80 coprocessor, CP/M-80, 10MB hard disk drive
Value: $17 to $65

The Victor 9000 ($17 to $65) was a well-designed business desktop that could run both MS-DOS and CP/M.

Video Technology Inc. (VTech) (Elk Grove Village, Illinois)

VTech was a significant producer of cheap home computers in the early and mid-1980s. Its VZ100 and VZ200 lines were sold worldwide under its own brand and many other brands such as Dick Smith, Dynasty, and Zeta.

The company also produced some of the best-known Apple II-compatible systems including the Laser 3000. Two custom designed LSI chips gave the Laser 3000 superior graphics and sound capabilities to the Apple II. Some might consider the Laser 2001 a game console, but its internals were similar to the Apple II-compatible Laser 3000.

Best known was the Laser 128, which was also sold under the Central Point Software brand in the U.S., VTech was the only maker of Apple clones to have reverse-engineered the Apple system ROMs, thus minimizing its legal liability with Apple. Laser 128s are not only common today, but one of the most collectible of the Apple clones.

VTech briefly sold several inexpensive PC-compatibles.

VTech VZ100 (1983, home computer)
Base Configuration: 3.58MHz Z80A CPU, 3K RAM (35K max), 8K ROM, integral Chiclet-style keyboard, cassette port, BASIC, AC adapter **Video:** 16-line x 32-column text **Size/Weight:** 11.3 x 6.25 x 1.95 inches, 3.3 lbs. **Important Options:** parallel interface
Value: $7 to $35

VTech VZ200 (1983, home computer)
Original Retail Price: $100
Base Configuration: 3.58MHz Z80A CPU, memory and peripheral expansion buses, 4K RAM (64K max), 12K ROM, TV video and monitor ports, integral Chiclet-style keyboard, cassette port, Microsoft BASIC, AC adapter **Video:** 16-line x 32-column text, eight colors **Size/Weight:** 11.3 x 6.25 x 1.95 inches, 3.3 lbs. **Important Options:** external 5.25-inch floppy disk drive, monochrome monitor, parallel interface, printer, joysticks, light pen, modem
Value: $8 to $35

Video Technology manufactured the VZ200 ($8 to $35) to be sold under other brands around the world in addition to its own.

VTech Laser 2001 (1983, Apple II-class desktop)
Base Configuration: 2MHz 6502A CPU, external expansion bus, 80K RAM (144K max), TV video port, integral Chiclet-style keyboard, parallel port, Microsoft BASIC, two joysticks, four-voice sound, AC adapter **Video:** 256 x 192 graphics, 16 colors **Size/Weight:** 13.3 x 9.4 x 2.3 inches, 6.6 lbs. **Important Options:** Expansion Module Interface, DR10 Data Recorder, floppy disk drive, PP40 Graphics Printer/Plotter, modem
Value: $10 to $40

An Apple II-compatible, the Video Technology Laser 3000 ($10 to $40) surrounded by its optional equipment.

VTech Laser 3000 (Apple II-class desktop)
Original Retail Price: $695
Base Configuration: 2MHz 6502A, 64K RAM (256K max), 24K ROM, RGB and composite video ports, integral keyboard/keypad, parallel and cassette ports, Microsoft BASIC, four-channel sound **Video:** 24-line x 80-column text, 560 x 192 graphics **Size/Weight:** 19.5 x 9.8 x 3.5 inches, 8.6 lbs.
Important Options: Z80A or 8088 coprocessor, CP/M, expansion box, one or two 5.25-inch floppy disk drives, cassette recorder, RF modulator, monochrome or color monitor, RS-232 port, modem, joysticks, printer, printer/plotter
Value: $10 to $40

VTech Laser 128/Laser 128EX
(Dec. 1985, Apple II-class desktop)
Original Retail Price: $479
Base Configuration: 3.6MHz 65C02 CPU, ProDOS or DOS 3.3, Apple-compatible expansion slot, 128K RAM (1MB max for 128EX), 32K ROM, 5.25-inch floppy disk drive, NTSC and RGB video ports, integral keyboard/keypad, RS-232C and parallel ports, Microsoft BASIC **Video:** 80-column text, 16 colors **Size/Weight:** 14.5 x 12.25 x 3.12 inches, 11.7 lbs. **Important Options:** expansion box, 3.5-inch floppy disk drive, monochrome monitor, mouse, joysticks
Value: $3 to $22

One of the best-selling Apple II-compatibles, the Video Technology Laser 128 ($3 to $22).

VTech Laser Turbo XT (desktop PC)
Original Retail Price: $1,099 to $1,599
Base Configuration: MS-DOS 2.1; eight ISA slots; 512K RAM (640K max); 5.25-inch floppy disk drive; composite video port; keyboard/keypad; RS-232, parallel, and game ports **Video:** Hercules, CGA
Important Options: 20MB hard disk drive, EGA card, 12-inch monochrome or 14-inch color monitor, mouse, technical reference
Value: $7 to $20

VTech Laser Compact XT (1987, desktop PC)
Original Retail Price: $599 to $699
Base Configuration: 4.77MHz 8088-1 CPU; MS-DOS 3.21; 256K RAM (640K max); 8K ROM; 3.5- or 5.25-inch floppy disk drive; composite video port; integral keyboard/keypad; RS-232, parallel, and game ports **Video:** Hercules, CGA **Size/Weight:** 14.5 x 12.5 x 2.12 inches, 11.7 lbs. **Important Options:** expansion box, EMS board, external hard disk drive, EGA card, 12-inch monochrome or 14-inch color monitor, mouse, joystick, technical reference
Value: $7 to $20

Visual Computer Inc. (Marlboro, Massachusetts)

The Commuter's small LCD was removeable so that a standard monitor could more easily be used with the system.

Visual Computer Commuter
(Nov. 1983, transportable PC)
Original Retail Price: $1,995
Base Configuration: 8088 CPU, MS-DOS 2.1, 128K RAM (512K max), 5.25-inch floppy disk drive, monochrome LCD, RGB, and composite video ports, integral keyboard/keypad, RS-232C and parallel ports **Video:** 16-line x 80-column text **Size/Weight:** 15 x 18 x 3 inches, 16 lbs. **Important Options:** expansion chassis, external 5.25-inch floppy disk drive
Value: $8 to $30

Visual Technology Inc. (Tewksbury, Massachusetts)

Unlike many of its competitors, the Visual 1050 offered bit-mapped graphics.

Visual Technology 1050 (1983, desktop)
Original Retail Price: $2,695
Base Configuration: Z80A CPU with a 6502 display processor, CP/M Plus with GSX Graphics, 64K RAM (128K max), two 5.25-inch floppy disk drives, monochrome monitor, keyboard/keypad, RS-232C and two parallel ports, CBASIC, application suite, VT100 terminal emulator **Video:** 25-line x 80-column text, 640 x 300 graphics **Important Options:** 5MB hard disk drive
Value: $15 to $45

The Visual Computer Commuter ($8 to $30) was PC-compatible, shown with an Epson printer of the same vintage.

Wang Laboratories Inc. (Lowell, Massachusetts)

Wang was one of the biggest players in the workstation/office automation industry when it introduced the Wang PC. In standard form, the Wang PC was not fully IBM-compatible. However, the company offered an expansion card in 1984 that it claimed provided full IBM compatibility.

Wang Professional Computer (PC)
(1983, desktop PC)
Original Retail Price: $2,445
Base Configuration: 8MHz 8086 CPU, MS-DOS 2.0, five expansion slots, 256K RAM (640K max), 5.25-inch floppy disk drive, keyboard/keypad, RS-232C and parallel ports, BASIC **Video:** 25-line x 80-column text **Size/Weight:** 23.1 x 14.9 x 6.5 inches **Important Options:** expansion card, second 5.25-inch floppy disk drive, 10MB hard disk drive, CGA card, monochrome monitor, dot-matrix or daisy-wheel printer
Value: $12 to $35

One of the more popular CP/M systems of its era, the Visual Technology 1050 ($15 to $45).

Wave Mate
(Gardena, California)

While most of its competitors offered bare-bones systems at an affordable price, Wave Mate decided to sell the Jupiter II fully decked out. Its customers got a much more functional system, but at a much higher price.

Wave Mate Jupiter II/Jupiter IIC
(1975, early micro)
Original Retail Price: $1,225 kit, $1,885 assembled
Base Configuration: 6800 CPU, 8K RAM, RS-232 port, BASIC and programming utilities in ROM, power supply, backplane, rack-mount cage, front panel **Important Options:** RS-232C conversion kit
Value: $85 to $200

What early computer hobbyist wouldn't like to have this Wave Mate Jupiter II ($85 to $200) and all the add-on boards shown here?

Wicat (Lindon, Utah)

Wicat 140 (1983, desktop)
Original Retail Price: $8,000
Base Configuration: 68000 CPU, MCS, 512K RAM, 5.25-inch floppy disk drive, 10MB hard disk drive, integral monochrome CRT display, keyboard/keypad
Value: $20 to $55

Xerox Corp. (Rochester, New York)

Given Xerox's reputation, earned with the development of the Alto, the 820 was a disappointment. Not that it was a bad computer; it was just a rather ordinary CP/M system that lacked the innovation found in Xerox's earlier systems. Xerox's code name for the 820 during development was WORM (Wonderful Office Revolutionary Machine).

Xerox sold the 6085 in standalone and network configurations.

The Xerox 1810 was developed by Sunrise Systems, a company founded with the help of Xerox. The full system was in two parts. The keyboard unit could be used by itself and had its own processor and a small LCD. A processor unit contained the Z80A-class and 8088 CPUs, as well as the floppy drives.

Xerox 820 (1981, desktop)
Original Retail Price: $2,995
Base Configuration: 2.5MHz Z80 CPU, CP/M, 64K RAM, 4K ROM, two external 5.25-inch floppy disk drives, integral 12-inch monochrome CRT, keyboard/keypad, two RS-232C and two parallel ports, BASIC-80 **Video:** 24-line x 80-column text **Size/Weight:** 12.88 x 13.5 x 15 inches, 30 lbs. **Important Options:** dual external 8-inch floppy disk drives, 630 printer
Value: $20 to $45

Xerox 16/8 (desktop)
Original Retail Price: $3,395 to $5,295
Base Configuration: dual processors (16- and 8-bit); CP/M, CP/M-86, and MS-DOS; 128K RAM (256K max, 16-bit); 64K RAM (8-bit); 5.25- or 8-inch floppy disk drive; integral 12-inch monochrome CRT; keyboard/keypad **Video:** 24-line x 80-column text **Important Options:** second floppy disk drive, 10MB hard disk drive, daisy-wheel printer
Value: $15 to $40

Xerox 6085 (1985, desktop)
Original Retail Price: $4,995
Base Configuration: 8MHz Mesa CPU, 80186 coprocessor, ViewPoint, 1.1MB RAM (3.7MB max), 10MB hard disk drive, 15-inch monochrome monitor, keyboard/keypad, mouse, two serial ports **Video:** 880 x 697 graphics **Important Options:** 5.25-inch floppy disk drive, 20MB to 80MB hard disk drive, PC-compatibility board
Value: $20 to $100

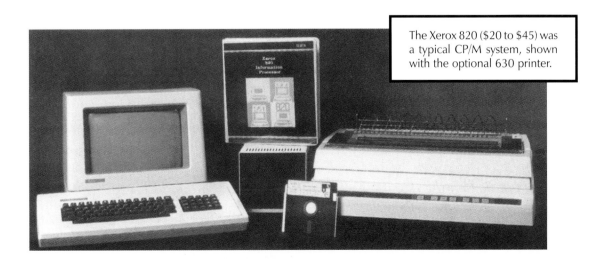

The Xerox 820 ($20 to $45) was a typical CP/M system, shown with the optional 630 printer.

Xerox 1810 (1984, notebook)
Original Retail Price: $2,195 to $2,495
Base Configuration: NSC800 CPU; MS-DOS, CP/M-80, or CP/M-86; ROM cartridge slot; 64K RAM (256K max); 16K ROM; integral microcassette drive; monochrome LCD; RGB, and TV video ports; integral keyboard; RS-232C and parallel ports; Microsoft BASIC; internal modem; NiCad battery pack; AC adapter **Video:** 3-line x 80-column text **Size/Weight:** 16 x 9 x 2 inches, 5 lbs. **Important Options:** 8088 coprocessor, 1850 expansion unit, external dual 5.25-inch floppy disk drives, integral printer **Value:** $20 to $70

Hard to find today, the
Xerox 1810 notebook computer ($20 to $70).

Yamaha International Corp. (Buena Park, California)

A YIS303 model had only 16K RAM and no parallel port. The CX5M could do everything that other MSX systems could, but had added features for composing and playing music.

Yamaha YIS503

(1984, MSX home computer)
Original Retail Price: $270
Base Configuration: Z80 CPU, two ROM cartridge slots, 32K RAM, composite video port, integral keyboard, parallel port, music synthesizer, MSX BASIC **Video:** 24-line x 40-column text, 256 x 192 graphics
Value: $10 to $40

Yamaha CX5M

(1985, MSX home computer)
Original Retail Price: $469
Base Configuration: Z80A CPU, ROM cartridge slot, 32K RAM, 32K ROM, integral keyboard, cassette port FM digital tone generator, MSX BASIC, MIDI port **Video:** 32-line x 24-column text, 256 x 192 graphics, 16 colors **Important Options:** music software, DX7 Voicing Program, mini and full-size piano keyboards
value: $17 to $75

Zeda Computer Systems (Provo, Utah)

The Zeda could function as a terminal or as a standalone computer. Its all-in-one design featured wooden sides.

Zeda Video Computer (desktop)
Original Retail Price: $4,500
Base Configuration: Z80A CPU; 48K RAM (58K max); 5.25-inch floppy disk drive; integral monochrome CRT; integral keyboard; two serial, parallel, and light-pen ports **Video:** 25-line x 80-column text **Size/Weight:** 12 x 15 x 18 inches **Important Options:** 5.25- or 8-inch floppy disk drive, keypad, light pen
Value: $17 to $45

Zeda 520/580 (desktop)
Original Retail Price: $3,995 (520)/$5,938 (580)
Base Configuration: Z80A CPU, Zedos, 64K RAM (520)/65K RAM (580), integral monochrome CRT, integral keyboard/keypad, RS-232C and parallel ports, BASIC **Video:** 25-line x 81-column text
Value: $17 to $45

Those are wood sides on this
Zeda Video Computer ($17 to $45).

Zenith Data Systems
(Glenview, Illinois)

Zenith first made a name for itself in the 1920s as a maker of radios, when it was called Zenith Radio Corp. Later, it would be a major producer of televisions and other consumer electronics. In 1979, it entered the computer business with the purchase of Heath Company from Schlumberger.

Heath produced several computers that were popular with engineers and hobbyists, and Zenith began selling one of them, the H-89, under its own brand as the Z-90. Zenith-branded systems were sold through retailers and value-added resellers, while Heath systems were sold via mail-order. This practice would continue through the 1980s. While Heath usually offered kit versions of its computers, all Zenith systems were sold already assembled.

The Z-100 was an appealing bridge system for developers and businesses transitioning from CP/M to MS-DOS. Its dual processors supported both operating systems (MS-DOS in the form of Zenith's licensed version, ZDOS).

A high level of PC compatibility and solid construction were the Z-150's main selling points. Zenith introduced the Z-159, a lower-priced version of the Z-158, in February 1987. It offered EGA video standard and accepted EMS memory chips to boost on-board capacity to 1.25MB.

In terms of technical specs, the Z-200 was typical of many PC AT-compatibles. However, Zenith had a deserved reputation for well-engineered and well-built systems.

Zenith's first portable was the Z-138 PC transportable, followed shortly by the Z-160. The disk drive bays on the Z-160 pop up from the top. The Z-171 had a "lunchbox" form factor and was the same system, with minor differences, as the Morrow Pivot and Osborne Encore. A Z-175 model featured a backlit LCD.

In the late 1980s and early 1990s, Zenith produced some of the best laptop and notebook computers available, including the SuperSport and MinisPort series. They have minimal collector value today, but are bound to be of interest in the future.

Zenith Z-90 (desktop)
Base Configuration: 64K RAM, integral monochrome CRT, integral keyboard/keypad
Value: $15 to $40

Zenith Z-100 All-In-One/ Z-100 Low Profile (1983, desktop)
Original Retail Price: $2,199 (kit), $3,499 to $5,599 (assembled)
Base Configuration: 5MHz 8085 and 5MHz 8088 CPUs, CP/M-85, five S-100 slots, 128K RAM (768K max), two 5.25-inch floppy disk drives, integral 12-inch monochrome CRT display (All-In-One), integral keyboard/keypad, two RS-232C and one parallel port, user manual **Video:** 24-line x 80-column text, 640 x 225 graphics **Size/Weight:** 13.5 x 19.5 x 19.5 inches, 50 lbs. (All-In-One)/7.25 x 19 x 19.25 inches, 40 lbs. (Low Profile) **Important Options:** ZDOS, 8-inch floppy disk drive, 5MB or 11MB hard disk drive, RGB CRT display (All-In-One), monochrome ZVM-121 or color ZVM-134 monitor (Low Profile), ZBASIC, Z-25 or Z-125 printer **Value:** $30 to $100

Zenith Z-148 (desktop PC)
Base Configuration: 8MHz 8088 CPU, MS-DOS 2.11 and 1.25, 128K RAM (640K max), 5.25-inch floppy disk drive, RGB and composite video ports, keyboard/keypad, RS-232C and parallel ports **Video:** 640 x 200 graphics **Size/Weight:** 16 x 4.8 x 16.1 inches, 22.5 lbs. **Important Options:** one-slot daughtercard, expansion box, second 5.25-inch floppy disk drive, Z-125 printer
Value: $12 to $40

The Zenith Z-100 Low Profile had a sibling with an all-in-one design called, appropriately, the Z-100 All-in-One ($30 to $100, both versions).

Zenith Z-150 (Feb. 1984, desktop PC)
Original Retail Price: $2,699 to $4,799
Base Configuration: 8088 CPU, MS-DOS 2.11 and 1.25, four ISA slots, 128K RAM (640K max), 5.25-inch floppy disk drive, RGB and composite video ports, keyboard/keypad, two RS-232 and one parallel port **Video:** 640 x 200 graphics **Size/Weight:** 16 x 6.25 x 16.5 inches, 42 lbs. **Important Options:** second 5.25-inch floppy disk drive, 10.6MB hard disk drive, Z-125 printer
Value: $15 to $40

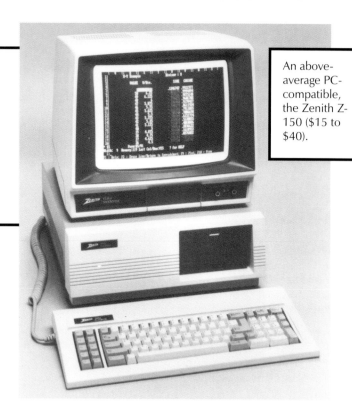

An above-average PC-compatible, the Zenith Z-150 ($15 to $40).

Zenith Z-158 (desktop PC)
Base Configuration: 8MHz 8088 CPU, four ISA slots, 128K RAM (640K max), 5.25-inch floppy disk drive, RGB and composite video ports, keyboard/keypad, RS-232 and parallel ports **Video:** 640 x 200 graphics **Size/Weight:** 16 x 6.5 x 16.5 inches, 42 lbs. **Important Options:** second 5.25-inch floppy disk drive, 10.6MB hard disk drive, Z-125 printer
Value: $7 to $27

Zenith Z-200 (1985, desktop PC)
Original Retail Price: $3,999 to $5,599
Base Configuration: 80286 CPU, MS-DOS 3.1, six ISA slots, 512K RAM, 64K ROM, 5.25-inch floppy disk drive, RGB and composite video ports, keyboard/keypad, RS-232C and parallel ports **Video:** CGA **Size/Weight:** 21 x 16.5 x 6.5, 38 lbs. **Important Options:** Xenix, one-slot daughtercard, expansion box, 20MB hard disk drive
Value: $5 to $25

Zenith Z-138 (transportable PC)
Base Configuration: 8MHz 8088 CPU, MS-DOS 2.11 and 1.25, ISA slot, 256K RAM (640K max), 5.25-inch floppy disk drive, RGB and composite video ports, integral 7-inch monochrome CRT, keyboard/keypad, two RS-232C and one parallel port **Video:** 25-line x 80-column text **Size/Weight:** 8.5 x 18 x 17 inches, 24.2 lbs. **Important Options:** Z-125 printer, carrying case
Value: $17 to $50

Zenith Z-171 (April 1985, transportable PC)
Original Retail Price: $2,699
Base Configuration: 4.77MHz 80C88 CPU, MS-DOS 2.11 and 1.25, 256K RAM (640K max), two 5.25-inch floppy disk drives, 10-inch monochrome LCD, keyboard, RS-232C and parallel ports, productivity software suite, AC adapter **Video:** 25-line x 80-column text, 240 x 200 graphics **Size/Weight:** 9.5 x 13 x 6.6 inches, 14.3 lbs. **Important Options:** expansion chassis, video board with RGB port, carrying case, battery pack
Value: $10 to $35

Zenith Z-181 (1986, laptop PC)
Original Retail Price: $2,399
Base Configuration: 4.77MHz 80C88 CPU, MS-DOS 3.2, 640K RAM, 3.5-inch floppy disk drive, monochrome LCD, RGB, and composite video ports, integral keyboard. serial and parallel ports, NiCad battery pack, AC adapter **Size/Weight:** 11.8 lbs. **Important Options:** external 5.25-inch floppy disk drive, BASIC, internal modem, bar-code reader
Value: $7 to $35

Zenith Z-160
(Feb. 1984, transportable PC)
Original Retail Price: $2,799 to $3,199
Base Configuration: 8088 CPU, MS-DOS, four ISA slots, 320K RAM (640K max), 5.25-inch floppy disk drive, integral monochrome CRT, RGB, and composite video ports, keyboard/keypad, RS-232 and parallel ports **Video:** 25-line x 80-column text **Size/Weight:** 19.5 x 8.38 x 19.13 inches, 38.6 lbs. **Important Options:** second 5.25-inch floppy disk drive, Z-25 or Z-125 printer
Value: $17 to $50

The floppy drives on this Zenith Z-160 ($17 to $50) popped up from the top when needed.